G000298695

Devon Libraries
D 12503634 X 0100

AT WAR IN DISTANT WATERS

AT WAR IN DISTANT WATERS

BRITISH COLONIAL DEFENSE IN THE GREAT WAR

PHILLIP G. PATTEE

NAVAL INSTITUTE PRESS
Annapolis, Maryland

Naval Institute Press
291 Wood Road
Annapolis, MD 21402

Library of Congress Cataloging-in-Publication Data
Pattee, Phillip G.
At war in distant waters : British colonial defense in the Great War / Phillip G. Pattee.
pages cm
Includes bibliographical references and index.
Summary: "At War in Distant Waters investigates the reasons behind Great Britain's combined military and naval offensive expeditions outside of Europe during the Great War. Often regarded as unnecessary sideshows to the conflict waged on the European continent, Pattee argues that the various campaigns were necessary adjuncts to the war in Europe, and fulfilled an important strategic purpose by protecting British trade where it was most vulnerable. Since international trade was essential for the island nation's way of life, Great Britain required freedom of the seas to maintain its global trade. While the German High Seas Fleet was a serious threat to the British coast, forcing the Royal Navy to concentrate in home waters, the importance of the island empire's global trade made it a valuable target to Germany's various commerce raiders, just as Admiral Tirpitz's risk theory had anticipated." — Provided by publisher.
ISBN 978-1-61251-194-8 (hardback) — ISBN 978-1-61251-195-5 (ebook) 1. World War, 1914–1918—Naval operations, British. 2. World War, 1914–1918—Economic aspects—Great Britain. 3. World War, 1914–1918—Campaigns. 4. World War, 1914–1918—Commonwealth countries. 5. Great Britain—Colonies—History, Military—20th century. I. Title.
D581.P28 2013
940.45941—dc23

2013020450

Maps created by Christopher Robinson.

♾ Print editions meet the requirements of ANSI/NISO z39.48-1992 (Permanence of Paper).
Printed in the United States of America.

21 20 19 18 17 16 15 14 13 9 8 7 6 5 4 3 2 1
First printing

To

my wife, Sally,
who endured this project for far too long

and

my mother, Dolores,
who inspired me to love learning

CONTENTS

MAPS

ACKNOWLEDGMENTS

I would like to acknowledge the archivists and clerks at the Western Manuscripts Reading Room, Bodleian Library, Oxford; the British Library, London; the Churchill Archives Centre, Cambridge; the Parliamentary Archives; and the National Archives, Kew Gardens. I truly appreciate their courteous and efficient service, without which this book would not have been possible.

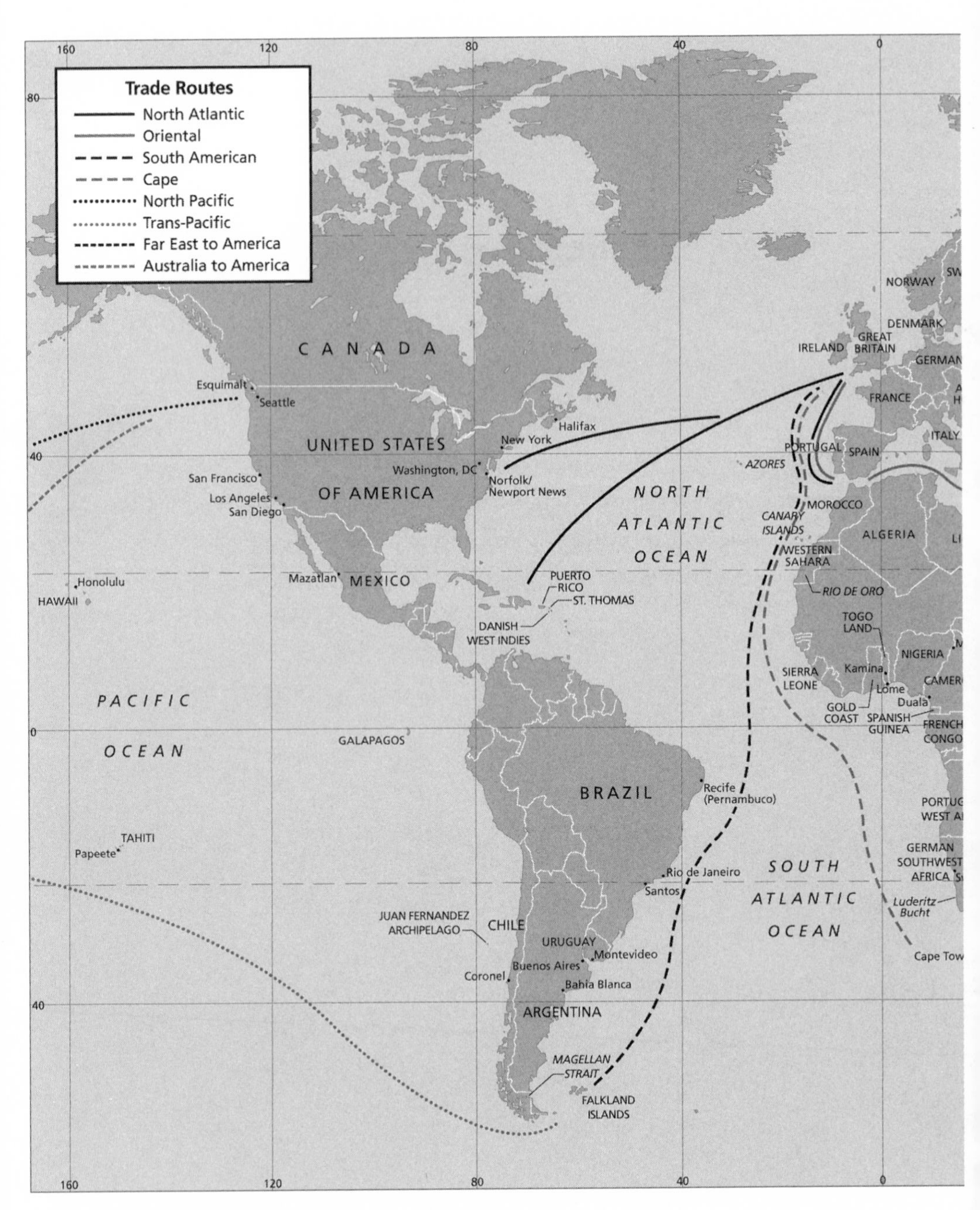

Map 1. *Trade Routes and British and German Colonies circa 1914*

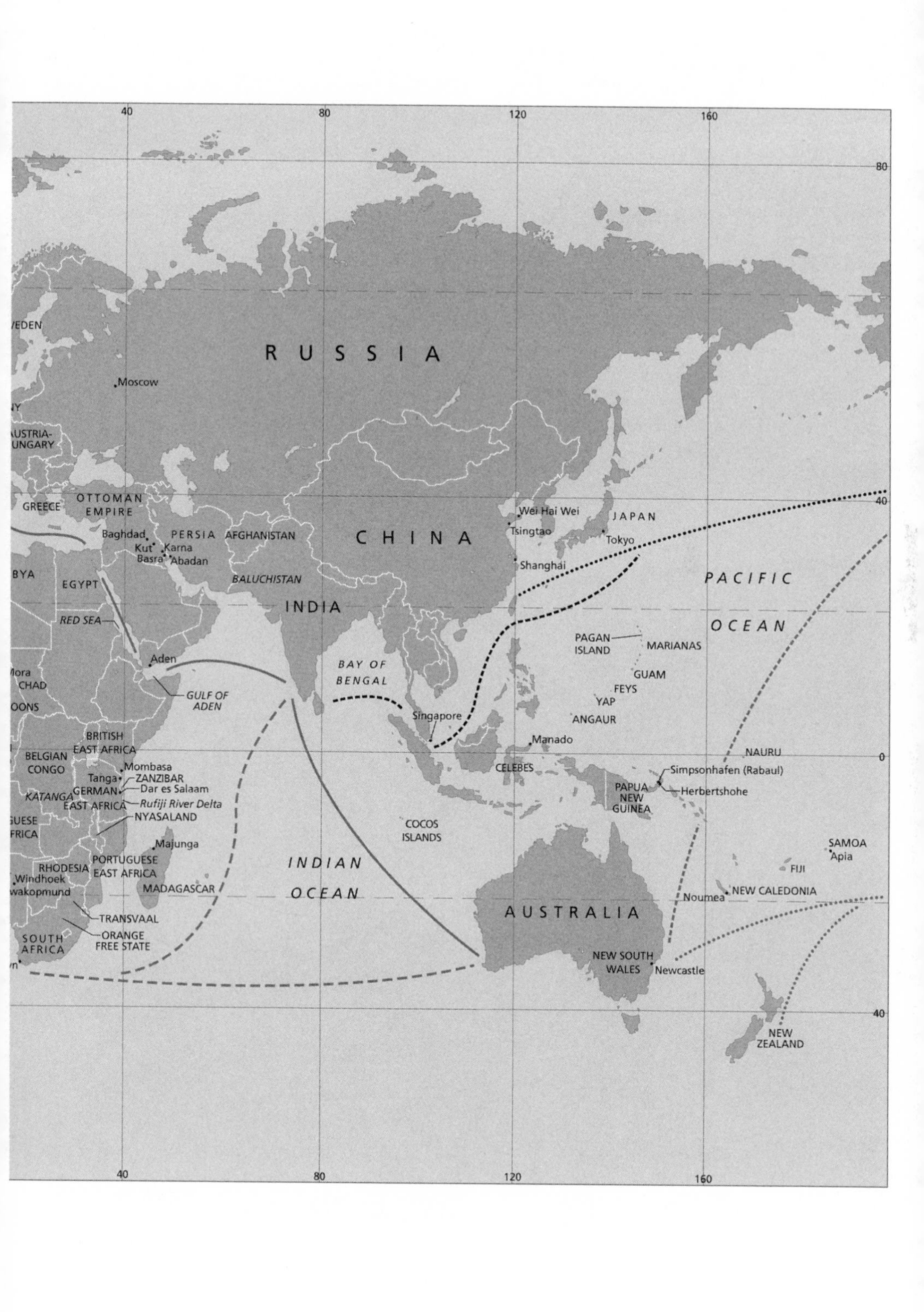

40
80
120
160
RUSSIA
Moscow
AUSTRIA-HUNGARY
GREECE
OTTOMAN EMPIRE
Baghdad
Kut
Karna
Basra
Abadan
PERSIA
AFGHANISTAN
BALUCHISTAN
CHINA
INDIA
EGYPT
RED SEA
Aden
GULF OF ADEN
CHAD
BRITISH EAST AFRICA
BELGIAN CONGO
Mombasa
Tanga
ZANZIBAR
GERMAN EAST AFRICA
Dar es Salaam
KATANGA
Rufiji River Delta
NYASALAND
Majunga
RHODESIA
PORTUGUESE EAST AFRICA
Windhoek
MADAGASCAR
TRANSVAAL
ORANGE FREE STATE
SOUTH AFRICA
BAY OF BENGAL
Singapore
INDIAN OCEAN
COCOS ISLANDS
Wei Hai Wei
Tsingtao
Shanghai
JAPAN
Tokyo
PACIFIC OCEAN
PAGAN ISLAND
MARIANAS
GUAM
FEYS
YAP
ANGAUR
Manado
CELEBES
NAURU
Simpsonhafen (Rabaul)
Herbertshohe
PAPUA NEW GUINEA
SAMOA
Apia
FIJI
Noumea
NEW CALEDONIA
AUSTRALIA
NEW SOUTH WALES
Newcastle
NEW ZEALAND

INTRODUCTION

On August 3, 1914, the eve of Great Britain's entry into the First World War, Foreign Minister Edward Grey delivered a memorable speech to the House of Commons. With heartfelt eloquence, Grey captured the threat that the looming conflict posed to the island empire:

> For us, with a powerful fleet, which we believe able to protect our commerce, to protect our shores, and to protect our interests, if we are engaged in war, we shall suffer but little more than we shall suffer even if we stand aside.
>
> We are going to suffer, I am afraid, terribly in this war, whether we are in or whether we stand aside. Foreign trade is going to stop, not because the trade routes are closed, but because there is no trade at the other end.[1]

With these words, Grey conveyed that his country's interest in the war sprang from more than loyalty to France or a treaty obligation to preserve Belgium's neutrality. Rather, it concerned Great Britain's way of life. Protecting the United Kingdom's political and economic independence would require British intervention in the war, not merely as a naval power—which Grey believed would suffice to prevent invasion and keep trade routes open—but also as a land power to preserve the vitality and economies of Great Britain's trading partners on the European continent.

The authors of the vast body of literature on the Great War have been mesmerized by the colossal human sacrifices on the western and eastern fronts of continental Europe. They depict the huge losses sustained by the opposing forces as the inevitable result of a war directed by incompetent generals and politicians, but the Great War was in fact a world war, with fighting in Africa, the Levant, Mesopotamia, China, and far-flung islands across the Pacific. The immensity of the military effort in Europe dwarfed operations conducted in the war's other theaters. This fact has led many historians to conclude that these distant campaigns were superfluous sideshows or opportunistic attempts at imperial expansion.

At War in Distant Waters: British Colonial Defense in the Great War investigates the reasons behind the combined military and naval offensives conducted outside Europe during the war. It finds that they fulfilled an important strategic purpose by protecting British trade where it was most vulnerable. Trade was not a luxury for the British; it was essential for maintaining their way of life and a matter of national survival. The United Kingdom required freedom of the seas in order to maintain its global trade. A general war in Europe threatened Great Britain's economic independence through the potential loss of its continental trading partners. The specific nature of the German threat also placed the British coast at grave risk. Military operations against German colonies were necessary to gain and maintain command of the seas while simultaneously protecting the British home islands. In Mesopotamia, overseas expeditions directed against the Ottoman Empire protected communications with India and British oil concessions in Persia. The various overseas campaigns that the British executed or encouraged constituted far more than frivolous adventurism. They formed part of a shrewdly conceived and frugally conducted grand strategy essential for British victory.

Great Britain's economic and physical survival rested upon trade with its colonies, its dominions, the European continent, and the United States.[2] The British imported as much as a third of their vegetables, half of their meat and dairy products, more than three-quarters of their cereals, and all of their tea, sugar, and cocoa.[3] Having created a specialized manufacturing economy, the British also depended on imported raw materials for their industries. Moreover, many of the Royal Navy's newest ships had been built with oil-fired boilers. With few domestic sources of petroleum, Great Britain had to import most of its oil.[4] To pay for imported foods and raw materials, Great Britain required consistent, worldwide outlets for manufacturers' goods and coal. British merchant ships generated additional revenues by transporting cargoes between foreign ports for third parties. British capital insured the cargoes and financed overseas industrial development.[5] Raw materials, finished goods, and capital all traversed the oceans either by ship or by telegraph. The system that enabled the British way of life was an elaborate combination of private and governmental enterprises. Naval squadrons, private merchant lines, insurance companies, telegraph cables and wireless stations, diplomats and generals, as well as treaties and international law worked together to maintain the free flow of capital and goods.

In the First World War, Germany posed the only credible threat to British security. If the German High Seas Fleet defeated the British Home Fleet, it could then bombard British cities and land raiding forces on British territory. First Lord of the Admiralty Winston S. Churchill later admitted that if the British Home Fleet had been decisively defeated by the Germans, Great Britain "could [have lost] the war in an afternoon."[6] Guarding against this possibility became Great Britain's most immediate concern.

To counter the German High Seas Fleet, Great Britain required a technologically and numerically superior battle fleet stationed at the entrance to the North Sea and in the English Channel. Technological advances in German ship design challenged Great Britain's ability to maintain a superior fleet. Nevertheless, the British prevailed. The great naval race between Great Britain and Germany entailed radical new designs incorporating armor plating, advanced gunnery, and new propulsion systems. By 1912 the British had won the arms race.[7] Oil-fired boilers provided the Royal Navy with an edge in speed that proved vital in attaining tactical superiority. Because Great Britain was already dependent on imports for survival, the government was willing to accept the risk in having to import oil for the newest ships in the Royal Navy.[8]

In the event of a general war in Europe, Great Britain's trade with the continent could be severed, particularly if Germany dominated France. So long as its naval supremacy was not compromised, Great Britain was little concerned about an invasion from the continent. If the British lost control of the seas, however, Germany could eventually amass a sizable army to possibly invade.[9] German occupation of the channel ports in Belgium and France would render defense of the English Channel precarious and thus poise a dagger at England's heart. The size and reputation of the German army as the world's best forced Britain to intervene with a large expeditionary force on the continent.

In light of the strategic situation, the Royal Navy juggled three major tasks: defend British shores against bombardment and military incursion; support an expeditionary force on the European continent; protect Great Britain's global commerce. Given the immediacy of the first two tasks, the third task proved challenging. A German system of raiders, ports, and communications comprised a serious threat to British commerce and potentially also to its colonies. A traditional view of sea control, as espoused by Alfred Thayer Mahan, is that it results from a powerful fleet imposing its dominance over the fleets of other nations. After a fleet has swept the seas of opponents, it has the use of them for its commercial and military purposes while denying such activity to the enemy.[10]

The German High Seas Fleet created the necessity to concentrate the bulk of British naval power in Scottish waters. That left the United Kingdom's trade routes vulnerable to interdiction by forces operating from Germany's colonies in Africa, Asia, and the Pacific. The threat to seaborne trade appeared quite serious because the Germans already had cruisers abroad, and the British thought they would outfit a large number of fast merchant liners as commerce destroyers at the outbreak of war.[11] Commerce raiders operating from German colonies in Africa and the Pacific could impede the flow of cargoes that the British needed to sustain themselves. This would eventually force British capitulation if losses or delays were heavy enough over a sufficient span of time.

Traditional methods of ensuring the safe transit of cargoes over the oceans required either a large number of naval vessels to protect trade routes for friendly and neutral merchant ships or a smaller number of warships to convoy select cargo vessels. The first option promised the least disruption and most efficient flow of cargoes. Adopting that strategy was problematic, however, because the Royal Navy had insufficient ships to patrol trade routes worldwide. The second option required merchant ships to sit idle while convoys formed and then proceed at the pace of the slowest vessel. The Royal Navy questioned whether convoys would guarantee the receipt of critical cargo in time to meet demand and also wondered if it had the authority to compel private merchantmen to follow convoy procedures.[12] Securing control of the seas against the German

High Seas Fleet and German commerce raiders seemed to be beyond the Royal Navy's capacity.

When Turkey entered the war as a German ally, Turkish threats to British trade routes and Mesopotamian resources compelled additional British action to protect its vital interests. Royal Dutch Shell and U.S.-based Standard Oil were Great Britain's two sources for the petroleum needed by its fleet. Since they were not British controlled, the Royal Navy did not want to rely exclusively on them to meet its wartime needs. In order to obtain a guaranteed source of oil, the British government purchased controlling shares in the newly formed Anglo-Persian Oil Company and compelled the company to accept contractual guarantees to supply the Royal Navy. Turkey's entry into the war forced the British to defend their new and undeveloped energy source.[13] Securing the Anglo-Persian oil fields in Mesopotamia required the British to initially commit the Indian Expeditionary Force D, which was slightly larger than a brigade.

The dual threat posed by Germany's High Seas Fleet was precisely that contemplated by its designer, Admiral Alfred von Tirpitz. According to Tirpitz's risk theory, the British had no choice but to acknowledge the threat posed by a concentrated German fleet in the North Sea and likewise concentrate their own fleet there. Tirpitz assumed that the British could not risk a loss in the North Sea and thus had to maintain a 33 percent numerical superiority, at the least, in ships there. This concentration of naval power in the North Sea would leave Great Britain's vast overseas empire only lightly defended. This would in turn grant Kaiser Wilhelm II latitude to conduct an overseas policy with which Great Britain would be hard-pressed to interfere.[14]

The combination of Britain's continental commitment and the nature of the German threat dictated that Great Britain quench the military potential of Germany's colonial empire in Asia, Africa, and the Pacific. The British cabinet appointed the Offensive Sub-Committee of the Committee of Imperial Defence to explore what overseas operations would best strengthen Great Britain's strategic posture. Subcommittee members recognized from the beginning that any planned operations could not interfere with the imperial troop and naval concentration in Europe or prejudice the safety of the major trade routes. These constraints produced guidelines for determining suitable objectives. First, no operation was viable that used more resources than were available locally from colonies, dominions, or allies. Moreover, if overseas expeditions were to have any effect on the subsequent course of the war, they had to enhance Great Britain's hold on sea communications. Operations observing these guidelines should tend to assist and strengthen the main concentration of effort in Europe rather than dissipate force. Without first establishing functional control of the sea, any operations for conquest of distant territory would have been ill-conceived.[15]

German commerce raiders required distant ports for coaling and repair. Moreover, the underwater telegraph cables and wireless stations linking Germany with its colonies provided a ready means of communications for directing raiders. The British solution to the threat entailed using available naval forces, acting in concert with colonial land forces and allies, France and Japan, in a series of expeditionary campaigns in Africa, the Middle East, and the Pacific. London therefore asked its dominion governments—the Union of South Africa, New Zealand, and Australia—and allies to capture nearby German colonial ports and wireless stations or assigned such missions to the various colonial governments, that is, India, Gold Coast, Nigeria, and Sierra Leone. The Offensive Sub-Committee determined that these objectives, if acted upon quickly, were within the capability of colonial military forces.[16] The offensives required rapid mobilization to overrun the German colonies before Berlin could organize an effective defense.

The immobilization of Germany's overseas military potential required Britain's home government to coordinate closely with its dominions, colonial governments, and allies to execute several simultaneous campaigns. Only two days after Great Britain entered the war, Lewis Harcourt, secretary of state for the colonies, placed the campaigns in motion. Immediately after receiving cabinet approval on August 6, 1914, Harcourt dispatched telegrams to the self-governing dominions asking them to plan and conduct expeditions against neighboring German colonies and outlining the specific objectives the cabinet wished each expedition to achieve. In the telegrams, Harcourt emphasized that each request from His Majesty's Government was "a great and urgent imperial service."[17] In quick succession, Harcourt also ordered the colonies to plan and execute expeditions. Foreign Minister Grey coordinated the campaigns with Britain's allies.

India, with the largest pool of available manpower, received two primary tasks: first, send a force into German East Africa to close the port at Dar es Salaam and seize the high-frequency radio station there, and second, secure the Anglo-Persian oil fields near Abadan.[18] The Indian army accomplished the latter by sending an expedition to seize the area around Basra. Although fighting continued in both of these theaters throughout the war, the British achieved the military objectives essential for controlling the seas and never suffered a setback serious enough to put their gains at risk.

In other operations in Africa, the Gold Coast was tasked with advancing from the west into the German colony of Togoland and by sea to subdue the port at Lomé and the wireless station near Kamina. This invasion was coordinated with a French thrust into Togoland from the east.[19] In a similar vein, a joint British and French expedition composed of land and naval forces from several colonies carried out a British request to attack the port of Duala and the wireless station in German-held Cameroons.[20] Great Britain enjoined South Africa to attack German Southwest Africa to close the ports and terminate radio operations at two wireless stations, in Swakopmund and Luderitzbucht.[21]

In the Pacific theater, Australia responded to the British call to seize the German ports and wireless stations at Rabaul, on the island of New Britain; Nauru, on Pleasant Island; and Yap, in the Caroline Islands.[22] The New Zealanders, with the assistance of French naval forces, cruised to Samoa and shut down German operations there.[23] The British required the help of their Japanese allies to curtail German operations out of Tsingtao, China. Foreign Minister Grey requested that the Japanese blockade the port and pursue Germany's armed merchantmen, and although the Japanese captured Tsingtao, it was with the intention of retaining it.[24] In addition, Japan occupied all the German possessions in the archipelagoes north of the equator.

British ministers at consulates and embassies consistently applied diplomacy in carefully built cases against German merchantmen engaged in supporting commerce raiding and pressured neutral governments to intern violators of international neutrality laws. The Germans eventually recognized that the British were their strongest enemy and could only be defeated through interdiction of the sea-lanes.[25] By the time the Germans realized this in late 1916, traditional methods of commerce raiding were denied to them due to the success of the earlier British-led expeditions. That left the Kriegsmarine no other choice but to resort to unrestricted submarine warfare.

The expeditions the British mounted or encouraged others to conduct outside of Europe constituted a global grand strategy essential for victory in the

Great War. Moreover, Great Britain pursued these non-European campaigns without jeopardizing its continental commitments by relying on the assistance of its dominions, colonies, and allies. These campaigns, the British hoped, would keep German commerce raiding disorganized and possibly curtail it altogether by denying advanced-base support to German naval operations. Success would enhance British control of the seas without drawing essential naval resources away from the North Sea; maintain the crucial flow of food, raw materials, and oil; and allow Great Britain to concentrate its professional army in Europe. In addition to applying an economy of force approach to protecting interests, the British strategy simultaneously struck a blow at Germany by curtailing its sea commerce. *At War in Distant Waters* makes an original contribution to First World War historiography by highlighting this essential but unappreciated facet of British grand strategy from 1914 to 1918.

This strategic concept stresses the linkage between the many operations Great Britain mounted or encouraged in the Middle East, Africa, and throughout the Pacific Ocean. Julian Corbett, the author of the Royal Navy's official history of the war, fails to note this connection, simply saying that a British campaign against Tsingtao was "too formidable an undertaking for the forces then available."[26] Corbett also states that the reduction of ports in German Southwest Africa "had to be ruled out as requiring too large a military force."[27] In both cases, however, the British eventually fulfilled their strategic goals with assistance from their empire and allies. In fact, Corbett never discusses overseas expeditions as part of a coherent grand strategy, but instead views them as distinct, combined operations.[28] The traditional parsing of historical study along national or regional lines and the common bifurcation of military history along military and naval lines mask, in this case, essential links among the consuls, government departments, and naval and military commanders that must be understood to appreciate the strategic significance of the expeditionary operations.

Corbett's analysis is nearly a century old, but the scholarship has not progressed much further since. Michael Howard, a Chichele Professor of the History of War and then a Regius Professor of Modern History at Oxford University, also undervalues the importance of the overseas colonial campaigns. In *The First World War* (2002), Howard devotes only a single paragraph to colonial warfare in his effort "to introduce the vast subject of the First World

War to those who know little or nothing about it."[29] He asserts that Germany's colonies were "too few to matter. . . . [T]he Germans had acquired overseas colonies mainly for reasons of prestige, to bolster their claim to the status of *Weltmacht;* but [the colonies] were if anything a drain on their economy." After succinctly describing which British colony, dominion, or ally had seized a particular German possession, Howard dismisses the overseas expeditions as irrelevant to the larger war, stating that "ironically, although all were to be the scenes of desperate fighting in the Second World War, in the First they hardly rated as sideshows."[30] Even though this particular view appears in a popular history aimed at a general audience, because of Howard's stature as an historian, his judgment of overseas expeditionary operations requires a vigorous rebuttal.

James L. Stokesbury also fails to discern the strategic importance of the overseas expeditionary operations in *A Short History of World War I* (1981). He explains the reasons for the expeditions in the Pacific as follows:

> German Pacific territories were dotted around the map of the China coast and islands here and there. All of these fell early in the war to a race between the Japanese and the Australians. Japan, who was not obligated by the Anglo-Japanese Alliance of 1902 to enter this war, immediately did so, not because Britain asked her to, but because she saw opportunities for herself to gain the German colonies. This was resented in Australia, where people feared the "yellow peril" a great deal more than they feared Germany. The upshot of it all was that the New Zealanders took Samoa, the Australians moved up into the Bismarck Archipelago, the island just east of New Guinea, and also occupied northeastern New Guinea, otherwise known as Kaiser-Wilhelmsland. As there were fewer than 2,000 German nationals spread all over the South Pacific, there was not much to all this.[31]

As for the expeditions conducted in Africa and the Middle East, Stokesbury contents himself with briefly describing the operations without presenting a strategic rationale behind them. This is fortunate for the reader because the reasons Stokesbury provides for the Pacific expeditions misinform rather than educate. While it is true that Japan was not obligated by alliance to assist Great Britain against Germany, Japan did not embark on any military activity until

British diplomats asked for assistance in blockading the German naval base at Tsingtao. Japan determined then that it would enter the war as an ally of Great Britain and make the best of the situation. Moreover, Stokesbury's analysis leads the reader to conclude that New Zealand and Australia, of their own volition, seized German possessions in response to Japanese expansionism rather than the purposeful execution of British strategy. Available historical evidence simply does not support such a conclusion. This book makes clear that Australia and New Zealand undertook their expeditions at the request of the British government.

In *British Strategy and War Aims,* David French describes British strategic planning early in World War I. He notes the British Army's desire to avoid committing a large force to the continent while the Royal Navy wanted to retain the flexibility to land a small expedition on the Baltic coast near East Prussia. In a brief passage, French asserts that the German colonies were important not simply because they added territory to the British Empire, but also because the Germans could no longer use them as bases for gathering intelligence and supporting commerce raiders.[32] French stresses, however, that Great Britain repeatedly modified its war aims as the war progressed in order to remain the strongest European power at its end. French's argument with respect to what he considers the minor point of capturing Germany's colonies is that doing so improved Great Britain's negotiating posture with respect to its allies, but Britain could not formally annex its prizes without inciting their jealousy.[33]

Other historians have also recognized the improved British negotiating leverage gained by capturing German colonies, but because their capture did not compel Germany's defeat, or because only comparatively small forces were involved, those historians concluded that Britain's overseas expeditionary operations were peripheral to the course of the Great War. Improved negotiating power is about all that could be gained from the conquest of any single German colony, but the cumulative effect produced by the conquest of all German colonies on the war's course was significant. *At War in Distant Waters* argues that military operations in these areas were of central importance to Britain's conduct of the Great War. They actually protected the empire from the incalculable damage that would have resulted from the loss of trade or economic collapse.

An alternative rationale for British offensive expeditions against German colonies is found in Hew Strachan's *The First World War* (2001). Strachan's explanation for Great Britain's campaigns outside Europe in 1914 is that they "were designed to restrict the war, to eliminate Germany as a global force, to drive its cruisers from the seas, to close down its African and Pacific colonies."[34] He contends that these efforts were not necessary to protect Britain's trade routes, but were instead meant to prevent the expansion of German *Kultur* and the further trammeling of small nations' rights. According to Strachan, "given Germany's naval inferiority, an alliance with Turkey seemed to be the only means by which to administer a direct blow to Britain's vital interests."[35] The threat to British interests, Strachan argues, came from a possible Turkish thrust from Syria to seize the Suez Canal, a move that would have threatened British lines of communication with India.

Some counterfactual historical analysis asserts that Great Britain would have best served its interests by remaining neutral in the Great War. In *The Pity of War* (1999), Niall Ferguson argues that Great Britain should have stood aside: "German objectives, had Britain remained out, would not in fact have posed a direct threat to the Empire; the reduction of Russian power in Eastern Europe, the creation of a Central European Customs Union and acquisition of French colonies—these were all goals which were complementary to British interests."[36] Other strategic options included keeping the colonies neutral and entering the war as a partner of the Triple Alliance of Germany, Austria-Hungary, and Italy. Ferguson also asserts that the primary reason Great Britain and Germany did not ratify a formal entente was "that Germany, unlike France, Russia, Japan or the [United States], did not seem to pose a serious threat to the Empire."[37] The conclusion Ferguson reaches is that Great Britain needlessly expanded a continental conflict into a world war by following a policy of appeasement.

The process used in *At War in Distant Waters* essentially follows that used by modern military strategic planners. Typically a planner develops an understanding of the situation, determines his or her organization's goals, and then proposes various policies or courses of action that the organization could pursue to achieve its goals. Once policy makers decide on a policy to follow, military planners execute the policies with modifications along the way in response to enemy activity. Chapters 1, 2, and 3 of this book provide a strategic assessment of the situation as British government officials understood it leading up to the war. Chapters 4, 5, and 6 discuss British deliberations about a wise policy, examining a variety of options (including neutrality), whether to immediately send an expeditionary force to the continent, and what operations might improve overall British strategic posture. These chapters go to the heart of the matter by describing why overseas expeditionary operations supported the British vital interest in sustaining its normal trading practices. Chapters 7, 8, and 9 demonstrate the effect of overseas expeditions on curtailing German commerce raiding and subsequent German attempts to disrupt British trade, which ultimately led to Germany's decision to pursue unrestricted submarine warfare.

At War in Distant Waters demonstrates how interdepartmental government cooperation and skillfully handled coalition warfare can yield maximum results from a relatively minor investment in material resources. In sum, the British undertook colonial operations as a way to secure their homeland from defeat and enhance command of the sea, rather than to add territory to the empire. At the same time, Germany had two choices: capitulate or use submarines to conduct a form of warfare that violated international law. The Germans had hoped to achieve victory without resorting to unrestricted submarine warfare, but in the end they had to resort to that expedient. At the war's conclusion, Great Britain sought to divest Germany of its fleet and colonies and place severe restrictions on submarines to ensure British security. Its insistence on dividing German colonies among the victorious powers is further evidence of how important these issues figured in British strategic calculations.

1 THE BRITISH EMPIRE'S DEPENDENCE ON GLOBAL TRADE IN 1914

By the end of the nineteenth century, the United Kingdom was not just one of Europe's great powers, but a global power. This particular circumstance was the result of Great Britain's geographic position and its economic system. Beginning in the late 1840s, Great Britain's economy experienced a dramatic transformation with the repeal of the Corn and Navigation Laws, which had imposed stiff tariffs on imported grain products and restrictions on imports not carried on board British ships. Prior to the repeals, British landowners had been protected against competition from cheaper imported grain. This resulted in overall higher food prices among the working class and consequently pressure on factory owners for higher wages. With labor's political rise, the laws benefitting landowners were repealed. Thus food prices dropped, and wages could be held lower, making British manufactured goods more competitive for export. The economic transformation was so pronounced that by the early 1900s Britons relied on imports for the majority of their food, and exported manufactured goods and capital to pay for it. With trade of strategic importance, its protection became a problem that the British government had to address.[1]

Trade protection was primarily the Royal Navy's concern, a responsibility facilitated by empire geography, which helped in protecting British trade and in time of war interfering with enemy trade. First Sea Lord Admiral John A. Fisher referred to this advantageous situation when he boasted that the United

Kingdom held "the strategic keys that lock up the world." His hubris rested on British possession of key choke points at the Strait of Malacca, the Suez Canal, the Strait of Gibraltar, the Strait of Dover, and the Cape of Good Hope.[2]

While Fisher's boast had a ring of truth, his perspective was one-dimensional, only considering the naval advantage offered by the empire's geography. The British Empire, however, consisted of a system of trade. As an empire, it was much more than geography. The empire comprised a political system with a metropolitan government, but it was also a conglomeration of mutually interdependent systems. Great Britain had five strategic keys—each one a system—for securing world trade: abundant finance, a preponderance of shipping, the empire's regions and waterways, secure methods of communication, and a robust navy. These five systems worked together to facilitate and protect British trade.

The British economy was based on a balance of imports and exports whereby imported food and raw material was paid for by the export of goods, services, and capital.[3] Imported food provided more than half of an average Briton's daily calories. The government protected fish, fresh milk, and vegetables from foreign competition to ensure their abundant production in Great Britain. Only about half of Britain's meat, cheese, butter, and eggs were produced domestically. All tea, sugar, and coffee were imported, as was 85 percent of all wheat and flour consumed in the home islands.

Grain made up the bulk of the working class diet, so its loss would have been particularly troubling. This was the driving force behind the study published by the Royal Commission on the Supply of Food and Raw Material in Time of War. In 1905, the commission released its findings in the *Economic Journal*, making them public reading for citizen and enemy alike.[4] The commissioners reported that other European powers had stockpiled grain but they were not in favor of doing so in Great Britain largely because wheat was available from multiple sources year-round; the Argentine harvest sold in February, India's in May, and Russia's large harvest came on the market in October, so regardless of the time of year, wheat could always be purchased somewhere.[5] Although this statement was true, wheat was not always available everywhere. It became available from specific sources at predictable times, which made supplies vulnerable to interdiction in wartime. Loss of grain supplies would directly affect other food sources. The livestock for domestic milk and meat depended on imported grain for its food.[6]

Argentina, Australia, Canada, and the United States all shipped wheat to Britain, but in Liverpool's futures market, Russia was Britain's most important supplier before 1914. In a general European war, the Russian and Danube region wheat harvests might be cut off completely. Because tensions in Europe threatened the loss of these sources of grain several times in the early 1900s, Great Britain had encouraged wheat production from sources outside Europe.[7] Because the new wheat sources lay farther away, however, importing it would impose increased strains on shipping resources. Longer voyages meant that a ship could make fewer trips in a season, thus hauling the same tonnage of grain from a distant source required more ships. Historian Avner Offer noted that somewhat surprisingly, the longer transit had the effect of mitigating the problem of storing wheat:

> Despite having to import four-fifths of its bread grains, Britain held a domestic stockpile that sometimes (especially towards the end of the harvest year) fell below seven weeks supply. By drawing on the staggered harvest of its different suppliers, on the American, Indian, and Russian winter—and spring—wheat harvest in one half of the year and on Australian, and Argentinean during the second half, Britain simply kept much of [its] stocks on the grainfields themselves. Three to seven weeks supply [was] afloat on merchant ships bound for Britain, which served, in effect as floating warehouses.[8]

A similar situation surrounded imported sugar, which British citizens considered an essential food item. The United Kingdom was the world's principal consumer of imported sugar, deriving 54 percent of its supply from German and Austro-Hungarian sugar beets. This source, unsurprisingly, became unavailable at the beginning of the Great War. As a consequence, shipping availability dictated that most sugar bound for the United Kingdom would come from the West Indies rather than the more distant East Indies.[9] Still the trip from the West Indies to English ports was far longer than that from a German port. Thus the rerouted sugar trade had the same effect on shipping as wheat. To import Britain's accustomed amount of sugar from the West Indies required more ships and generally higher freight rates. An even longer journey from the East Indies would tie up even larger numbers of ships. Hence the market shifted to the West Indies.

For British trade and security, it mattered immensely when and where food and raw materials were produced. In a farsighted move, Prime Minister A. J. Balfour created the Committee of Imperial Defence in 1902 to consider complex issues affecting imperial security. The committee consisted of the heads of most cabinet offices so that the various government departments could act in concert on the great issues of their time. It could also form various ad hoc and permanent subcommittees to investigate specific issues and make recommendations for the full cabinet to consider. The Committee of Imperial Defence produced "Supplies in Time of War," a study on wartime trade. The report, which appeared in February 1914, discussed the types and amounts of foodstuffs, raw materials, and manufactured articles that came into the United Kingdom via the Baltic and North Seas countries and from Mediterranean countries (including food and materials from India and Australia shipped via the Suez Canal).[10] Since there were no comparable studies done for Atlantic, Pacific, or Cape Horn routes, this report indicates that the committee was particularly concerned about the possibility of war with Germany or the Triple Alliance (Germany, Austria-Hungary, and Italy). The report also demonstrated the extent of British dependence on certain imports and how its dependence affected trade patterns.

"Supplies in Time of War" confirmed that more than half of British sugar originated in central Europe and was transported via the Baltic and North Seas. The same was true for butter, margarine, and condensed milk. Significantly more than a third of British-consumed yeast products, eggs, and bacon arrived via this route. From Mediterranean countries, Great Britain received more than half of its imported corn (for feeding livestock), half of its wine, and another 20 percent of its condensed milk. In total, Great Britain depended on these two routes for more than half of its corn, butter, margarine, and eggs; for condensed milk and sugar, more than 70 percent.

The report also presented evidence that only 14 percent of British wheat and flour transited the North Sea (1.7 percent) or the Mediterranean (12.3 percent).[11] This means that Russia was not one of Britain's substantial grain providers, because grain from Russia bound for Great Britain would have primarily originated from ports in the Black Sea, Sea of Azov via the Mediterranean, and to a lesser extent, the Baltic and North Seas. Those implications are at odds with the report of the Royal Commission on Supplies of Food. This is explained by the fact that wheat exports from Russia to Great Britain had declined steadily since 1904, when the Royal Commission had conducted its study. Data for the Committee of Imperial Defence report was taken from 1911. The data indicating that Russian wheat was important in the Liverpool futures market reflects how much Russian wheat was available for purchase, not that it was in fact purchased for consumption in Great Britain. By 1911 Russian wheat exports to Great Britain accounted for only 15.7 percent of the total wheat Russia sent abroad. This commodity had been specifically grown and marketed to supply a continental European market, with the most significant quantities destined for France, Italy, and the Netherlands.[12]

Britons depended nearly as much on Baltic and North Sea countries and Mediterranean countries for raw materials as they did for food. The British imported more than 86 percent of their flax. They used spun flax fibers to make small line and fine lace, while coarse fibers were used for rope and heavy line. Britain imported 100 percent of its esparto, which was chiefly used with wood pulp for manufacturing fine-quality paper for books. Britain also imported more than 60 percent of timber and wood. Pit timber from the Baltic was used for mine shaft structural support by the coal industry. Moreover, Britain imported more than 50 percent of its required seed oils and 33 percent of its iron ore. This list represented only those items that would be lost if trade were interrupted from either the Baltic and North Seas and Mediterranean routes.[13] For physical reasons, many other raw materials, including cotton, silk, jute, petroleum, India rubber, and tobacco, were not produced in Great Britain.[14] The country imported about three-quarters of its total consumption of wool, timber, hides, and leather.

The steel sector was entirely dependent on imported materials. Engineers in the United Kingdom believed that to produce superior steel, iron ore had to be phosphorus free. All domestic iron ore, however, contained phosphorus. Thus, imported iron ore of a superior quality accounted for more than 40 percent of the pig iron produced in Great Britain. Moreover, steel making required manganese, which also had to be imported.

In many cases, Great Britain derived the raw materials on which it relied from only a few points of origin: nearly all cotton came from the United States; flax, for linen products, originated in Russia; jute, the key fiber in burlap gunnysacks used to package goods for transport, came exclusively from India; silk originated in China; India rubber came from Brazil; petroleum was produced mainly in Russia and the United States.[15]

Relying on a few sources for essential raw materials placed British trade at risk. A December 1914 report by the Board of Trade concerning the availability of pit timber, which served for props in coal mining, reflected the same conclusions as the earlier Committee of Imperial Defence report. The Board of Trade pointed out that more than 60 percent of timber was imported from the Baltic region. At the same time, coal was one of Great Britain's most important exports, but Britons depended on imported timber to shore up their mines, as well as imported grain to feed the coal miners. The report showed that because imported timber came mainly from the Baltic region, Germany might be able to completely stop exports via the Baltic Sea. The outbreak of war validated that concern.

All British imports of pit timber after September 1, 1914, barely kept pace with consumption. Increased supplies came from Norway, Spain, and Portugal, while still more timber was obtained from France. Britain also sought additional sources to mitigate the risk associated with the loss of trade via the Baltic Sea. Across the Atlantic, Canada and Newfoundland could provide ample supplies, but like transporting food from farther afield, going across the ocean for timber meant fewer annual trips and more ships to import the same tonnage of timber.[16]

Great Britain also imported significant amounts of manufactured goods via the Baltic and North Seas. Steel billets and crude zinc imports exceeded 50 percent of total British imports of these goods. Cotton goods from the Baltic region exceeded 80 percent, with cotton trimmings and dyed cotton piece goods at about 86 percent. Britain imported more than 50 percent of its silk ribbon from the Baltics and more than 82 percent of its coal tar dye. Most paper for wrapping and packing came from this region as well. Dressed skins and furs were also predominately from the Baltics as were toys and games.[17]

Beyond demonstrating how much Great Britain depended on imports, these figures also show that the British Empire was not a closed economic system whereby the metropole received raw materials from its colonies and then exported finished goods to them. Many foodstuffs and raw materials essential for British survival came from sources outside the empire. Moreover, the British exported most of their goods to destinations outside the empire.

To pay for imports, Great Britain relied on exports, payment for various services (such as shipping and insurance), and interest on investments. In addition, Britain's industries provided employment for the bulk of British subjects. Without exports, a typical Briton's livelihood would have been threatened.[18] It is not surprising then that Great Britain's share of exports for 1913 was 13 percent of the value of the world's total. Europe constituted Britain's oldest market and remained its largest and most stable.[19] For the decade 1904 to 1914, Belgium, France, Germany, and the Netherlands ranked as Britain's steadiest customers, absorbing about 35.5 percent of the kingdom's visible exports, meaning goods that can be touched and seen, as opposed to capital, which is an invisible export. Australia, North America, and South America took another third of British exports. The remainder streamed to the rest of the world.[20]

Another analyst, assessing British exports differently, showed that those for 1913 broke down as roughly 34 percent going to continental Europe, 37 percent to destinations in the British Empire, and the remaining 29 percent to the rest of the world.[21] By either method, the share of British exports to Europe exceeded a third of the total, and more than 60 percent of British exports were to customers outside the empire. This demonstrates that global, and particularly continental, trade was necessary to sustain Great Britain's economy.

On the continent itself, Germany controlled the preponderance of trade with Austria-Hungary, Belgium, Bohemia, Denmark, the Netherlands, Norway, Russia, Sweden, and Switzerland. German trade dominated in these countries because of interior lines and extensive rail networks that made transport costs cheaper than those of competitors. Bulgaria, France, Greece, Italy, Portugal, and Spain traded most with Great Britain because access was easiest by sea, and shipping was the cheapest transport.[22] While Belgium, France, Germany, and the Netherlands industrialized, they accounted for more than half of Britain's sales to Europe, totaling approximately 18 percent of all British exports.[23]

Coal, Britain's most abundant raw material, constituted 10 percent of its aggregate exports, while manufactured exports accounted for 78.8 percent. In order of monetary importance, the latter goods were cotton, iron and steel, wool, and machinery. Cotton products, the largest group in this category, made up 24 percent of exports.[24]

Great Britain's considerable exports, valued in 1913 at £525,000,000 were well below the value of its imports, valued at £659,000,000. These values represent visible imports and exports.[25] During the three years immediately preceding the Great War, the average value of goods annually imported into the United Kingdom for home consumption was £623,000,000, which includes about £263,000,000 for food, drink, and tobacco and £205,000,000 for raw materials used in factories. Exported produce and manufactures totaled nearly £489,000,000 annually. The difference, about £134,000,000 annually, was made up for through services and income on investments. A considerable part of the £623,000,000 worth of goods consumed in Great Britain was received as payment for interest on British investments abroad or in return for shipping, banking, and insurance services rendered to foreigners. This means that the actual value of services and investments exceeded the £134,000,000 figure. In addition, foreign and colonial produce valued at £108,000,000 a year was consigned to Great Britain and subsequently reexported to other destinations.[26]

To the visible commodities and goods bartered, one must add invisible imports and exports, that is, non-merchandise items, mainly of capital and services. Great Britain's largest invisible source of income came from foreign investment, while the second largest income flow derived from the merchant marine carrying cargoes for foreign businesses. The third largest, actually an invisible export, was capital in the form of loans made to other nations and foreign businesses.[27]

C. Ernest Fayle, in his history of oceanic trade during the Great War, observes, "It was only by the uninterrupted flow of exports that imports could be paid for, and unemployment and distress amongst the industrial population avoided, without incurring crushing indebtedness to the producing countries."[28] Great Britain owed a great deal of its power to the fact that it was a lender country rather than a debtor country, the key point being that the British economy was solvent because of income generated from services connected to trade. Shipping services, whether freight or passenger, were paid for at once. Thus the income generated by the merchant marine could be turned around immediately to pay for more imports. Other smaller sources in this category included insurance premiums, credit interest, fees generated from sales transactions in various commodity exchanges, and fees for other services, such as telegraphic communications.

International credit was an essential lubricant to trade. Given the volume of global trade, the capital held by merchants was relatively small compared to the value of the goods bartered. Growers still sought to be paid at harvest time or soon thereafter, while consumers were only willing to pay when goods were delivered. Shipping between ports of origin and market usually took weeks. To bridge the gap between when growers needed to be paid and when consumers bought goods, bankers and large discount houses provided credit through a mechanism called a bill of exchange.

The purchase price of any cargo resided in the bill of exchange, which had for its collateral a hold against the bill of lading and the insurance policy for the cargo. Bills of exchange might be held in many countries having little to do with the point or origin or final destinations of the cargo and might each have passed through several financiers in the adjustment of international exchanges. Creditors gained their principal back plus interest on the sale of the cargo, or in the event of loss, when the insurance policy was paid. There were very few cases where the merchant or a single entity (such as a grower) wholly owned a cargo; at any given time, the greatest proportion of cargoes afloat belonged to the holders of the discounted bills of exchange. Great Britain held a surplus of capital and was a major stakeholder in the international credit market.[29] Moreover, insurance generated considerable income. The London insurance market covered most cargoes carried in foreign merchant vessels.[30]

Loans were different. When Great Britain made payment to a country as a loan or extended credit for a business venture, that investment typically would not produce a return for several years or even several decades. Such investment income was the result of repayment of the balance plus profit from interest or profit from dividends gained in foreign business. In this, British investors dominated. In 1914, British overseas investments totaled $19.5 billion. This represented about 43 percent of the world's total foreign investment.[31] As Britain increasingly spent investment income to pay for imports, less capital was available to reinvest in the form of new loans.[32] Such a practice tends to shrink future income from investments. Great Britain's future economic vitality would increasingly depend on a healthy and growing service industry.

The flow of goods and finance for services rendered was tied to the types of ships available, seasons, and trade routes. The steamships worldwide that made overseas transport possible in the early twentieth century numbered only about 8,000. In addition to these larger transoceanic ships, there were slightly more than 14,000 smaller ships engaged in coastal trade, but incapable of making overseas voyages. In all cases, vessels plying the seas flying the British flag outnumbered those of other nations. The proportion of ships greater than 1,600 gross tons that were British owned totaled 49.4 percent in number and 51.7 percent by tonnage. In ocean-going ships less than 1,600 gross tons, the British share was 42.3 percent in number and 36.2 percent by tonnage. As a proportion of total oceangoing ships, the British held 45 percent of them and 49.1 percent of the world's carrying capacity. Britain's nearest competitor was Germany, which held less than one-quarter as much shipping as did Great Britain.[33]

The consequence of uneven shipping distribution was that most industrialized nations depended on foreign shipping—the preponderance being British—to conduct their trade. For example, in peacetime 60 to 70 percent of French imports and exports came and left by sea. Of this seaborne trade, about 60 percent of the imports (36 percent of total trade) traveled in merchant vessels under foreign registry. In a similar vein, foreign-flagged vessels carried about 40 percent of French exports (25 percent of total trade). The remainder of French trade, 30 to 40 percent, moved via land routes. Most of overland trade to and from France could be cut in the event of a war with Germany and Austria-Hungary. In such a case, France's dependence on seaborne trade would become more acute.

Russia, even more so than France, relied on foreign merchant vessels to carry its trade, while Belgium leaned almost totally on foreign vessels for trade. With so many nations dependent on maritime commerce, British shipping operated globally. The historian Fayle argues that British shipping was only slightly less important to Great Britain's allies and trading partners than it was to the British. All nations depended to varying degrees on seaborne trade, and none of them possessed a merchant marine of its own sufficient to carry it out. Only the British merchant marine held a surplus of shipping that could be withdrawn from general service to carry its own trade should an emergency develop. Other nations relied on the British merchant marine's ability to sustain the general carrying trade to facilitate their own participation in the global economy.[34]

The ships used to transport the world's goods varied considerably in size, speed, and purpose. Not all vessels had refrigeration or the configuration necessary to safely carry liquids. Only a few concentrated exclusively on carrying passengers. Many carried passengers as well as cargo, but most were strictly cargo ships. When one ship dropped from a route, another ship could not necessarily replace its cargo-carrying capacity.

In general, the merchant ships engaged in overseas trade in 1914 fell into two categories: liners and tramps, the latter also known as general traders. Speed varied from the swift, large liners, which could exceed 20 knots, to the slow tramp steamer, some of which could barely attain 7 knots. About a third of the vessels, comprising half the tonnage available in 1914, belonged to the liner type. Liners traveled regular routes according to consistent schedules. The practice of keeping to a schedule between specific ports made liners suitable for transporting passengers as well as cargo. Liners carrying passengers and a variety of cargoes were, as a rule, the largest, fastest, and best-built ships. By keeping to regular ports on a schedule, liners could maintain stable rates over periods of time. This was particularly advantageous to merchants who required only a portion of a ship's capacity to transport their cargoes to market. In addition to regularly shipping manufactured goods, such as cotton items and machinery, liners could easily meet the transportation requirements for such food items as cheese, eggs, meats, condensed milk, and grain.

To maintain consistent shipping rates, owners of the liners required consistent customers and efficient operation. As a hedge against competition from tramp steamers, owners of the liners would form mutual associations, called conferences, and would often offer deferred rebates to customers who shipped exclusively with them or another liner of their international conference. At the end of the rebate period, customers who shipped exclusively with the conference's liners would see a substantial portion of their freight charges refunded to them. A single shipment made on a merchant vessel outside the conference could suffice to forfeit the rebate. This practice caused customers needing regular shipments of part cargoes to rely on liners to meet their needs and had the effect of keeping liners' holds filled with such cargoes from several reliable customers. The international conferences controlled about one-half of the world's transport under this form of limited financial control, enough to sustain regular service but also to allow for effective competition. Fewer than twenty large companies owned these liners. In contrast, a tramp might be individually owned or make up part of hundreds of variously sized companies.[35]

Tramps were twice as numerous as liners, but smaller and generally slower ships. They made up the other half of available tonnage. Tramps would typically ship bulk cargoes, such as ore, coal, sugar, and timber. They could shift routes as needed to meet market demands and seasonal requirements.[36] When a harvest was due to enter the market, brokers would generate a demand for shipping that increased freight rates. The rates for tramps reflected these changes most quickly. Available shipping then moved to the region in response to higher freights. Increased shipping in a region generated increased fuel consumption there as well. The harvest signaled the approach of winter and cooler temperatures. Colliers, the ships transporting coal for industries, heating homes, and fueling other ships, also moved about to meet the fluctuating demand.

The freight market allocated the world's tonnage by an automatic process operating outside of government control through a system of exchanges. This system secured shipping for supplies without any overarching understanding or survey of the world's need. As historian J. A. Salter explained, "All that the system needed in order to allot the transport exactly to the supplies for which there was the strongest effective demand was that the offers of merchants with goods and owners with ships were brought together in the big freight markets, such as the Baltic in London, or the Collier Exchange in Cardiff. The brokers in these exchanges would know the current freights offering in their own line of business, and something about the seasonal changes likely to raise or lower them in the near future."[37]

The various commodities exchanges for wool, wheat, coal, cotton, and so on estimated the markets for their commodities and made purchases, the majority of which would be completed with a bill of exchange. Then brokers would look for the best rates of available tonnage through freight exchanges. Knowing the strengths of their markets, some were willing to pay a premium rate for freight while others waited for rates to fall by either canceling or postponing shipment. The brokers bid for freight in tonnages for specific quantities, dates, and prices. Then freight exchange agents accepted on behalf of owners with disposable tonnage those bids within specified conditions that offered the best rates. By virtue of the exchange systems for commodities and tonnage, those cargoes that consumers were most willing to pay for got priority movement; those that consumers wanted least were left behind.[38] Tramps moved about in response to the best prices to keep the system going. Liners also adjusted routes based on the exchange mechanics of consumer demand, only much more slowly. Tramps provided for surge in shipping demand and liners made the system less volatile while meeting most routine shipping requirements.

Neither the merchant nor the broker knew the entire world system, nor did they set the prices. They were only part of the mechanism by which the world's economic demand affected adjustments.[39] The freight allocation was set up to maximize profit and serve the economic interest of merchants, ship owners, financiers, and insurers. In other words, the system supported private economic interests, but not necessarily the public interest.

Because of the value and nature of cargoes transported, some trade routes were more essential to the British economy than others. The North Atlantic route was the most important. It had branch routes to the Mediterranean and the Caribbean and West Indies. Of nearly equal importance was the Oriental route—from Australia and India through the Suez Canal, the Mediterranean Sea, and the Strait of Gibraltar to the home islands. The third most important was the route from South America. This route went north from Cape Horn along the coast of Argentina and Brazil. It also connected trans-Pacific routes from New Zealand.

The so-called Cape route, named for the Cape of Good Hope, at the southern tip of Africa, was important for trade to African colonies and some outbound goods headed to Australia. Its importance declined when the Suez Canal opened, but if the canal were to be closed—thus affecting the Oriental route—the significance of the Cape route would be revived. From the British perspective, the North Pacific, the Far East to America, and Australia to America routes were the least important.[40]

Every one of these trade routes touched somewhere on a portion of the British Empire, which consisted of vast land tracts in the Northern Hemisphere (India, Canada, Halifax, and Nova Scotia) and Southern Hemisphere (Australia, New Zealand, and South Africa) in addition to hundreds of islands around the globe that served as coaling stations and connections for underwater telegraph cables. Admiral Fisher's five geostrategic keys offered effective control over most of, but not all, the important sea routes. The Strait of Malacca, near Singapore, and the Suez Canal, connecting the Mediterranean and Red Seas, were adjacent to the important Oriental route. The Strait of Gibraltar, separating the Mediterranean from the Atlantic Ocean near the coastal African route, commanded all trade to and from the Mediterranean and transiting north-south along the Atlantic coast of Africa. The Cape of Good Hope dominated all shipping traffic around South Africa. Fisher's last key, the Strait of Dover, easily allowed naval forces to prevent coastal traffic up and down the western European coast and control or block all traffic in and out of the United Kingdom's key port, London.

Great Britain had but little power to control trade between the Americas and continental Europe. The Royal Navy simply could not interfere with trade where it had no presence and no bases, but the British did have a naval presence in important locations that Fisher omitted in his boast—the Falkland Islands, near Cape Horn; the West Indies stations (which could control traffic into the Caribbean Sea and the proposed Panama Canal, which officially opened on August 15, 1914). The British Empire also extended into the Northern Pacific with bases at Esquimalt, on the west coast of Canada, and at Wei-Hai-Wei and Hong Kong, in China. These Pacific possessions along with Australia and New Zealand were obviously important connectors on the Oriental, Far East to America, and Australia to America routes. The trade routes connecting countries across the Pacific Ocean may not have figured as significantly in British trade, but they were certainly important to Japan, Russia, and the United States.

A purposefully designed global communications system, with submarine telegraph cable and later wireless telegraphy as the backbone, connected the British Empire geographically and economically. Great Britain's policy-making elite recognized early on the strategic benefits of what originally was strictly a commercial operation. The carefully planned communications network facilitated not only trade, but military operations as well. By 1910, the Colonial Defence Committee, a subcommittee of the Committee of Imperial Defence, was adamant that "[t]he maintenance of submarine cable communications throughout the world in time of war is of the highest importance to the strategic and commercial interests of every portion of the British Empire."[41]

The first cables across the English Channel were for private, commercial use. Britons welcomed the electromagnetic telegraph as another innovation that contributed to progress and trade growth.[42] Stockbrokers, businessmen, journalists, and diplomats all benefited from rapid long-distance communications.[43] British companies were the foremost financiers of the new commercial network centered on London. The cables increased the city's dominance in the service industries—such as banking, insurance, business, and news—that relied on rapid and reliable communications. "It was an advantage," observed historian Paul M. Kennedy, "not lightly to be thrown away."[44]

As early as 1898, Great Britain held a preponderance of underwater telegraphic communications with more than 60 percent of the world's cables. Much in the same way that Great Britain dominated shipping, it also possessed an overwhelming capacity in terms of specialized ships and expertise to lay and maintain cables. British cable ships numbered twenty-eight, with no more than thirteen of these specialized vessels sprinkled among the rest of the world's nations. Only one other power, France, with five cable ships, had the potential to build an extensive communications network. So dominant was Britain in cable laying and repair that most other nations simply relied on British companies for this service.

Because of British preponderance in cable ships and so little capability throughout the rest of the world, it would take an impossible combination of foreign powers to isolate the United Kingdom from communications with its colonies.[45] This advantage greatly increased the security of Britain's global business communications. By May 1902, British-owned cables carried 80 percent of the world's telegraphic traffic outside Europe.[46] Other powers of course noticed and resented Great Britain's control over communications. The French government, when beginning its own cable-laying program in November 1900, noted, "England owes her influence in the world perhaps more to her cable communications than to her navy. She controls the news, and makes it serve her policy and commerce in a marvelous manner."[47] A modern counterpart exists in U.S. dominance over the underlying technology that connects computers to form the Internet. Many foreign nations also resented that control, which as of September 2009 was beginning to be eased.[48]

Dominating commercial communications still did not provide the security British cabinet members, diplomats, and military leadership desired. Most of the commercial cables followed the trade routes, connected important commercial centers, and ended in foreign capitals. Many countries participated in the system, even defraying portions of the cost, and enjoyed its commercial benefits. The access and openness of the system was what made it commercially successful, but that also made information transmitted via the cables at each telegraph station available to persons of unknown loyalty.

To provide secure and reliable communications, the British government determined to build a system that only touched land at locations fully controlled by it. The scheme, named the "all red" route, likely because of the famous

1897 map of the world that showed British possessions in red, broke with the earlier practice of laying cable along commercial routes to weave the telegraph network into one international system. From this decision, the network evolved into parallel networks where an all-red route existed alongside a commercial system. The goal was for every important British colony or naval base to possess one cable that did not touch a foreign shore. If this were impossible for a particular location, then cables would be connected through a friendly neutral. Otherwise each colony or base would have as many alternative cables as commercial considerations rendered expedient.

Government all-red cables were subsidized with funds from the public coffers and generally traversed long distances. Commercial cables were normally unsubsidized and were shorter.[49] The British fully anticipated that an enemy would cut their cables at the outbreak of war. This consideration led Whitehall to spend millions subsidizing British cable companies to lay cable and maintain stores of spare cable overseas for repairs.[50] By 1911, the all-red system was worldwide.[51]

Calculating that an enemy could not easily cut British communications, the Colonial Defence Committee had decided in 1898 that in times of war it would be useful to cut enemy cables. This committee comprehensively listed all the alternative routes for communications on British and foreign cables for all the feasible permutations of belligerents and neutrals. Where a cable landed in a British possession, it would of course not be necessary to cut the cable since British censorship would effectively isolate the line. With all this information, the committee determined the "number of cutting operations required to isolate each country."[52]

By 1911, Whitehall considered the only real prospect of a war being one against Germany, and therefore other members of the Triple Alliance and the possible addition of Turkey. This simplified matters for British planners. Germany realized that its communications were at risk and sought to improve its own cable network. Without the acquisition of more colonies, however, it was not possible for Germany to create its own version of an all-red route. To mitigate against this, Germany placed its lines to the extent possible between neutral stations. This served to avoid dependence on the British and to preserve the cables in times of war.[53] From the British perspective a combination of cable cutting and censorship would mostly eliminate the hazards and expense of assaulting enemy stations.

British military planners believed that Berlin relied on a Russian line to communicate with the German naval base at Tsingtao and French lines to link to the German colony of Togoland. If France remained neutral, Germany could connect through it to maintain telegraphic communication with the United States. If Germany were at war with France and Russia, and Great Britain were allied with the two of them, effective action against Germany's cables at the island of Yap, in the Pacific, and Germany's cables emanating from Emden would, according to historian Paul M. Kennedy, "isolate Germany from practically the whole world, outside Europe."[54]

The Standing Subcommittee of the Committee of Imperial Defence warned that cutting cables between an enemy and a neutral would probably be followed by reprisals. Nevertheless, the subcommittee approved cutting cables in wartime, arguing:

> But even if the United Kingdom abstained from cable cutting, it would probably have no effect on influencing Germany, who in view of the great strategic value to this country of the cable system connecting the overseas dominions, would undoubtedly do all in [its] power to render useless as many of the cables as possible.
>
> In these circumstances, and seeing that there are places which it would be desirable for naval and military reasons to cut off from telegraphic communications in a war with Germany, or with Germany and [its] allies, the Subcommittee are of the viewpoint that the right to cut cables, whether connecting neutral ports or not, should be exercised whenever the exigencies of war demand it.[55]

But the subcommittee also noted the need for discretion because cutting of certain cables, such as the one connecting the United States and Germany via the Azores, would pique the powerful neutral nation across the ocean.[56]

New technology rapidly rendered British scheming over these submarine cables obsolete. In 1897, Guglielmo Marconi demonstrated a machine that made wireless high-frequency radio communication practical. British interest in wireless telegraphy was that it promised the ability to direct movements of warships over long distances, something that could not be done with underwater telegraph cables. The new wireless telegraphic technology also presented a problem in that other powers would also immediately adopt the technology.[57] Once wireless communications matured, cable cutting would no longer sever other powers' international communication (particularly with their fleets), so assaulting enemy stations had to be reconsidered.

No one at the Royal Navy was more interested in the potential of wireless telegraphic communication than Admiral Fisher, who had become First Sea Lord in 1904. Fisher was enthusiastic about wireless, and his administration invested heavily in the technology and the supporting infrastructure to create what was at the time the world's most extensive network.[58] Fisher began outfitting British warships with wireless sets and constructing navy-owned wireless stations. The initial equipment consisted of 1.5-kilowatt transmitters for smaller cruisers and more powerful, longer-range 14-kilowatt sets for battle cruisers. When integrated with the submarine telegraphic cable system, the limited range of wireless transmitters could be surmounted, and the network would have built-in redundancy making it suitable for wartime service. Global communications could continue even with a loss of several stations.[59]

By late 1904, less than half the fleet was wireless capable. Moreover, the navy possessed only its original eight short-range (fifty miles) naval wireless stations. Until the naval budget permitted more construction, the Admiralty would rely on privately owned wireless transmitters to meet its wartime needs. As an interim measure, in 1903 the navy leased time on the Marconi Company's 35-kilowatt transmitter in Poldhu, Cornwall, that had sufficient power to bridge the Atlantic.[60] The Royal Navy initially paid £20,000 with an annual subsidy of £5,000 payable for eleven years. Under the terms of the contract, the navy acquired the use of all developments and improvements made by the company and special rights to use Marconi's facilities for communications.[61]

The Admiralty began encouraging British companies to develop wireless networks, reasoning that the navy would commandeer them in times of war. Starting in 1901, prior to Fisher's tenure, the Admiralty had secretly paid Lloyd's of London a subsidy to upgrade the latter's global network of semaphore signal stations with a wireless installation at each site. Each sat where it could see and communicate with passing ships and nearby an underwater telegraph station where information could be passed back to London.[62] Fisher worked to establish closer links with Lloyd's, which agreed to build four overseas wireless stations at locations that the Navy requested when the treasury denied the latter funds to build its own; the Royal Navy secretly subsidized two-thirds of the capital cost to build the stations. In return for the navy's capital, Lloyd's agreed that the Admiralty could use the network when necessary. It copied telegrams from the signal stations to the Naval Intelligence Division (NID), and the Admiralty covertly established a direct phone line to Lloyd's.[63]

Fisher realized that the remarkable improvements in communications capabilities had fundamentally altered the conduct of naval warfare. To exploit the potential that would be gained by Britain's lock on global communications, Fisher first had to build the necessary infrastructure. By 1906, the Admiralty could keep in contact with large warships operating within 500 miles of Gibraltar, Malta, and Cleethorpes and any ship with a transmitter within 100 miles of its overseas bases. The Admiralty still relied on submarine cables to connect bases outside the 100-mile range. In 1908, upgrades to the Cleethorpes and Horsea stations extended wireless range to 1,000 miles.[64]

Around 1908, a crude but workable system was in place for directing Royal Navy operations. With it, the Admiralty could gather, process, and apply global intelligence to control naval operations centrally in London. The communications network became essential for imperial defense and commerce protection.[65] This process constituted the first global command and control system of its kind.[66] According to historian Nicholas A. Lambert, the system made London "the commercial hub of the world."[67] Britain dominated banking, insurance, and shipping—that is, industries that flourished on information. The Royal Navy benefitted from the information the cable and wireless network provided, and British trade benefitted from the security provided by the Royal Navy. Nearly two years into the Great War, the naval strategic wireless system was complete and independent of the imperial wireless chain.[68]

The intelligence system using the global communication network eventually tapped many information sources, including private parties benefitting from the trade protection the navy provided. The local managers of British-owned cable companies would forward copies of any foreign military and diplomatic communications relayed over their lines.[69] The Board of Trade pooled economic intelligence with Admiralty intelligence. The Post Office, which controlled most of the world's telegraphic communications, shared intercepted and decrypted foreign communications with British intelligence services. The NID Trade and Intelligence divisions pooled their efforts and daily created a record of every ship of war, foreign and British, worldwide. Moreover, they tracked some 100 ships an enemy might likely convert into auxiliary cruisers.[70]

Sighting reports—from regional intelligence officers, customs, consular, and diplomatic sources, and, of course, the Lloyd's signal stations—were collated with other relevant data and the results plotted on a large wall chart in what quickly became known as the "war room." This was not all. War room plotting factored in predictions of likely movements based on analysis of ship logistics. The Admiralty also tracked the world's colliers, about 75 percent of them being British; coal supply largely governed the destination of any ship and assisted the Admiralty in forecasting a potential enemy's strategy.[71] In 1905, the plot was updated daily; in 1908, every four hours; and by 1914, close to real time.[72]

Wireless telegraphy helped British war vessels acting in concert run down threats to commerce. Merchants also benefitted because wireless hastened warnings of danger to British shipping in particular theaters.[73] Because the British were heavily invested in international credit and marine insurance, early warning would seem to be a boon; a threat to trade anywhere affected the credit and insurance sectors of the British economy. The communications network, however, was a double-edged sword. It warned the navy early on of threats, but those working in the credit and insurance markets would also immediately know of threats and possibly react by withholding their services. Loss of trade anywhere decreased revenues, increased insurance rates, and created scarcity of certain commodities.[74]

The marvelous communications revolution that provided the British with so many benefits also enabled their enemies to warn their shipping that war had broken out and that the moment had arrived for mounting guns and operating against British commerce. Moreover, it assisted commerce raiders to locate and intercept lucrative targets while avoiding British cruisers.[75] On the whole, advantage accrued to the nation that could maintain its own global communications while simultaneously vitiating an enemy's network.

The Royal Navy not only had to be sized appropriately to protect Britain's global commerce, but also to defend the British Isles from invasion and safeguard overseas territories from attack.[76] The Naval Defence Act of 1889 defined the problem in terms of a fleet of battleships numerous enough to defeat the combined fleets of the second- and third-ranking naval powers, the so-called two-power standard. The reasoning was that the battleship fleet would command the seas in home waters and suffice to deter invasion. The imperial territories and trade routes would be protected by flotillas of cruisers, gunboats, and second-tier, obsolescent battleships. Beginning in 1895, the British government also determined that the Royal Navy required twice as many armored cruisers as the number possessed by the second-ranking naval power.[77]

Since 1890, the French had developed improved armored cruisers specifically to compete with and overwhelm the lighter British cruiser used for trade protection outside European waters. The French plan called for systematically deploying these cruisers from overseas bases against British commerce and the use of greater speed to avoid engaging superior British naval forces. By 1900, both France and Russia had significant numbers of cruisers and building programs for more such ships. Because Britain maintained a two-power standard, the French and Russian programs stressed British budgets. Four years later, in 1904, Fisher believed that the two-power standard was unaffordable. He also concluded that safeguarding oceanic trade was the Royal Navy's biggest strategic problem in the event of war with France and Russia.[78] In defending Britain itself, Fisher was satisfied with mutual sea denial in home waters—in other words, Britain could not invade nor could Britain's enemies invade the British Isles. This freed up the bulk of the Royal Navy's modern ships for service at the periphery of the empire.[79]

For example, Fisher surmised that Britain's rivals, France and Russia, would not seek a decisive fleet engagement or attempt to invade the British home islands. Instead, he believed that those two powers would interfere with British trade along imperial trade routes. For developed nations, participation in the global trading system was vital. Fisher, recognizing this, believed that Britain's next war would be more about control of transoceanic trade than traditional sea battles between grand fleets.[80] In 1905, the Board of Admiralty and the cabinet approved recalling older fleet units from overseas stations and replacing them with modern battle cruisers.[81]

Fisher's vision to change from a station fleet system to the battle cruiser concept represented a strategic paradigm shift from forward presence to maneuver. Arthur Wilson, who succeeded Fisher as First Sea Lord, thought that Fisher's ideas to attack an enemy's economy rather than directly attacking its naval power would not be an effective strategy, so he did not fully support Fisher's system. He kept the communications network in place and added to it, as did his two successors. Planning to rely on victory through a decisive battle, however, Wilson built more battleships and cut the submarine and cruiser programs.[82]

With the veritable destruction of Russia's fleets in the Russo-Japanese War in 1905, and an entente with France, the Triple Alliance became the signal factor in British defense planning. The Colonial Defence Committee's report "Principles of Imperial Defence," nevertheless maintained the two-power standard.[83] Thus was the state of the Royal Navy at the beginning of the Great War in 1914. It was not fully committed to Fisher's strategy of maneuver warfare, yet not wholly ready to renounce it for an alternative strategy.

On the eve of war in July 1914, the Royal Navy possessed a comfortable superiority in dreadnought battleships over the German High Seas fleet with twenty-one to the German's thirteen.[84] Added to Britain's modern dreadnoughts were twenty-nine second-tier battleships, ten battle cruisers, about thirty-five modern cruisers of several designs, one hundred fifty other cruisers built prior to 1907, about two hundred destroyers, and various smaller craft. This considerable navy had to prevent invasion and raids against the home islands and overseas territories and protect more than four thousand British-owned ocean-going merchant ships engaged in global trade.

The extent of the British Empire served to promote trade by providing convenient and multiple harbors for refueling, communications, and ship repair. The British Empire possessed key geographical positions astride trade routes, which its naval forces could use as bases from which to operate against enemy trade. The Royal Navy, however, was more interested in protecting Britain's overseas possessions and trade than it was with interfering with enemy trade. By holding vital territory along key trade routes, naval forces could move from one trouble spot to another more quickly than could opposing navies.

The British dominated world trade, accounting for 50 percent of the world's shipping tonnage. Likewise, Britain controlled access to approximately 80 percent of the international communications network. Traders worldwide received the preponderance of their credit and purchased insurance in the London market. British shipping, communications, and financial systems mutually supported each other, but ultimately relied upon the Royal Navy for protection.

British naval strength, however, equaled only the next two naval powers combined. Compared to British advantages in merchant shipping, communications, finance, and geographic position, the Royal Navy's margin of superiority over potential enemies was thin. Moreover, Britain's naval superiority was not solely devoted to protecting international trade but also to preventing invasion at home and protecting imperial possessions abroad. Accomplishing all that was required of the Royal Navy stretched its resources to the limit.

Trade was Great Britain's lifeblood. Fisher's boast that Britain held the keys that could lock up the trade of the world was true, but his strictly geographic and naval interpretation of trade was incomplete. The Royal Navy could have blockaded foreign ports and resorted to commerce raiding to prevent a nation from trading. But Great Britain could also have prevented trade simply by withholding its services—refusing to grant credit or provide insurance, restricting communications, or passing laws forbidding merchant ships from carrying cargoes to and from specific nations. Although the British government could have severely curtailed any nation's trade, to do so would not have been in its economic interest. The more global trade freely circulated, the more Great Britain prospered. When trade suffered anywhere, Great Britain felt it.

2 GERMAN FOREIGN POLICY, 1880 TO 1914

Germany's shift from continental politics to world politics as the basis for its foreign policy fundamentally challenged Great Britain's vital interests. Three key manifestations of Germany's *Weltpolitik* produced threats. First, by building a large navy, Germany created a threat of invasion, bombardment, and blockade of British seaports. Second, by accumulating colonies, Germany threatened to establish naval bases near key shipping lanes that could interfere with Great Britain's imperial trade and communications. Third, Germany developed a fleet of fast, liner merchant ships capable of being transformed into commerce raiders in time of war; merchant ships commissioned as auxiliary cruisers thus gave Germany the potential to disrupt British shipping worldwide.

During Otto von Bismarck's tenure as chancellor, Germany formed an alliance with Austria-Hungary, in 1879. Italy joined it in 1883, as did Romania albeit secretly.[1] When Germany became a major European power, it also acquired the requisite colonies in Africa and the Pacific. From the perspective of other European governments, Bismarck appeared to be following a pattern of colonization: first, provide a pretext for a claim; second, establish a German protectorate; and third, formally annex the territory. Several instances of German expansion fit this pattern, although ministers working on Berlin's Wilhelmstrasse denied any pretext. According to the Wilhelmstrasse's point of view, the flag simply followed trade, extending its protection over a territory inhabited by citizens over which it already had authority.[2] Nevertheless, by the early twentieth century, other European powers had interpreted these signs as Germany's intention to acquire additional colonies.

In November 1882, the German businessman Adolf Luderitz sought imperial permission and protection to establish a trading post for his German West Africa Company along the coast of modern-day Namibia.[3] Once Luderitz had established a presence, the German gunboat SMS *Nautilus* visited the region.[4] Luderitz later sold his interest to the government-chartered German West Africa Company. Meanwhile, Bismarck's son, Herbert Bismarck, negotiated with the British government to establish Germany's undisputed claim to the area. Germany officially claimed the territory in August 1884 and hoisted its flag in a ceremony witnessed by the corvette SMS *Elisabeth*.[5]

In a similar manner, Carl Peters, a German businessman, signed agreements with several chiefs on the African mainland opposite Zanzibar in the Rufiji River region. In March 1885, Germany granted an imperial charter to Peters' German East Africa Company with the intention of converting the region into a German protectorate. The sultan of Zanzibar, who claimed sovereignty over the African coast along the eastern seaboard opposite Zanzibar, protested the Germans' move. Bismarck dispatched a naval squadron that took station within gun range of the sultan's palace and opened negotiations. Despite the overt threat, the sultan only yielded when he lost the support of Britain, which made a deal with Germany to divide the disputed territory between themselves.[6] The European powers signed the Helgoland-Zanzibar treaty in 1890. As part of the agreement, Great Britain ceded Helgoland, an island off the German coast in the North Sea, to Germany in return for control of Zanzibar, the large island directly adjacent to German East Africa's main port, Dar es Salaam. The treaty established the extent of German East Africa and formalized what for five years had been a fait accompli.[7]

In another example, in 1868 the Hamburger Shipping Company had established a trading post at the mouth of a river that is now the location of Duala, present-day Cameroon. In 1884, Germany used this foothold to establish colonies in West Africa. Kaiser Wilhelm I commissioned famed German explorer Gustav Nachtigal to inquire into the condition of commerce in western Africa with a secret mission to annex territory to the German empire. Nachtigal accomplished his mission under the guise of the German West Africa Company, which was granted an imperial charter in 1885. Germany then established a protectorate over the region, which they called Kamerun, ostensibly to guard against British encroachment on German business interests.[8]

In the Pacific, Germany tried to execute the same plan to acquire German New Guinea. In 1884, the imperial-chartered New Guinea Company staked a business claim to the northeastern quarter of the island of New Guinea. Germany attempted to annex the Caroline Islands, portions of the Solomon Islands, and Nauru, but Spain had rights to the chain based on the principle of first European discovery. As a result, Europe's other powers refused to accept Germany's claim. Spain later sold these possessions to Germany, which formally annexed the territories in April 1899.[9]

After 1900, Germany's colonial acquisition slowed because of changes in the chancellor's office. In 1888, Wilhelm II became kaiser after Friedrich III, who had succeeded Wilhelm I, died from cancer three months after his ascension. As chancellor, Bismarck never enjoyed the trust and confidence of Wilhelm II to the same degree that marked his relationship with Wilhelm I. By 1890, the friction between Wilhelm II and his chancellor grew so acute that Bismarck had to resign.[10] Bismarck's replacement, Leo von Caprivi, was moderately successful at managing the German empire. It was Caprivi who secured the 1890 Helgoland-Zanzibar treaty with England. He also added to Germany's colonial territories with a strip of land connecting German Southwest Africa to the Zambezi River, which empties into the Indian Ocean on Africa's east coast.[11] This offered Germany the potential to establish a desirable trade route across central Africa. By this time, European powers surmised that when Germany claimed a business interest in a region, it represented a prelude to annexing the territory. At the same time, German authorities simply believed that government had a duty to follow trade in order to regulate commerce and protect it. In other words, private commercial interests initiated the quest for colonies, not the government.[12]

Beginning in 1897, Kaiser Wilhelm II and several close advisers—Bernhard von Bülow, Alfred von Tirpitz, and Johann von Miquel—pursued a new foreign policy to magnify the greatness of the German nation. The kaiser appointed Bülow as foreign minister, Tirpitz as naval secretary, and Miquel as Prussian minister of finance. The advisers' reenergized approach to foreign policy was in part designed to slake the kaiser's ambition to personally play a major role in world affairs, but they also believed that domestic political divisions would be relieved by convincing the German people of the benefits inherent in establishing a powerful empire.[13]

Berlin's uneasiness with the international status quo stemmed from London's announcement in 1896 that it intended to form a flying naval squadron capable of responding to trouble anywhere in the world. Should the Royal Navy acquire such a squadron, British warships could arrive off Germany's North Sea coast within a day. This concerned the kaiser's advisers, who considered war with Britain a distinct possibility.[14] Germany also desired to break the cycle of diplomacy that had forced Berlin to acquiesce to London's wishes, as had happened when it yielded half of East Africa to England in the showdown with the sultan of Zanzibar. German weakness with respect to the United Kingdom was palpable. The kaiser sorely wanted a way to check the British.[15]

German strategy also had to address the naval problem in the North Sea. It needed to devise a plan with some prospect of success in a war with England with the numeric and geographic balance in the north seas tilted heavily in England's favor.[16] According to the American naval strategist Alfred Thayer Mahan, the weaker naval power should adopt a strategy of *guerre de course,* or war against commerce.[17] In 1897, Tirpitz categorically rejected commerce raiding and proposed instead that Germany build a fleet that could not only defend the German coast but also challenge Great Britain for dominance in the North Sea. Such a fleet would also create the added value of making Germany an attractive alliance partner.[18] This fleet became known as the Risk Fleet, and his naval policy was referred to as risk theory.[19]

Historian Herbert Rosinski sharply criticizes German naval policy in the Tirpitz era, branding the admiral as a man without insight. Citing the results of World War I, Rosinski and others argue that because Germany's High Seas Fleet was effectively blockaded in the North Sea, it could not contribute much to the country's war effort. These scholars claim that the resources Germany used to create the fleet could have been used more profitably to bolster the army.[20] Tirpitz reasoned, however, that Britain's many overseas commitments, and the threats posed to British colonies by the fleets of France and Russia, would force the Royal Navy to disperse its strength. A sizable German fleet poised to threaten the British Isles would therefore present Whitehall with a dilemma: If the Royal Navy had to concentrate in home waters, it would deprive London of the freedom of action to thwart Germany's overseas ambitions. Thus the presence of

Tirpitz's Risk Fleet could deter the British from effectively using their vast naval power. In such a situation, perhaps London's diplomats might concede, without resort to war, to the kaiser's aspirations.[21]

As the sixth strongest naval power, Germany's navy was far weaker than its potential rivals, Great Britain, France, and Russia. Germany, however, desired to alter the status quo. In this respect, several questions are relevant: What size fleet would Germany require to defend itself? What were Germany's requirements to protect its trade? Would a fleet of this size threaten Great Britain?

Guerre de course was initially not a good option for Germany because of its geographic position relative to the British Isles. Great Britain could enforce a blockade against Germany's coast. Moreover, Germany possessed only a few cruisers, and even fewer overseas bases with which to sustain a concerted campaign against British commerce. Even if Germany had built cruisers to raid England's commerce in case of war, the Royal Navy would have blockaded them in the North Sea.[22] The outcome of a naval battle pitting German cruisers against the British Home Fleet, with its impressive line of battleships, would have been certain humiliation for Berlin.

If Great Britain remained neutral in a European war, then Germany would not have to fret over the size of the Royal Navy. In such a case, Germany would require a navy sufficient only to hold off the combined efforts of France and Russia. In fact, Tirpitz claimed that this was the basis for his plans for a battle fleet.[23] Great Britain would use a similar "two-power standard," to justify the size of the Royal Navy. London's rationale held that Great Britain should have a fleet equal in size to the combination of the next two ranking naval powers, France and Russia.[24] If Germany determined that its needs were similar, then it would have to build a navy second only to Britain's.

During this period, Germany's merchant marine grew in proportion to expanding trade. Second in tonnage and numbers only to Great Britain's, Germany's merchant fleet was far larger than those of France and Russia.[25] France had colonies in North Africa, East Asia, and the West Indies that could support its overseas cruisers. This gave Paris the potential to interdict German trade with impunity. Also of importance, British ships carried more goods for France than did French ships.[26] Thus, German retaliation against French commerce raiding was likely to provoke the British because it would probably involve intercepting cargo carried by British ships. For Berlin to protect German trade, it needed cruisers and bases at least equal to those of the French. Irrespective of Great Britain, and because of the Russo-French alliance, the kaiser needed a naval force larger than the French navy to protect German shores and trade. Mahan assessed Germany's naval construction as follows:

> In this direction also we may seek a proper comprehension of what the size of a navy should be. It should be so great, and its facilities for mobilization and for maintenance of supplies should be such, that a foreign country contemplating war should feel instant anxiety because of the immediate danger that would arise from that navy, either to itself, or to its dependencies, or to its commerce. Such effect would be deterrent of war; and to deter is simply to practice diversion in another form. This has been announced, with military brevity and emphasis, as the official purpose of the German government in its naval programme adopted in 1900.[27]

The preamble of the German naval law stated, "Germany must have a fleet of such strength that, even for the mightiest naval power, a war with Germany would involve such risks as to jeopardize its own supremacy."[28] Tirpitz's first priority was to put a battle fleet in the North Sea, but Germany also required bases abroad.[29] The history of Germany's Far East squadron illustrates Berlin's frustration with its dearth of overseas naval facilities.

The Prussian and Chinese governments signed the Treaty of Peking in September 1861. Article 6 of the treaty allowed Prussian warships to operate in Chinese waters to protect trade; Article 10 provided a mandate to protect missionaries. The treaty also warned China that crimes committed against Prussian nationals by Chinese subjects would be met with swift naval retaliation.[30] Even after German unification in 1871, the treaty remained in force. Kaiser Wilhelm II created a cruiser division of four ships under Rear Admiral Paul Hoffman with specific orders to protect German interests and locate sites in China suitable for a German base.

In 1895, Germany revitalized the squadron with modern ships. Without a base of their own, German warships depended for repair and replenishment on facilities provided by the British at Hong Kong, the Chinese at Shanghai, and the Japanese at Nagasaki. During the Sino-Japanese War, the Chinese and Japanese refused logistical services to the German division at Shanghai and

Nagasaki, respectively. Hoffman used this to punctuate to the German Imperial Admiralty their country's need for a base in East Asia. He emphasized that the Japanese and Chinese actions inhibited the cruiser division's ability to protect German interests.

At the end of the Sino-Japanese War, the kaiser had planned to seize Wei-Hai-Wei in the Shantung peninsula to use as a German naval base. When informed that the Japanese intended to occupy it, the kaiser backed away. Kiao-Chou bay, near Tsingtao, had also been considered as a possible base. The location lacked modern infrastructure and was somewhat distant from the inland centers of trade, so Germany would need to build costly facilities and railroads to make it truly useful.

When Tirpitz replaced Hoffman as commander of the cruiser division on June 15, 1896, his orders were to determine a location on the Chinese coast where Germany could establish a permanent military and economic base.[31] Tirpitz's evaluation favored Kiao-Chou. Based on Tirpitz's advice, Wilhelm directed the Admiralty Staff to prepare a plan to seize the location. Germany would begin the operation when a *casus belli* presented a reasonable justification. When Tirpitz read a report in the *North China Daily News* that China was preparing to lease Kiao-Chou to Russia, Germany shelved its plan to seize the port.

The kaiser summoned Tirpitz to Berlin before he could secure a permanent base and dispatched Rear Admiral Otto von Diedrichs to replace him. Diedrichs left Berlin on May 1, 1897, with specific orders to find a suitable base in China. As the third officer with orders to procure a base, Diedrichs was prepared to force events if necessary. He also preferred Kiao-Chou as a location.

Two incidents related to provisions in the treaty of Peking finally prompted Wilhelm to allow Diederichs to seize Kiao-Chou. First a Chinese mob pelted officers from SMS *Comoran*. Later, the kaiser deemed a report of a German missionary murdered on the Shangtung peninsula, with another missionary missing, sufficiently provocative and therefore gave Diederichs the order to proceed. Diederichs advised General Chang, the Chinese official in the area, that Germany intended to occupy the entire Kiao-Chou region as compensation for the murder of two German missionaries. Under threat of bombardment, Chang withdrew. Germany formally occupied Kiao-Chou on November 14, 1897.[32]

Fearing that a partition of China would harm British trade, Great Britain attempted to reach an accord with Germany after the kaiser seized Kiao-Chou.

Colonial Secretary Joseph Chamberlain led the effort. Bülow, the German foreign minister, balked at an alliance, claiming that Britain's form of government would make it an unreliable ally; he charged that a subsequent Parliament could reverse any agreement between the two nations. Chamberlain's diplomatic overture coincided with Tirpitz's submission of Germany's first naval law to the Reichstag.[33] Chamberlain made two more attempts to reach agreements with Germany so that the two powers might avoid conflict. Both failed. Germany took these overtures as evidence that an aggressive foreign policy might force Great Britain to make concessions.[34]

When Wilhelm and his advisers contemplated building Germany's navy, they knew it would arouse apprehension in London. Without the ability to replenish along trade routes, German cruisers would have had little staying power. Therefore, Germany needed additional colonies near these routes as bases for supplies. The British would find German attempts to acquire such bases threatening, so adding territory to the German empire would be impossible without checking British interference. The kaiser believed that London would continue to meddle in German foreign policy as it had done in the past,[35] so building Tirpitz's Risk Fleet could possibly deter the British. Berlin believed this was the key to acquiring German colonies and developing German trade.

Tirpitz's risk theory addressed the imbalance between Great Britain and Germany by playing off the tensions among Paris, St. Petersburg, and London. Moreover, with Great Britain's requirement of defending its many overseas commitments, Westminster might balk at the expense of matching the Germans ship for ship in the North Sea. Tirpitz estimated that with shrewd planning over a period of about ten years, Germany could transform its fleet from the sixth-ranked naval power to the second.[36]

Given that Kaiser Wilhelm found the status quo unacceptable, the alternative to challenging Great Britain was to become its ally. In that case, the Royal Navy would have to protect German trade.[37] The pitfall of such an alliance was that Great Britain, with the ability to project military and economic power worldwide, would naturally take the lead in foreign policy decisions. For Germany to have deliberately adopted a subordinate role, in effect become Britain's Teutonic sidekick, would not have convinced the German people of the greatness of their nation.[38] With these issues considered, the German government adopted a strategy appropriate to its worldview. Tirpitz's Risk Fleet and risk theory were rational methods for achieving German aims. Moreover, the progress Germany would make over the next decade would give the kaiser and his court ample feedback that Germany's foreign policy, of which risk theory formed only part, was effective.[39]

Beginning with laws passed in 1898 and 1900, Germany began an ambitious naval construction program. The 1898 law provided for a defensive fleet, but the 1900 law was more ambitious, calling for a doubling of fleet size by 1907 with the goal of rivaling Great Britain's battle fleet. The German Imperial Naval Office ultimately set a goal of sixty modern battleships and battle cruisers. It estimated that the British treasury could not bear the financial stress nor could Britons supply the manpower to crew the ships that it would take to sustain a decisive superiority over the German fleet.

The German Imperial Naval Office likely presumed that Whitehall would continue its long-standing policy of maintaining Britain's naval strength at the two-power standard. Moreover, Germany assumed that France and Russia would continue their building programs. Germany doubted that Great Britain would drain the king's treasury by building naval vessels against a three-power standard and was therefore more likely to accept risk somewhere. Given the traditional animosity between France and Britain, Germany calculated that it would take its chances with German policy. The kaiser looked to gain colonial possessions from Denmark, Portugal, or possibly France. German planners assumed that London's relationship with Paris and Moscow would remain cool. Consequently, they surmised that an aggressive foreign policy toward France would not unduly provoke Great Britain. Even if it did, Berlin's scheme was to placate London by terminating German naval ships authorized in naval legislation. If it became necessary, Berlin would scrap ships under construction.[40]

Chamberlain's second diplomatic overture to Germany came in November 1899. After years of challenging Germany for control over the Samoan Islands, Great Britain offered to relinquish all claims to them in exchange for exclusive influence in the Fiji Islands and the German Solomon Islands. The United States, which also had a claim in Samoa, and Germany were amenable to a split, with Germany gaining the greatest share of the landmass and an excellent harbor at Apia. On the occasion of Kaiser Wilhelm's visit to Great Britain that same month, Chamberlain reiterated Britain's desire for an understanding with Germany at a banquet held at Windsor Castle. Thinking that relations had improved with the resolution of the Samoan Islands, Chamberlain argued that a British, American, and German alliance would combine to check France and Russia. Bülow was not persuaded and considered British assistance of little value in the event of war with Russia. Nevertheless, Washington, Berlin, and London signed their treaty over Samoa on December 2, 1899.

Tirpitz wanted to push his second navy bill forward at that time to take advantage of anti-British sentiment built up since October 1899 over the Second Boer War. On December 11, a week after signing the Samoa treaty, Bülow appeared before the Reichstag to garner support for the bill. He possessed full knowledge of the discussions that had taken place in London between Chamberlain and the kaiser. In his speech, he derided Great Britain as a declining power envious of German progress. By doing so, Bülow summarily and publicly repudiated Chamberlain's second attempt to reach an agreement with Berlin.[41]

Great Britain had feared European intervention during the Boer War. To forestall aid to the Boers, England had promised Germany territory from Portugal's African colonies in return for its neutrality. Britain also pledged, however, to uphold the integrity of Portuguese colonies if Portugal permitted the British to use its territory as a staging area for military operations against the Boers. London was counting on a financial crisis and Portuguese financial collapse that would force Lisbon to relinquish territory as payment on loans made by British financial institutions against Portuguese colonial receipts.[42] Britain could then in good conscience fulfill its bargain with Germany.

Britain did not realize that for Germany to maintain a "free hand" during the risk period before its fleet was ready, Berlin could not allow itself to be constrained in a pact against Great Britain. This prevented a European coalition against Great Britain during the Boer War. Germany's plan was to foster amicable relations with Russia and England after the Boer War and build a strong fleet that would make the Reich an attractive alliance partner. It would then wait for developments to exploit diplomatically.[43]

Wilhelm promoted Bülow to chancellor in October 1900. Bülow and his successor, Theobald von Bethmann-Hollweg, and officials from the Foreign Office believed that battleships being built at German shipyards were useful bargaining chips for extracting British political concessions. What Germany sought was British neutrality in the event of a war with France or Russia, and British support for German colonial expansion.[44]

When the Boer War turned in favor of the British, Chamberlain initiated a third attempt for an alliance with Germany. In January 1901, Chamberlain, accompanied by Spencer Compton Cavendish, Lord President of the Council, approached Hermann von Echardstein, first secretary to the German ambassador in London and proposed joining the Triple Alliance of Germany, Austria-Hungary, and Italy. Bülow received the news in Berlin, and elected to proceed cautiously. The negotiations bogged down in February. Bülow proposed terms certain to make London balk, including a five-year defensive alliance between Germany and Britain to be ratified by the Reichstag and Parliament, thus ensuring that it would be public at a time when other alliance provisions among nations were secret. Moreover, Bülow's proposal went beyond the standard pledges of non-aggression, mutual goodwill, and benevolent neutrality in the event of a war with a third party. By including a clause requiring London to commit to the defense of Austria-Hungary instead of merely remaining neutral, Bülow proposed a relationship that tied London's hands in foreign policy and would have thus made Great Britain a junior partner in the alliance's foreign policy decisions. Meanwhile, the British press stoked public fears about Germany that made it difficult for Westminster to contemplate any sort of treaty with Berlin. Naturally, London declined Bülow's proposal.[45]

Despite the effort invested in forming an alliance with Great Britain prior to 1901, the evidence indicates that Germany did not actually desire one. Rather, Berlin was using Britain's diplomatic overtures to gauge the effect of German foreign policy. Each time London sought better relations with Germany, Berlin responded with a diplomatic rebuff and increased naval expenditures.[46] Germany played this game for another decade, generally furthering its interests.

Two particular events in 1904 gave Germany opportunity and cause to advance its foreign policy goals. The first was the Russo-Japanese War. Because of this conflict, the tsar diverted Russian troops toward the Pacific to confront the Japanese. This diminished Russia's potential to fight Germany. Two Japanese naval victories left the Russian fleet smashed and demoralized. Bülow recognized that Russia was temporarily useless as an ally to France. The cause for German action was that Britain and France had reached an understanding, the Entente Cordiale, about their respective rights in Egypt and Morocco. France controlled Algeria and Tunisia, but Great Britain had consistently opposed a European power controlling Morocco because of its location on the shore opposite Gibraltar. The Treaty of Madrid, signed by all major European powers and the United States in 1880, guaranteed Morocco's independence. After years of sending advisers and offering incentives attempting to reform the sultan of Morocco's corrupt government, London simply had had enough. Unwilling to invest more in the sultanate, Britain hoped France would; the French government had always been interested in Morocco. For a free hand in Morocco, France agreed to British primacy in Egypt. As part of the deal, France and Britain each had open commercial access to ports and each agreed that they would cooperate for free passage of the Strait of Gibraltar. London was particularly interested in prohibiting fortifications being built on the Moroccan coast. Paris likewise desired that no power establish a strategic position along Morocco's coast.[47] Germany would test this latter aspect of the agreement twice in the coming decade.

Germany did not protest when the Anglo-French agreement on Egypt and Morocco became known, but at the end of March 1905 Bülow seized an opportunity to test the limits of the Anglo-French entente and to humiliate the French. Paris had earlier that year sent a mission to Fez; its actions and language presaged making Morocco a French protectorate. Germany insisted that this would be a violation of the Treaty of Madrid, and used it as a pretext to assert its rights, to demonstrate to France that it still had to avoid antagonizing Germany, as well as to probe the Anglo-French relationship.[48]

Bülow set events in motion by orchestrating a visit by Kaiser Wilhelm to Tangier. Wilhelm arrived in Tangier on March 31, 1905, transported in the steamship *Hamburg*. Once ashore and having been received by the sultan's delegation, Wilhelm read a speech that Bülow had prepared for him. In it, he promised the sultan that Germany would not stand for the French trampling on Moroccan rights, and that to establish a more harmonious relationship between Europe and small nations, an international conference should be held to establish the limits of European influence in Africa.

The French recognized that they had gained advantages in Morocco, but they wanted to avoid a conference by negotiating disputes with Germany directly. The German ambassador rejected a French offer to negotiate and insisted instead that France submit to a conference. Germany's tone became more bellicose. To the French, Germany made it clear that the alternative to a conference was war. This conference-or-war dilemma forced a showdown inside

Map 2. *The Mediterranean Sea*

the French parliament over foreign policy. Foreign Minister Theophile Delcassé believed Berlin was bluffing. The proper course then would be to call the bluff and wait out the Germans. Prime Minister Maurice Rouvier argued that France was in no position to go it alone against the German army so a war over the status of Morocco was out of the question. Parliament voted in favor of Rouvier. Defeated and humiliated, Delcassé resigned.

On June 6, 1905, Rouvier notified Germany that Delcassé had been removed from office in the belief that the foreign minister's humiliation would mollify Bülow. Thus, acting as if Delcassé's fall was what Germany desired, the prime minister then proposed direct bilateral talks with Germany to settle the dispute. The German ambassador flatly refused and insisted on a conference. Bülow's goal was to reverse the progress Delcassé had made settling colonial disputes with Great Britain. Had Germany negotiated directly with France, the kaiser may have gained some concessions, but it would have left colonial agreements between Paris and London in force. An international conference, however, held the prospect of revisiting the status of colonial spheres of influence in Africa and might have had the potential to undermine the British position in Egypt. Bülow's design was to push Great Britain and France apart.[49] Germany had the strength to bully individual nations, but to manipulate alliances was a different matter altogether. The kaiser's foreign policy relied on keeping Britain and France antagonistic toward one another. This was a key assumption underpinning risk theory.

Germany's hawkish diplomatic strategy had gone well up to this point. France had been compelled to submit to German demands, and the minister who had negotiated the entente with Great Britain had resigned. To avoid a conference, Rouvier went as far as reneging on the French agreement with Britain to prohibit any other power from gaining a strategic position in Morocco. When he notified Germany of Delcassé's ouster, his emissaries to Germany offered a concession on Morocco's Atlantic coast where Germany could place a coaling station.[50] The Germans, firmly focused on destroying the Anglo-French entente, refused to accept the concessions.

On July 8, 1905, the European powers agreed to the conference. The British prime minister, Henry Campbell-Bannerman, authorized Edward Grey to back the French at the conference. His concern was that if Germany planned to force a war on France over a transparent agreement between the French and British, then Great Britain could not adopt the position of an interested observer and remain neutral. Britain also supported France in order to retain its influence in Egypt. In fact, article 9 of the Entente Cordiale stipulated that the two contracting powers would lend one another their diplomatic support in order to execute the declaration's various clauses.[51] Campbell-Bannerman authorized Grey to seek retrenchment and reform of Britain's relationship with France and to begin military conversations between the British and French General Staffs with a view toward acting in concert should war break out.[52]

The conference convened in Algeciras, Spain, on January 16, 1906. Representatives from each of the countries participating in the original treaty of Madrid attended the conference, but only Austria-Hungary clearly supported Germany. One of the two German diplomats, Christian von Tattenbach, made matters worse when he attempted to usurp the agenda; the other representatives simply found him rude and bellicose. Great Britain assumed a leading role and fully supported France.

With clever procedural maneuvering and a timely visit from the British home fleet at Gibraltar, Great Britain and France were essentially able to secure what they had agreed to bilaterally. The combined British Mediterranean and Home Fleets at anchor in Gibraltar—directly across from Algeciras bay—presented a picture of British power that the delegates could not ignore. In addition, the British wined and dined the delegates on board His Majesty's ships. Britain and France corralled the votes they needed with this show of power and hospitality.

Germany and Austria-Hungary, left looking for a way to quickly end the conference, ultimately conceded. The key sticking point was over control of Morocco's police force. The police were corrupt, and whoever controlled the force would undertake its professionalization and supervision. Furthermore, whoever controlled the police essentially controlled Morocco. The participants agreed in the end to French and Spanish supervision of Morocco's police with oversight by a Swiss commissioner.[53]

Although Tirpitz and some other high-ranking German officials believed that Germany had maintained its prestige throughout the crisis, in reality it suffered a political defeat. In the kaiser's favor, France and Britain were put on notice that they must consult Germany in important matters of foreign policy. The world also recognized that Germany had forced a conference on two great powers that did not want one. Moreover, the French diplomat responsible for the Entente Cordiale had been humiliated and drummed out of office. On the other hand, France and Great Britain were not driven apart. Their agreement stood, and in addition, Germany's threats provoked the British into discussing military cooperation with the French.[54] In the end, Germany's humiliation of Delcassé cemented the Anglo-French relationship.

The Entente Cordiale between Great Britain and France dealt a severe blow to Tirpitz's risk theory, based as it was on British estrangement from other European powers. The entente should have been enough to check Germany's ambitious foreign policy, except that in October 1905 the British laid down HMS *Dreadnought,* a battleship of revolutionary design that included steam turbines for propulsion (giving the ship a speed of twenty-one knots), a uniform main battery of 12-inch guns that could fire in a battery against a target with a central fire-control system, and improved armor protection. When the battleship was completed in December 1906, all naval powers judged that pre-dreadnought ships, lacking *Deadnought's* speed and armament, were of inferior design.

Germany completed the two pre-dreadnought battleships it had under construction, but started no new ships until 1907. Then, in June, July, and August, German shipyards began building *Rheinland, Nassau,* and *Westfalen,* respectively, all three of which mimicked the dreadnought design.[55] Germany planned to build dreadnoughts at the same rate as Great Britain. In his memoirs, Tirpitz insists that coincidence explains why Germany's shipbuilding program matched Britain's planned procurement of the radical new warship. Nevertheless, in the course of several years, Great Britain's previous lead in obsolescent pre-dreadnought battleships would be irrelevant. The kaiser had modified his policy. Instead of having to rely on a balance between Great Britain and other great powers, Germany launched a naval arms race that challenged British naval strength directly.[56] Whether a direct challenge is precisely what Berlin's ministers had intended or was coincidence, as Tirpitz claimed, is beside the point. Building the ships, for whatever purpose presented a challenge to British naval superiority.

Seeking better relations with the British, the Germans made overtures to London between 1907 and 1912 hoping to reach an entente, though not a formal alliance. Berlin wanted the British to accede to its completion of the Baghdad railway, accept the status and size of Germany's fleet as the second-ranking naval power, and acquiesce to more German colonies so that Berlin could have a "place in the sun." Every effort, however, failed.[57] Germany got another opportunity to exercise its foreign policy muscle when on October 5, 1908, Austria proclaimed that it had annexed Bosnia-Herzegovina. The independent Kingdom of Serbia immediately contested the annexation because the area was populated by a large number of ethnic Serbs. Britain, France, Germany, Italy, Montenegro, the Ottoman Empire, and Russia also all had an interest in the peaceful resolution of the crisis The announcement came while Austria was in negotiations with Russia over the status of the territory, former Ottoman provinces that had been under Austrian administration since 1878. The purpose of Austria's move was to signal to the leaders of the Young Turk revolution that the status of Bosnia-Herzegovina had been settled. Russia was also interested in Bosnia-Herzegovina's future because of its Slavic population, and it appeared to the British that Austria had made the declaration unilaterally, before having procured an agreement with the tsar on a suitable concession.[58]

Germany cowed Russia when the former declared that Austria would have its full and complete support in a war with Serbia. Germany insisted instead that Serbia was to give way to the annexation without compensation. Germany pressured Russia to advise Serbia to yield or it would mean war. Russia, faced with a prospect of fighting against Germany and Austria-Hungary, backed down.[59] Thus, in 1908, Germany had threatened a second European power with war, as it had with France in 1904, and made it blink. Berlin rejected offers by several powers to mediate the dispute over Bosnia-Herzegovina in a general European conference, having previously been outmaneuvered at Algeciras over Morocco, it sought to avoid a repeat.[60]

A truculent Germany established itself as Europe's bully. Russia, France, and Great Britain reacted by strengthening their preparations for war. Russia revamped its army just as France had done following its retreat from conflict over Morocco. Moreover, the Germans had steadily built warships under their existing laws and accelerated construction with the new naval law of 1908. According to Winston Churchill, this new law caused the British Admiralty "the greatest anxiety."[61] In 1909, First Lord of the Admiralty Reginald McKenna requested Parliament to fund six dreadnought battleships in order to answer the rapid growth of the German fleet. Had Great Britain not acted, Germany certainly would have challenged its naval primacy. Including the initial three dreadnought-style battleships, Germany would commission a total of thirteen battleships and four battle cruisers prior to the Great War. Four more battleships and an additional battle cruiser were completed within months after the war began. Before the armistice, Germany would build four more battleships and three battle cruisers.[62]

The impetus for a second Moroccan crisis came when the French sent an expedition to Fez in January 1911, during which several French military personnel were killed. Paris claimed that military action had been necessary to quell disturbances and protect Europeans. They followed up with a military deployment to Rabat, from which they could supply an expedition inland to deal with the rebellion. The German government protested France's actions, suspecting that Paris would by these military measures incrementally increase its hold on Morocco.[63] Eventually, Berlin would claim that a significant German business interest in the small port town of Agadir required protection. Agadir was regarded by the British and French as having the best natural harbor on Morocco's Atlantic littoral and a prime location for a naval base.[64] The Mannesmann Brothers, a German firm engaged in the fabrication of seamless steel tubes, had been pursuing an iron ore mining concession for years without successfully gaining official recognition from their efforts.[65]

German Foreign Minister Alfred von Kiderlen-Wachter raised the firm's problems with France. The French government acknowledged that Mannesmann Brothers had sought mining rights and that no specific right had been granted. Trying to protect its advantages in Morocco, Paris proffered that Germany be compensated with a colonial concession in the Congo area. The German press carried stories indicating that popular sentiment was behind pushing German interests in Morocco's milder climate rather than exchanging them for more disease-prone tropical areas, plenty of which Germany already held.[66]

The French resigned themselves to long-drawn-out negotiations in order to settle the Morocco issue and despite the Mannesmann's activity, eventually denied any German business interests at Agadir. They argued that the harbor was little more than an undeveloped sandbar, there was no German property there, and no trade being conducted. The French urged a visit by representatives of both governments to verify this assessment. Without warning, on July 1, Kiderlen-Wachter sent the gunboat SMS *Panther* to Agadir to uphold and protect German business interests, in keeping with the pattern Germany had established to gain colonies in Africa. With the announcement of *Panther's* dispatch, governments across Europe became alarmed, worrying about Germany's intentions.[67] According to several historians, Kiderlen-Wachter wanted to nudge the French in the direction of conceding portions of the Congo to Germany while leaving Morocco to the French.[68] Others contend that Kiderlen-Wachter sought a concession in Morocco but decided to back down after Chancellor of the Exchequer David Lloyd George delivered a threatening speech to the Banker's Association at Mansion House on July 21.[69]

Members of the British Admiralty Staff consulted charts and observed that a naval base at Agadir would allow the German navy to operate where it could interfere with the South American and African trade routes. Shipping along those routes converged near the African coast. A German naval base at Agadir would also have facilitated impeding shipping traffic though the Strait of Gibraltar. Foreign Minister Edward Grey informed the German ambassador, Paul Wolff Metternich, that Great Britain could not be ambivalent on the outcome of the crisis. Germany maintained a disquieting silence until July 21.[70] France too found the prospect of a German military presence in Morocco alarming.[71]

The British and French reactions to German posturing suggest their concern was that Germany intended to establish a protectorate in Morocco. Germany was likely attempting to gain the concession for a port on the Atlantic coast as offered during the previous Moroccan crisis, in 1905. Britain and France, however, had no intention of making such an offer. During the first crisis, Germany had not established a reputation for a bellicose foreign policy or built a fleet sufficient to make it the world's second-ranking naval power.[72] By 1911 it had, however, making the potential threat of a German naval base on the Atlantic coast near the entrance to the Mediterranean Sea too great a risk.

On the evening of July 21, Lloyd George, delivered a stern warning to Germany when he declared before the Banker's Association that if a situation were forced on Great Britain in which preserving peace could only be purchased by surrendering its great interests, then peace at that price would be too costly. The United Kingdom would surely side with France.[73] Lloyd George's remarks provoked a strong German reaction. Metternich told Grey that if France rejected the hand that Kaiser Wilhelm had offered, then his government would compel France to acknowledge German rights by all means necessary. When this news reached England's shores, Great Britain mobilized the fleet, a move that Berlin had not anticipated. Wilhelm's agents had led him to believe that the liberal imperialists and the radicals that composed the British cabinet were divided. The Germans thought the radicals led by Lloyd George stood firmly for maintaining peace. Lloyd George's speech indicating otherwise shocked Berlin. As a result, the kaiser lost faith in Metternich.[74]

Metternich had once told Winston Churchill, home secretary at the time, that Germany had no thoughts of rivaling the Royal Navy. All Germany wanted was a fleet to protect its commerce and colonies. Britain believed that allowing the Germans into Morocco would be a threat to France in much the same way that German domination of France or the Low Countries—the Netherlands and Belgium—would imperil the survival of Great Britain.[75]

The Agadir crisis ended peacefully, with France angrily ceding territory in West Africa, something Paris would likely have done even prior to Berlin's provocation. The French prime minister, Joseph Caillaux, was dismissed from office. Germany considered the whole affair a diplomatic humiliation; the colonial secretary, Friedrich von Lindequist, resigned his post to avoid signing the agreement. Because London mobilized for war during the crisis, Berlin perceived that Great Britain had not been sufficiently convinced of Germany's ability to prevent its interference in the kaiser's foreign policy ambitions. Tirpitz used Britain's response to the Agadir crisis to justify another boost to the German navy.[76]

All things considered, Germany's policy goal could not simply have been to gain a concession in the Congo, a version of events that Kiderlen-Wachter's memoirs attempted to justify years later. If it were, Germany would have believed its policy a success, yet this was not the case. What Germany wanted—and what Britain and France feared—was a partition of Morocco. This would have given the kaiser's fleet a menacing naval base on the Atlantic coast outside of the North Sea, where it was boxed in by Britain's dominating geography.

Following the Agadir confrontation, Germany noted a change in British policy. London began sending messages through prominent business contacts that it sought rapprochement. King Edward's emissary, Ernest Cassel, knew Albert Ballin, president of the Hamburg-America Line and a friend of the kaiser. Cassel was granted an audience with Wilhelm, whereupon he produced a letter prepared with the approval of the British government presenting three proposals that could lead to amicable relations between the two nations. First, Germany had to accept Britain's superiority at sea with no further augmentation to the Kriegsmarine's shipbuilding program (although London would have preferred a reduction in the building program). Second, Great Britain would not interfere with Germany's colonial expansion and would even undertake discussions to promote the kaiser's imperial ambitions. Third, the two nations would not enter into aggressive pacts against the other. Wilhelm received the message favorably and promptly drafted his reply. This led Great Britain to send former war minister Richard Burdon Haldane to Berlin for formal negotiations.[77]

The Haldane mission, though initially promising, yielded nothing. Haldane met with Kaiser Wilhelm, Tirpitz, and Bethmann-Hollweg to discuss the tensions between the two nations. On the ratio of capital ships, Tirpitz proposed three British vessels for every two German battleships. Haldane countered that Great Britain, as an island nation, must be superior at sea to any potential combination of enemies and therefore would not deviate from the two-power standard. Haldane suggested that Germany slow its shipbuilding: instead of proceeding with three dreadnoughts in 1912, build only two and push the third out to 1913 and delay adding the additional ships planned in 1914 and 1916 until 1916 and 1919, respectively. The kaiser and Tirpitz agreed to Haldane's proposal. Wilhelm presented Haldane with a draft of the 1912 navy bill, and Haldane returned to England.[78]

While Haldane was on his diplomatic mission in Berlin, Churchill, now First Lord of the Admiralty, delivered a speech of his own, during a trip to Glasgow inspecting shipbuilding, with the intention of firmly spelling out British priorities and bolstering Haldane's diplomacy. In the speech, Churchill explained that as an island nation, a strong fleet was a strategic necessity for Great Britain, while for Germany a fleet was not strictly speaking necessary, but an option. To quote him, "[T]he German Navy is to them more in the nature of a luxury."[79] In the German translation, the term *luxury* was interpreted as akin to "decadence" rather than "unnecessary" or "optional." Churchill's speech infuriated the Germans. The German press' reporting of it created an uproar among readers.[80]

When Haldane returned to London, the Admiralty scrutinized the German's draft naval bill and found that Berlin's interpretation of "no augmentation to the shipbuilding program" only applied to capital ships. Germany considered it a significant concession that it had agreed to spread the building of battleships over several years. The bill still proposed adding a third battleship squadron, albeit over a long time span. The bad news for London was that the bill also included substantial increases in destroyers and submarines plus adding 15,000 naval personnel to active duty rolls. The bill, when implemented, would have enabled the German navy to stand at wartime strength year-round.[81]

Grey told Metternich that Great Britain could not proceed with such proposals as the offer to cede Zanzibar to Germany without substantial reductions in its shipbuilding program. Grey also made clear that the navy bill meant that Great Britain would lay down two hulls for every German ship and likely transfer more ships from overseas stations back to home waters. Germany, however, had been hardened by Churchill's speech and refused any reduction in ships. Bethmann took the initiative to break the impasse, asserting that Germany needed a guarantee that Great Britain would observe neutrality when Germany became involved in a war. If Britain were to assure its neutrality, he was certain that Germany would pay the price in ships.

Grey counteroffered: "England would make no unprovoked attack upon Germany and will pursue no aggressive policy towards her." He also stipulated that Great Britain had no treaties, or relationships with other powers that had any aggressive intent toward Germany. Metternich responded that the proposal had to contain the word *neutrality* for Berlin to accept it, insisting on "England will therefore observe a benevolent neutrality should war be forced upon Germany." These positions represented the bottom lines of the two governments.

Metternich had been instructed that the naval bill would go forward unless Britain guaranteed absolute neutrality toward Germany,[82] but Grey could not grant the Germans' terms. Improving Britain's relationship with France was Grey's highest foreign policy priority. To pledge unconditional neutrality with Germany in any war would mean the end of the entente with France and dire consequences for future relations with Russia as well.[83] Berlin still desired an end to the entente and a pledge of British neutrality; it would get neither. The talks broke down. Metternich relayed the information to Berlin and added that London was committed to laying down two keels for every one that Germany laid down. The kaiser recalled his ambassador and replaced him with Karl Max Lichnowsky. Germany soon began to receive more indications that Great Britain was seeking better relations and relief from the high cost of shipbuilding to stay ahead of Germany. Taking up Haldane's line, First Sea Lord Churchill suggested that both nations cease building ships for a period of time. He announced in Parliament that if Germany would build only three ships, Great Britain would build five—a 6:10 ratio.[84]

During the two Balkan wars—the first from October 1912 until May 1913, the second from June until August 1913—Grey had met with Europe's great powers in London and kept the eruptions there from turning into broader European wars.[85] These British initiatives signaled to Berlin that London had come closer to war over Agadir than it had wanted and was seeking ways to avoid a confrontation with Germany. In the minds of Berlin's policy makers, this amounted to Britain reeling under German pressure—an indication that Germany's foreign policy compass was pointed in the right direction. Nevertheless, German diplomacy toward Great Britain softened, as the kaiser needed to mollify the British while he strengthened the navy and army.

The German Admiralty Staff and General Staff believed in January 1912 that Great Britain would support France in the event the French became involved in a war with Germany. Both observed British war preparations during the Agadir crisis and planned for London to send about 170,000 troops to the continent in support of France if war were to break out. Moreover, they believed that Britain would have ships available immediately to embark the troops because of their preparation during the increase in tensions.

The German Admiralty Staff estimated that the Royal Navy was capable of protecting its transports from German submarine and torpedo attacks. Because of the threat submarines posed, Great Britain would likely disembark in Dunkirk, Calais, and Boulogne-sur-Mer, the three French ports closest to England. Helmuth von Moltke the Younger, chief of the German General Staff, suggested, however, that the British might land in Belgium or Holland to prevent Germany from taking the Rhein and Schelde estuaries. If Germany possessed these decisive points, it could render British control of the channel tenuous. German submarines and torpedo boats operating from there could seriously threaten British trade.[86] Moreover, the German Admiralty realized that Britain would likely implement a blockade to prevent the German fleet and merchant shipping from entering the North Sea. Germany did not have sufficient naval strength to assume an offensive posture, so planning assumptions called for a defensive option.[87]

On November 5, 1912, the German Admiralty Staff submitted a revised plan, with updated assumptions, to Kaiser Wilhelm. The new document discussed the possibility that in a European war involving Germany and France, Britain would assume a waiting posture, so Germany would only have France and Russia as opponents. The staff claimed their assessment was the result of a newly arisen situation, but Germany could not be certain of British actions; they could not dismiss the possibility that Britain might ally with Germany's opponents.[88] Although the staff did not elaborate as to the specific situation, the timing suggests ministers in Berlin had interpreted several diplomatic initiatives as signs of a rapprochement. British overtures to Germany preceding the failed Haldane mission, and the British reaction to the Balkan wars appear to be the newly arisen situation to which the staff referred. Germany's ministers found additional encouragement for their policies when Berlin and London resumed discussion over naval issues during 1913–14. Despite the fact that the status of the ratio between the German navy and the Royal Navy was still unresolved when war broke out in 1914,[89] during that two-year period the pair had resolved their disagreements over the Baghdad railway, and London supported Berlin's colonial acquisitions in southern Africa.[90] Britain still, however, opposed German colonies in the Mediterranean and along the North African coast. Step by step, Germany and Britain came together on all of the issues discussed during the Haldane mission. This prodded the Wilhelmstrasse to believe that much progress had been made toward an accord with Great Britain. Tirpitz even claimed after the war that he had acquiesced to the fixed 6:10 shipbuilding ratio proposed by Churchill in February 1913. Historian Robert Massie disputes Tirpitz' claim, pointing out that each nation had built the capital ships it could afford.[91] Nevertheless, Berlin's hopes that London would remain neutral in a Franco-German war were based on the history of their mutual relations over a decade, especially the years of improved relations beginning in 1911.[92]

The Risk Fleet, the Germans' shipbuilding plan that Tirpitz had worked out for the Kaiser, was supposed to shore up political support for a German empire. Moreover it was supposed to attract minor naval powers as allies, and threaten Britain's European security with a massive fleet near its eastern shores. The threat to Britain would allow the German empire to acquire additional colonial concessions without opposition from London. Tirpitz believed his policy to be successful, even gloating at one point after the war that Britain had to virtually withdraw the Royal Navy from the Mediterranean and the Far East in order to have an effective counter to the German High Seas Fleet. Therefore, Great Britain's control over those portions of the world had virtually ceased.[93]

Beginning in 1904, Germany improved the military usefulness of its colonies. It had developed the ability to communicate with each of its colonies via submarine telegraph cables, but most of the cables were British owned. The German government exercised initiative by building modern port facilities and adding wireless telegraphy. Generous subsidies provided by Berlin helped build neat and thriving cities, such as Dar es Salaam in German East Africa, and Rabaul in German New Guinea. For access to independent and reliable communications, Berlin had wireless stations erected in these locations as well as other Pacific locations: Angaur (Caroline Islands), Apia (Samoa), Nauru, and Tsingtao (Kiao-chau).[94] A series of relay stations—at Duala (Cameroons), Kamina (Togoland), Windhoek (German Southwest Africa), and Yap in the south Pacific—connected these more distant locations to the main transmitting station in Nauen, Germany. These stations provided global coverage with the exception of areas in the Indian Ocean and the southernmost Pacific Ocean. Germany planned major transmitting stations in Tabora (German East Africa) and Sumatra to fill in these gaps.[95]

Germany provided several shipping lines with subsidies to compete for trade in Africa and the Pacific.[96] The German merchant marine, however, was the world's second largest and no longer needed subsidies to compete with British firms for a fair share of the freight market. The effect of the subsidies therefore was to keep merchant vessels in a region of the world that they would otherwise vacate in search of more profitable trade.

Germany's improved port facilities in its colonies served as coaling stations and important communications links. They were not major naval bases as in Tsingtao, but in a pinch they could serve as support bases for naval operations. This increased Germany's naval potential in geographic areas where the Royal Navy presence was weak. German naval planning leveraged this advantage.

Germany's plans for ships outside the North Sea became more elaborate over time. In the event of war with Great Britain, the East Asiatic Squadron was to attack Australia and to conduct cruiser warfare against British commerce along Australia's northwestern coast, in the seas around Colombo, and in the China Sea. Cruiser warfare tactics stressed that ships were to operate in one area only for a short time and then move to another region, always evading large forces and attempting to retain the element of surprise. When Vice Admiral Graf Maximilian von Spee assumed command of the East Asia squadron, his mission after April 1913 was to damage British shipping. His secondary mission was to attempt to divide British East Asiatic naval forces and defeat them in detail.[97] In 1907, ships on the East African and West African stations were instructed to avoid being blockaded so they could conduct cruiser warfare. On the East American station, German cruisers were to intercept British food imports from Argentina. In 1909, guidance to vessels on the East American station changed to a more general task: intercept food imports to Britain coming from South America, the Caribbean Sea, and around the horn from Asia. The Admiralty Staff now considered the aging ships stationed in West Africa obsolete, so their orders directed the ships to proceed to the Brazilian coast to give up their guns to specified merchant ships that would become auxiliary cruisers.[98]

Germany had begun making better arrangements to provide its commerce raiders with cash and coal in 1906. In 1908, it equipped passenger ships as auxiliary cruisers to replace obsolete naval vessels and augment the activities of modern cruisers. Merchant ships used for this purpose had to be capable of a minimum speed, have dual propellers, a submerged rudder, engine rooms below the waterline, and a double bottom with coal chambers located to protect the engines and boilers. Each also required provisions for mounting cannons and conveyance of below decks ammunition to the guns. Ships of the East Africa, Hamburg-America, and North German Lloyd lines met these requirements. Suitable ships had orders to depart any overseas port in which they found themselves at war's outbreak, head for Brazil for conversion, and begin operation as auxiliary cruisers in the North Atlantic.[99]

By April 1913, Germany's naval staff believed that the best shipping lane to disrupt was the North Atlantic route between the United States and Great Britain. Since the most important route would also be the best protected, the German plan was to use the converted liners as commerce raiders. The staff reemphasized these orders in March 1914.[100]

Berlin developed the Etappen system—a group of bases at communications hubs and other cities where Germany had a strong diplomatic presence—to support commerce raiding.[101] The system's major centers were in Batavia

(Sud Etappe), San Francisco (Etappe Nordwest Amerika), Valparaiso (Etappe Sud Amerika) Rio de Janeiro (Etappe Brasilien), the Caribbean (Etappe Westindien), New York (Etappe Nord Amerika), Duala (Etappe West Afrika), Dar es Salaam (Etappe Ostafrika), and the Mediterranean (Etappe Mittlemeer). Others included Tsingtao, China, Japan, and Manila, in the western and southern Pacific. In South America centers were also established at Callao, Peru, and La Plata, Argentina. Germany staffed the Etappe centers with naval officers and agents, arming them with plenty of money and contacts. Their mission was to keep the kaiser's navy operating.

At war's outbreak, colliers were to be dispatched from these stations to meet cruisers at prearranged locations in the open seas as chartered adjuncts to the cruisers. Colliers would then ply back and forth from various centers with coal and supplies. Hundreds of Germany's merchant ships were chartered for this purpose. To function properly, the scheme obviously relied on a benevolent interpretation of neutrality laws by neutral countries. Germany expected that South American nations and the United States would take little action to prevent colliers from supplying commerce raiders. The overt presence of a warship in a neutral port would push neutral countries to abide by international convention, so Germany planned to minimize this. On the other hand, an unscheduled merchant ship entering port could justifiably be ignored, especially if the neutrals expected to profit from the transaction.[102]

The fast merchant liners designated to become auxiliary cruisers were to proceed to neutral ports to meet aging German gunboats. The gunboat would transfer its guns to the liner and then accept becoming interned. The liner would receive a commissioned officer and a small naval crew to provide oversight. When the ship left port, the commissioned officer would assume command; the liner would hoist a military pennant and become a commissioned warship. The sole purpose of these auxiliary cruisers was to inflict maximum damage on enemy trade. In no case were they to attempt to engage an actual enemy warship because they would certainly be destroyed. The idea was that the liners' speed would permit them to flee an enemy warship and also easily run down and capture unarmed, slow tramp steamers.[103]

By 1914, Germany had reinvented itself as a major sea power. Kaiser Wilhelm's foreign policy was an aggressive one. Twice in a decade, Germany had threatened other major powers with war and caused them to back down.

The first instance occurred in 1905 when Germany bullied France and forced the Algeciras conference, where ironically German diplomacy showed itself wanting. The second threat, issued in 1908, deterred Russia as Germany successfully supported Austria-Hungary's annexation of Bosnia-Herzgovina. In the German colonies, Berlin improved the port facilities and built modern communications. All of this would support German trade, but it was also meant to support the kaiser's navy in the event of war.

With the rapid construction of its modern navy, Germany positioned a serious threat near the British homeland. As Germany intended, its imperial fleet compelled Great Britain to concentrate its own fleet in home waters. As a result, the Royal Navy was only thinly represented in the Mediterranean and the Pacific. Germany also implemented plans to turn its merchant fleet into support ships for its regular navy cruisers and into auxiliary cruisers that could operate against enemy trade during war. The three initiatives, when combined, presented a significant danger to British world trade and the security of the British Isles.

3 THE BRITISH RESPOND TO GERMAN POWER

Whitehall interpreted Imperial Germany's aggressive foreign policy, colonial expansion, and naval buildup as potential threats to the British homeland and its worldwide trade. Although Germany repeatedly claimed that it had no intention of challenging Britain's naval supremacy, its colonies and a newly acquired large, modern fleet provided Kaiser Wilhelm II the capability of harming Britain's global interests. Accordingly, London modified its foreign policy and military posture in response to these developments.

In the decades following the Napoleonic Wars, Europe's major powers pursued their interests independently. In doing so, they maintained a relative balance among themselves known as the Concert of Europe. As an island nation, Britain remained comparatively free of continental entanglements, intervening when and where it chose, such as its temporary partnering with France in the Crimean War. In contrast, Germany and Austria-Hungary formed an alliance in 1879. Italy joined them in 1883, creating the Triple Alliance. To counterbalance the Triple Alliance, France and Russia drew closer and formed the Dual Alliance in 1892. At this point, the two powerful alliances balanced, and deterred, each other. A shift by Great Britain to one side or the other would alter the balance. London, however, opted to remain detached from both alliances to retain its freedom of action.[1] Only a menace to Great Britain's national survival could stir the British from their continental detachment. Germany's 1900 naval law declaring its intent to double the size of its navy within seven years supplied it.

In the view of First Sea Lord Winston Churchill, Germany's decision to become the second-ranking naval power, when its army already dominated the continent, constituted a world-changing event. Berlin's pronouncement, according to Churchill, shook Britain out of its splendid isolation from the European alliance system. London first sought to dissuade Germany from its course by pursuing an alliance. Joseph Chamberlain, with a leading role in British foreign affairs although colonial secretary, extended an offer of friendship to the kaiser three times, in 1897, 1899, and 1901. On the third approach, Great Britain proposed Germany join an alliance in conjunction with Japan and also participate in a resolution of the Morocco situation.[2] Germany rebuffed every attempt. With Germany intent on being Europe's strongest land power as well as a peer to Britain in naval power, London had to find some friends. Having been spurned by Germany, Britain looked elsewhere—to Japan.

Because Russia, Germany, and France had pressured Japan to relinquish the territory it had gained on the Liaodung Peninsula (Port Arthur) during the Sino-Japanese War, Tokyo acutely felt its diplomatic isolation. Japan also feared Russian encroachment in the Korean peninsula. Initially, Tokyo sought its own agreement with Russia by offering Tsar Nicholas II hegemony over Manchuria while Japan sought to dominate Korea. When Russia rejected Japan's proposal, Tokyo turned to London as a security partner. Japan reasoned that other European powers would remain neutral rather than risk war with the British by siding with Russia in a potential Russo-Japanese conflict.[3] Great Britain wanted to thwart Russia's ambition to expand southward, which threatened the security of India. The Anglo-Japanese treaty took effect on January 30, 1902.[4]

The treaty specified that Great Britain's primary interest lay in China, but not India. While Japan shared this interest in China, it also had a major interest in Korea. Each party acknowledged the right to protect its own interest in the event of an aggressive attack against it. If either country became involved in a war, the other pledged to maintain its neutrality. Should the war involve more than one aggressor, the other would aid the attacked party.[5]

What benefit London might derive from this treaty is not as clear. As written, the document did not invoke Japanese support for any case other than a war between Great Britain and two or more powers over British interests in China.[6] Should war erupt between Britain and the French-Russian Dual Alliance, or against Germany and Austria-Hungary in either India or Europe, Japan had no obligation to join the fight. The alliance did, however, serve as a warning to Russia that Great Britain had friends in Asia. More important, the treaty guaranteed a solid ally in the event that France, Russia, and Germany attempted to claim territory in China.[7] With Japan invested as an ally, Great Britain maintained its naval presence in East Asia, protected its position in China, and began to strengthen its presence in the North Sea.[8] Great Britain and Japan's primary means of preventing future partitions of China was naval.

In 1903, the Russo-Japanese War broke out. Just as Japan had hoped, its alliance with Great Britain diplomatically isolated Russia. Tsar Nicholas received no assistance from other European powers. Great Britain remained neutral during the conflict to avoid coming to blows with France. France did the same. Britain and Japan renegotiated their treaty so that it extended to British interests in India. In addition, it also reduced the requirement for invoking aid to attack by any single power instead of two. Likewise, France's treaty obligation to Russia did not extend to a war with any party outside the Triple Alliance. Moreover, France, having escaped a war with Britain—over the incident at Fashoda, where British and French military forces met while trying to solidify their respective governments' territorial claims in Africa—sought to avoid one over Russian interests in the Far East as well. French Foreign Minister Theophile Delcassé ardently desired to improve relations with the British. The potential for conflict between France and Britain because of their respective alliances with Russia and Japan caused the old enemies to reconsider their grievances.[9]

Japan's drubbing of Russia strengthened Germany, as Russia's large army constituted Germany's principal threat in Europe. The war with Japan exhausted and diminished the Russian army, producing a new balance of power in which Germany became the dominant military force on the continent. Russia's decline also sapped the potential might of the Franco-Russian alliance. Isolated again, Paris became eager to repair relations with London. Moreover, with Germany's strength burgeoning, Britain could not afford to allow dangerous quarrels to fester, so Prime Minister Arthur Balfour and Foreign Secretary Henry Lansdowne determined to settle their nation's ongoing disputes with France. In 1904, London and Paris signed the Entente Cordiale, which fell short of an actual alliance but meant that Great Britain had abandoned its policy of "splendid isolation," at term coined by First Lord of the Admiralty George Goschen in 1896 to popularly describe Britain's policy of remaining aloof of continental alliances.[10]

Russia's decline strengthened Great Britain's position in East Asia and made Britain's ally Japan the dominant naval power in the Pacific. London used the opportunity to safely bring portions of its Asiatic fleet back to home waters.[11] This helped preserve the balance of naval power in the North Sea in the Royal Navy's favor. Germany's fleet was still under construction. Great Britain viewed its strategic position in Central Asia differently. At first, Russia's decline aroused hope at Whitehall that Britain's defense burden in Central Asia could be reduced. Several prominent policy makers believed that Russia no longer posed a menace, but others, such as Charles Hardinge, Britain's ambassador to Russia, feared that Russia might seek to restore its prestige with an attack on India to gain territory. Claude MacDonald, Britain's head diplomat at the legation in Japan, expressed similar thoughts.

Even though the consensus at Whitehall held that Russia's true policy aims with respect to India were benign, those with the responsibility of defending the Indian frontier had reason for concern. Despite Russia's defeat by Japan in the Russo-Japanese War (1903–5), the tsar could still send more than 250,000 men some 3,000 miles along a railway to oppose British forces in India. Moreover, in 1900 St. Petersburg proceeded to build two railroads that would connect northern Russia with its south Asian provinces. When completed in 1906, the railways provided Russia with the capacity to quickly transport troops toward India's northern frontiers along two distinct avenues of approach. Horatio Herbert Kitchener, British commander in chief in India at the time, and the War Office recognized that Russia could mobilize and seize most of Afghanistan without even a modicum of interference from the British Army. Kitchener advocated, as the only practical method for providing security in the region, maintaining near the Afghan frontier an army commensurate with Russia's capability.[12]

The cabinet realized that accommodating such a large military presence in northern India would strain the public coffers to the point that Parliament would certainly balk at the proposal. Moreover, money spent to defend the Indian frontier reduced funding available to recapitalize the Royal Navy. Whitehall considered the latter a priority because of Germany's naval buildup.[13] Great Britain faced a policy conundrum: should it improve security in India against possible Russian encroachment or ensure that the Royal Navy matched Germany's High Seas Fleet? Tirpitz's risk theory had sought to create just this type of dilemma.

Persia, where Russia was increasingly gaining business concessions, was another area of potential Anglo-Russian conflict. Russia had lost its all-weather port in the Pacific to Japan, so Britain's concern was that it would push eventually for a port concession on the Persian Gulf as an alternate outlet for trade. Lansdowne, in a speech to the House of Lords, warned Russia that an attempt to acquire and fortify a port on the Persian Gulf would be met with stiff resistance.[14]

Prime Minister Balfour established the Committee of Imperial Defence in 1902 following the military and naval drawdowns at the end of the Boer War. Balfour chartered the committee to consider Britain's strategic position and find ways to improve it. It brought the heads of the military services together with cabinet ministers, key civil servants, and at times the leaders from the dominions to provide the prime minister and cabinet with advice. The committee's virtue lay in discussing emerging trends, threats, and opportunities, which helped move Britain's security planning from ad hoc responses toward overarching, coordinated strategy.[15] Over time, the full committee evolved to include standing subcommittees responsible for long-term issues as well as various ad hoc committees assigned to consider specific problems. Reports generated by and for the Committee of Imperial Defence figured prominently in most of Great Britain's policies for a decade.

As Great Britain reconsidered its strategic posture, the Committee of Imperial Defence twice broached the idea that the potential existed for an enemy to invade the home islands. In each case, in 1905 and 1907, Germany was the antagonist. The studies concluded that as long as the Royal Navy dominated the English Channel and North Sea, there existed no credible threat of invasion.[16] Of course, Britain bore a significant expense maintaining its naval superiority as Germany increased its own naval capacity. Additional expenses were incurred in responding to many of Kitchener's recommendations to reform the British army in India.[17]

In 1906, Great Britain could no longer maintain its superiority over Germany's navy and at the same time fortify the Indian frontier against Russia. A choice had to be made. Choosing the latter course required troops that the British did not have; moreover, those troops would have been tied down in India and thus unavailable for use elsewhere. Whitehall's planners drew comfort from knowing that while Russia had the potential to invade Afghanistan, St. Petersburg was not taxing itself to prepare for such a contingency.[18] This fact reduced Britain's need to deter Russia. The renegotiated Anglo-Japanese treaty of 1905 extended its protective umbrella to India further mitigating the threat posed by Russia.[19] Meanwhile, Germany had set about making every exertion, at least as it appeared to authorities in London, to rival British naval mastery. In contrast to Russia's foreign policy, German aggression toward France had created the first Moroccan crisis, tested the Anglo-French entente, and highlighted the risk in Europe. Theoretically, the status quo could have existed indefinitely as long as Anglo-Russian relations and Anglo-German relations remained benign. If the relationship with either great power had soured, however, Britain would have been unprepared. In the end, Britain found that the pragmatic solution to its security needs lay in reaching an entente with Russia.

France, already allied with Russia, welcomed settling the British-Russian rivalry. Russia had also felt the weight of German power. When Russia supported Serbia in its dispute with Austria-Hungary over the annexation of Bosnia-Herzegovina, Kaiser Wilhelm had threatened Tsar Nicholas with war. Russia, France, and Great Britain each had reason to balance Germany's growing strength. At the end of August 1907, after eighteen months of negotiations, Great Britain and Russia agreed to separate spheres of influence in Persia and settled their disputes over the frontier areas in Afghanistan and Baluchistan. Russia's sphere extended to the north, from a line drawn along Isfahan, Yezd, and Kakhk and ended at the intersection of the Russian-Afghan border. Britain's sphere extended to the south, beginning at the Afghan border along a line from Gazik, Birjand, Kerman, and the port at Bandar Abbas.[20] The Anglo-Russian entente relieved the pressure Britain felt over the India frontier and completed what became the Triple Entente of Britain, France, and Russia.

Great Britain understood that Italy's relationship with the Triple Alliance was limited because Rome refused to engage in a war against Russia and France if that war involved fighting the greatest naval power and its major trading partner—Britain.[21] Britain's entente with France had weakened the Triple Alliance, and the Anglo-Russian entente had an even bigger impact. Therefore, Whitehall calculated that likely combinations in war would have been Britain, France, and Russia opposed to Germany and Austria-Hungary whereas earlier the combinations would have been Russia and France opposed to Germany, Austria-Hungary, and Italy.[22] This shift reduced Germany's threat to the continent.

In hindsight, Churchill held that Germany's two great mistakes that led ultimately to the Great War were that it let the reinsurance treaty with Russia lapse and it began a naval rivalry with Great Britain.[23] This allowed France to recover from its isolation and harmed the good relations Germany had with Great Britain. It also completely changed London's strategic posture. In 1900, London was aloof from the continent. By 1907, London had negotiated two treaties with Japan and had settled its decades-old disputes with France and Russia. Britain's security relied on the pillar of good relations with France and Russia. After 1907, protecting the British home islands from invasion and Britain's vast overseas commerce constituted London's vital security concerns. In both cases, Germany's burgeoning navy represented the only significant menace. This focused Whitehall on ensuring that the Royal Navy remained in all cases superior to the German Imperial Navy.

According to historian Bryan Ranft, in the early 1880s British elites and policy makers plunged into debates on methods for protecting trade after William H. Stead published "The Navy of Old England: Is It Ready for War?" and "The Truth about the Navy" in the *Pall Mall Gazette.* The back and forth involved protecting trade as a choice between naval cruisers patrolling trade routes transited by fast merchants or by convoying merchants assembled in groups by speed. Offensive actions aimed at enemy ports and coaling stations, while also hunting down enemy commerce raiders, provided a third alternative but was not considered at that time. Ranft argued that the convoy strategy represented the Royal Navy's best option. He explained that naval planners recognized convoying afforded greater security because they intended to move troops from the colonies to Europe in convoys rather than permit troop transports to venture the oceans unescorted. For protecting merchants, however, Ranft derided British thinking as so offensive minded that the navy preferred hunting down raiders to the more effective defensive convoy system. The slower, tramp merchants that carried Britain's food supply, Ranft argued, could only have been protected by convoy.[24]

Ranft was correct in that convoys afforded greater security for ships than patrolling trade routes. There were, however, relatively few troop ships to convoy compared to thousands of merchant vessels. Moreover, to have organized merchant ships into convoys would have had the effect of forcing shipping into regular routes at prescribed intervals, while cutting off all other potential trade, and compelling Whitehall to assume responsibility for directing all British trade. This meant acting as though all ships were liners, instead of a combination of liners and tramps. Thus, the world's trade—deprived of the lion's share of tramp steamers that made essential connections for seasonal trade and completed circuits between trading nations without their own merchant marine—would have been dislocated. Britain derived significant income from freights, commissions, investments, and insurance; all of these revenues would have been lost. In short, immediately implementing a convoy system would have been nearly as detrimental to British security as cumulative shipping losses.

Convoying remained an extreme measure aimed at survival rather than prosperity. For Britain to have implemented draconian convoy measures before circumstances necessitated would have been unwise. Enacting a convoy system would have been expensive, and ruinous, to a free market economy. Britain needed to safeguard its income, not just its ships, to effectively wage industrial war. To that end, Whitehall strove to prevent disruption to its global economic system.

With convoying eliminated as an option, the Admiralty experimented with another, equally problematic, approach. In naval maneuvers conducted in 1889, cruisers playing the role of commerce raiders had repeatedly evaded their hunters. The Royal Navy's inability to bring raiders to action, even in the relatively narrow confines of the English Channel, demonstrated that offensive patrols against enemy commerce raiders were unlikely to provide adequate protection to merchant ships.[25] The Royal Navy proposed an increase in the number of cruisers through an aggressive building program to rectify the problem. The Admiralty's reasoning held that more cruisers patrolling trade routes would diminish commerce raiders' ability to evade capture or destruction. Budget conscious officials opposed the idea, but the government, however reluctant to increase expenditures, could not long ignore the potential threat to the nation's existence via interrupted trade.

If the navy had insufficient numbers to protect trade, even in home waters, something more had to be done. Britain thus sought improvements in international law, fiscal policy, and the quality of its naval vessels and intelligence to provide the needed edge. The Treaty of Washington (1871) between the United States and Great Britain created the historical precedent for much of international seafaring law and greatly expanded the body of international law.

Beginning with the Hague Conventions (1907), and later the Declaration of London (1909), Britain attempted to create universal rules with respect to maritime war that the world's major powers would understand and follow.

The Treaty of Washington settled disputes between the two powers over fishing rights, the Pacific Northwest boundary between Canada and the United States, and most important for this discussion, the *Alabama* claims.[26] The United States had accused Great Britain of lending material support to the Confederacy during the Civil War (1861–65) when Whitehall permitted British shipyards to build several ships destined for the Confederate navy. One of these vessels became CSS *Alabama*, a highly successful scourge to the Union merchant marine that claimed sixty-nine victims.[27] The Treaty of Washington established a precedent for neutral behavior with respect to support for belligerent naval powers and commerce raiding.

To settle the *Alabama* claims, each power agreed to appoint commissioners to present its case for arbitration to a tribunal in Geneva, Switzerland, consisting of five arbitrators, one each appointed by Britain, the United States, Italy, Switzerland, and Brazil. Guiding principles, agreed to by Britain and the United Stated, formed the basis on which the tribunal would decide the claim. Britain denied that these principles were in effect at the time *Alabama* roamed the seas, but accepted them in order to settle the claim. Moreover, the two countries vowed to observe these rules between them in the future and sought "to bring them to the knowledge of other maritime powers and to invite them to accede to them."[28] They held that any government wishing to remain neutral in war must do three things to preserve its neutral status. First, it must do its utmost, within its jurisdiction, to prevent a belligerent's fitting out and arming any vessel it had reason to believe the belligerent intended for warlike use against another power. Along this line, it should act to prevent any such vessel, having made a conversion to a warship or auxiliary, from departing. Second, the neutral government should not permit a belligerent to use the former's ports or national waters as a base for naval operations. The neutral should prohibit any belligerent from recruiting, resupplying, refitting, or rearming for future naval operations. Third, the neutral government must diligently exercise its authority in its ports and waters to prevent violations.[29]

By agreeing to these precepts, Britain guaranteed that the United States would win the case. The tribunal awarded the United States $15,500,000 in punitive damages.[30] The ruling established, however, that any nation intending to attack an enemy's commerce must support its raiders using only its own ports and resources. As to the facilities required to prosecute a global campaign against commerce, coaling stations, dockyards, telegraphic communications, and so on, Great Britain held the lion's share and could readily attack an enemy's commerce. The ruling effectively made it illegal for a neutral power to aid one of Britain's potential enemies, if that enemy entered a neutral's port or territorial waters, and thereby helped to protect British trade. An enemy vessel on the high seas, however, could provide assistance to a commerce raider, so danger had not been entirely eradicated. The treaty remained a bilateral arrangement. Britain then pushed conventions in order to extend bilateral rights into the realm of international law and set up courts for arbitration. The Hague Conventions highlighted the different views that the powers held concerning maritime war. In particular, the powers disagreed over the criteria governing capture of merchant ships and other private property at sea. Without such criteria, they had no basis upon which to establish an international prize court. Negotiations in this area broke down.

In 1908 British foreign secretary Grey, wanting to firmly establish international law covering maritime war,[31] invited representatives of Austria-Hungary, France, Germany, Italy, Japan, Russia, Spain, and the United States to London to discuss rules governing maritime warfare. The proceedings of the London conference became known as the Declaration of London. Grey proposed the conference consider specific topics where the practice of the major maritime countries diverged. The delegates discussed what constituted contraband cargo and methods used to declare and enforce blockade. The delegates also debated the doctrine of continuous voyage, which when determined allowed a merchant ship to maintain its peacetime status if its voyage had begun prior to the outbreak of hostilities.

The delegates also hoped to rule on the practice of destroying neutral vessels prior to their having been condemned in a legitimate prize court and transfer of merchant vessels from a belligerent power to a neutral power after hostilities. The rules regarding neutral persons or vessels rendering hostile assistance to a belligerent, and rules for converting merchant ships into warships on the high seas, formed more disputed points. Another topic over which the conference contended was whether a property owner's citizenship or domicile determined the property's status as enemy or neutral.

To facilitate the conference's work, each government first laid out its view as to the correct interpretation of international law on each of the conference topics. On most topics, the powers found common principles and agreed on what constituted international law for conducting maritime war. The interpretation and application of the resulting Declaration of London greatly affected conduct of the coming war. Areas about which the powers disagreed sharply and could not devise rules also played out in the subsequent war.

Maritime powers conducting war had long held that enemy property in ships and cargo constituted targets liable for seizure. One method certain powers, especially weak naval powers, used to circumvent risk to their trade was to rely on neutral shipping to transport their goods. Much of the Declaration of London's substance pertained to the rights of neutral shipping and what unneutral service created liability for seizure. The powers understood that blockades declared and notified were legal and applied equally and impartially to vessels of all nations. Blockades applied only to the enemy coast and could not extend to neutral ports. Merchant vessels that could not have known of the blockade prior to an interception were innocent and allowed to pass. All other vessels that breached the blockade, risked condemnation of the vessel and cargo.

Cargo liable to seizure and condemnation fell into two categories, absolute contraband and conditional contraband. Absolute contraband consisted of items readily used in war, such as arms of all kinds (including sporting rifles) and their components, all types of ammunition, and parts for military equipment. The blockading power held authority to seize absolute contraband bound for enemy territory or territory occupied by enemy forces. Conditional contraband included foodstuffs and forage for animals. Textiles and footwear suitable for use in war also made the conditional contraband list. Money, vehicles or vessels, railway materials, and any fuel or lubricants also constituted conditional contraband. When a power seized conditional contraband, it was not enough that the cargo was destined for enemy territory. The blockading force had to prove that the cargo was consigned to the belligerent's armed forces or the government in order to retain or condemn it. The powers also prohibited each other from considering certain items, for example, raw materials, as contraband. The conference delegates also had the foresight to exclude articles used to aid the sick and wounded from contraband lists.

Enemy vessels were liable to capture on the high seas or in any belligerent's territorial waters at anytime, anywhere. Neutral vessels faced the same risks when they carried contraband cargo. The vessel itself faced condemnation if it could be substantiated that contraband formed greater than half the cargo. In a rule that clearly sought to discourage unneutral service, the captor determined what constituted half the cargo based on any one of the following: weight, volume, value, or freight charged. The rules also entitled a captor to seize any non-contraband goods found on board that belonged to the owner of contraband.

The delegates found it necessary to create a distinction between property in ships and property in cargoes. Merchant vessels flying the flag of the enemy defined an enemy vessel. Simple enough, but the delegates added supplemental rules to close loopholes regarding flight from the flag to avoid enemy status. Enemy vessels, however, often carried neutral goods, so determining the enemy or neutral nature of cargo formed a more complex problem. Three separate opinions emerged among the delegations. The basic formula held that enemy goods were those owned by an enemy. One position held that an owner's citizenship determined enemy status. Another opinion considered the owner's domicile as the prime determinant of neutral or enemy status. If the goods' owner resided in enemy territory, irrespective of citizenship, then the goods' status was enemy. The other conception postulated that neither citizenship nor domicile covered the complexity of the issue. During transit, when goods were liable for capture, the majority of cargoes were actually owned under bills of exchange, so ownership fell to a limited liability company or joint stockholding company. In this case, the location of the national headquarters should prevail as the determinant of a cargo's status.

A special committee assigned to follow up on the ownership dispute proposed a three-tiered approach to determining the enemy or neutral status of goods. First, the citizenship of the good's owner determined status. If the owner's citizenship remained indeterminable, then the domicile held sway; if neither the good's owner nor domicile were evident, the location of the holding company's national headquarters would be the determining factor. The delegates could not agree on this proposal either, so the only salient, albeit unhelpful, determinant became that enemy goods belonged to an enemy owner. The German opinion stated that neutral goods on an enemy vessel could be treated as enemy goods, even if they had no enemy character, provided the government making the capture indemnified the owner for the loss.[32] In practical terms, if this action were allowed, a belligerent power could seize any cargo and pay for it simply to deny its benefit to an enemy.

An even more contentious debate arose when delegates attempted to set a precedent for how and where a nation could convert merchantmen into ships of war. The problem was not one of vague definitions, but because of sharp differences in practice. Germany asserted its right, as it had earlier during the 1907 Hague Conventions, to convert merchants into warships inside its own territorial waters and on the high seas. The French position held that because a nation's sovereignty extended to all vessels flying its flag, a nation could do as it chose. Austria-Hungary proposed that with restrictions applied, conversion on the high seas might be justified. All the remaining delegations opposed the practice of conversion on the high seas.

Great Britain, which expected to remain neutral in European conflicts, believed that converting a merchant into a warship on the high seas placed too much power in the hands of belligerents with respect to the rights of neutrals. British merchants traded heavily with continental powers in goods that fell under the rules for conditional contraband. The rules for determining the cargo owner's neutral or enemy status remained vague, and when the cargo neutral character could not be conclusively proved, the captor presumed an enemy status. A belligerent's right to visit and search neutral vessels had already been asserted, with neutrals resisting search subject to seizure and condemnation. Whitehall's delegation argued that a belligerent merchant converting into a warship, perhaps within close proximity to a neutral merchant it wished to search, would so prejudice commerce as to bring other nations into war. The powers granted to belligerents against neutrals already greatly favored belligerents. The British government regarded it of highest importance that warring nations restrict converting merchant vessels into warships to only within their own territorial waters. The delegates remained divided over this issue throughout the conference.

Interested British citizens urged their government to ratify the declaration. They argued that replacing the existing uncertainty with law and practice would benefit all neutral shipowners and merchants faced with their property at the mercy of belligerents. Raw materials would have entered freely in neutral vessels and the declaration also placed limits on food that could be considered contraband, both valuable measures that would have protected British trade.[33] Britain's policy-making elite, however, disagreed. Ultimately, of all the nations participating, only the United States voted to ratify the Declaration of London.

In Great Britain, most interested parties expressed disappointment that the declaration created no precedent for determining the neutral or enemy status of goods and left the question of converting merchants into warships open. Without settling these issues, establishing the international prize court, the key to protecting neutral rights, became improbable. If Germany asserted a right to transform a merchant into a warship on the high seas, then British planning must presume that Germany would do so. Moreover, Germany could perpetrate the fraud of reconverting a warship into an innocent merchant to take advantage of refitting and resupplying in a neutral port. Great Britain had to prepare for that contingency as well.

On the whole, Great Britain had good reason to feel concern over its ability to protect commerce with international law. A belligerent nation had much more power to assert its rights over shipping than did a neutral power. To remain neutral, a maritime nation had to acquiesce to a vague and somewhat arbitrary set of rules, while a belligerent could take full advantage of the ambiguity to protect its interests. The rules had a pronounced effect on the commercial sector. The insurance market balked at covering the potential liability. Without adequate insurance against loss, most owners would send their ships to a safe place and await a war's end. Whitehall had investigated the merits of government insurance for shipping in 1908, at which time the Committee of Imperial Defence determined that the number of potential commerce raiders remained small and decided to rely on the private sector to insure shipping. Because a change in fiscal policy held the possibility of rectifying the situation, Britain revisited the idea again in 1911. To investigate the likely wartime actions of shipowners, the government approached Charles Brighton, chairman of the British Shipowners' Association, and Raymond Beck, chairman of Lloyd's. The government queried them as to the "course probably taken by shipowners in the event of outbreak of war between Great Britain and another power possessing a strong fleet?" Both agreed that a ship's owners would detain the vessels in any friendly or neutral port that they might occupy at war's outbreak. Ships under way would proceed to the nearest friendly or neutral port for safety. The ships would remain in port until the owners obtained adequate insurance for them to proceed, unless the danger was so obviously low that insurance became unnecessary.[34]

The reason for ships to lay up in the nearest safe port was straightforward: War risk insurance was difficult to obtain at a reasonable rate in the private insurance market. Shipowners found a remedy for war risk, beginning around 1906, by forming mutual associations, or clubs, to self-insure against war losses. The club's rules varied in particulars, but all of them stipulated that if Great Britain were a belligerent, ships would take the actions that Brighton and Beck described to minimize risk. If Britain were a neutral power, the ships were fully covered throughout their voyage. The open private insurance market provided ample coverage for cargoes that a merchant obtained separately from the ship's insurance. This, however, provided little comfort to Whitehall officials. The cargoes were vital to Britain's survival, so the ships had to sail.

In 1912 the government, desiring a scheme to provide war risk insurance at reasonable rates so ships would complete their voyages, appointed members to the Standing Subcommittee on Insurance of British Shipping in Time of War to produce such a scheme. The shipping associations agreed that vessels would sail if insured appropriately. As a goal, the planners sought to ensure that the shipping industry paid its fair share of any insurance premiums, but that rates would not rise to the point where the prices of ordinary goods were grossly inflated. Building on the study completed in 1908, the subcommittee recommended an 80-20 percent split. The crown assumed 80 percent of the liability for loss while the shipowners associations carried the remaining 20 percent liability. The premiums collected split along the same share as for liability. The associations would sell the policies and administer the program, which made sense because the associations already had mechanisms in place to issue and maintain policies. Standing up a government office to accomplish the same task would have unnecessarily extended the time for issuing an adequate policy, because the associations could do so immediately. The government also could have elected to maintain an office for the exigency, but that would have entailed an overhead expense that would be passed along to the purchaser, making insurance more costly.

Since cargoes moved when ships moved, the government sought to let the private insurance market handle as much of the war risk as it could without ratcheting up consumer prices. The subcommittee determined not to meddle with cargoes and to allow insurance to fluctuate at war's outbreak. The time between the beginning of war and the need to insure passage of subsequent cargoes allowed ample time to establish a government insurance office in London whose purpose was to provide alternate insurance at a flat rate—determined by a committee of various insurers and government representatives—slightly higher than prevailing rates in the general market. The idea held that cargo owners purchased insurance from the market in most cases. When a route became particularly dangerous, market forces would drive up insurance premiums. This, in turn, made the government flat rate the lowest available, so cargo owners would purchase their insurance from the government. Under this mechanism, the government only insured the highest risk cargoes while in most cases allowing normal market forces to function. The plan called for offering cargo insurance irrespective of the origin or ownership of the cargo. Since routes often formed a circuit involving several ports, the intermediate transport usually involved a foreign-owned cargo transported from one foreign nation to another. The only British interest in the cargo was the freight. Nevertheless, if the vessel could not obtain insurance for the intermediate sailing, the entire voyage would be scrapped.[35]

When the subcommittee reported its recommendations in February 1913, several key factors had changed since the study in 1908. Wireless telegraphy, the committee argued, could potentially give an initial advantage to commerce raiders by directing them to attack shipping prior to a British-government warning. In addition, oil propulsion, which several nations were developing, potentially increased the range and speed of commerce destroyers. The Royal Navy's strength relative to other nation's fleets had diminished, so at the outset of a war, a larger proportion of British warships would be required in the main theater of operations; thus, fewer such ships could be spared for the local protection of trade routes. Most important, Germany's intent to arm merchant cruisers exponentially magnified the threat to British commerce. At war's outbreak, commerce destroyers would likely operate along trade routes. In 1913, complete protection of trade routes by means of British cruisers could only be provided at prohibitive cost.[36]

The Committee of Imperial Defence made the subcommittee's report a central topic at its 122nd meeting on February 6, 1913. The committee members' initial debate focused on the threat posed by Germany. Prime Minister H. H. Asquith reminded the members that the previous study completed in 1908 by Austin Chamberlain's committee had concluded that the only real guarantee against war risk was a strong navy. That report had recommended against national indemnity insurance, but in 1913 the Royal Navy was relatively weaker than it had been in 1908. Lord President of the council Robert Crewe remarked that given Britain's refusal to acknowledge a right to convert merchants to auxiliary cruisers on the high seas, German merchant vessels so converted could be considered as privateers or pirates. He noted, however, that if London conceded the right, following suit could prove an effective remedy to deterring Germany given Britain's superior numbers in ships. Here, Crewe seemed, however, to miss the point. Britain acknowledged that any nation had a right to convert merchant vessels into auxiliaries; it was conversion on the high seas that Britain contested. The idea that Great Britain could convert more merchants into auxiliary cruisers than could Germany remained true irrespective of where the conversion took place.

Eyre Crowe, the senior clerk in the Western Department of the Foreign Office, who had been at the London naval conference, admitted that Britain's delegates had lacked a firm basis on which to oppose conversions on the high seas. They had been instructed to oppose the principle, so they did. Lord Chancellor Richard Burdon Haldane saw no reason to oppose conversions on the high seas so long as they were carried out transparently, and the ships' status did not change throughout the war's duration. The two also seem to have missed the point: A nation would most likely elect to convert merchant ships into cruisers on the high seas because it could not effect the conversion in its own waters and then avoid blockade when trying to proceed into open seas. To convert in a neutral's port invited the host's enmity. If the practice were prohibited under international law, then the transformation from peaceful merchant to hostile raider simply would not take place. Had the nations agreed on this matter, an international prize court would have been possible. If a nation violated the statute, its auxiliary would be treated as a pirate, with any captures ruled illegal and full restitution demanded from the enemy at war's end. Britain, with its many overseas ports, could transform and sustain auxiliary cruisers without violating international norms. The island nation clearly gained an advantage if conversion on the high seas was prohibited.[37]

First Lord of the Admiralty Churchill stated at the meeting on February 6 that the Admiralty had evidence that Germany had armed a considerable number of its merchant ships, but could not tell definitely which ships were armed. As a countermeasure, the navy had 150 4.7-inch guns available and proposed to pay for mounting these on British steamers. The Admiralty also anticipated providing for magazines and naval reserve crews. "The prospect of 40 German merchant vessels being converted into warships," he stated, "with orders to prey upon [British] commerce was serious." He believed the only suitable expedient entailed arming British merchants to defend themselves.[38] Moreover, Churchill argued that the Admiralty should dictate routes and delivery ports to obtain efficient use of naval assets engaged in commerce protection. Ensuring the British people's food supply demanded such measures. He believed that the Admiralty could secure merchant marine cooperation via the national guarantee insurance by stipulating in the policy that vessels must follow Admiralty instructions.

Churchill emphasized that "the navy could not protect the ships if they did not start." Without the national guarantee insurance, vessels had no incentive to put to sea except for the prospect of high prices. The navy did not dispute that most ships making the attempt would safely complete their voyage. The Admiralty feared, however, that most would not make the attempt without additional incentive. The people's choice consisted of exorbitant prices or a national insurance program. Minister of Agriculture Walter Runciman argued that the insurance costs exposed the government to "a leap in the dark financially." The plan's proponents provided no basis for estimating the government's cost, and the system presented opportunities to plunder the treasury. To this, Churchill replied that the government's first responsibility was to "secure the food supply of the nation. Without that, the successful prosecution of war was impossible."[39]

Prime Minister Asquith agreed, adding that the same people would pay either through taxes collected and subsequently paid out as indemnity for shipping losses or in high food prices. At this point, Churchill remarked that the state's exposure to loss probably could not exceed 5 to 6 percent of total shipping and cargoes. When Home Secretary Reginald McKenna questioned whether it could really be that high, Churchill responded that a German liner in the South Atlantic that received orders by wireless could become active on the Cape route and make numerous captures before being destroyed.[40]

Germany naval developments posed a dual threat to Britain's security. German navy light cruisers and armed merchantmen poised to attack British merchant shipping constituted the first serious threat. The German High Seas Fleet prowling the North Sea also threatened bombardment and potential invasion if it defeated the Royal Navy. Britain's naval building program provided the Royal Navy with the material edge required to retain its superiority at sea. Advancements in armor plate and gunnery played an important role, but the Admiralty also determined that in order to assure victory in the North Sea its fastest warships had to attain a speed advantage over the German fleet. The high speeds the Admiralty desired were attainable with coal-fired boilers, but only if the ship were lengthened to accommodate the larger engine room boilers and machinery. The required extension made the design too long for existing docks. Admiralty cost projections to rebuild docks at shipyards and naval bases, as well as the added expense for armor plate and steel, proved exorbitant. The case against using coal as the fuel for cruisers was similar. The added length on the cruiser meant additional cost and so much weight that it would restrict top speed by 3 to 4 knots. In smaller ships, such as torpedo boats and destroyers, coal systems did not provide the speed or endurance needed. Oil-fueled boilers packed more power than coal could into a similar sized engine room for a comparable construction cost in any size ship. The Admiralty felt compelled to use oil in warship construction to increase speed and endurance without driving up ship size and cost.

For the 1911–12 building program, the Admiralty recommended that all future construction include oil-fueled propulsion in all types of naval ships. In the big battleships, oil was only required when battle necessitated top speeds. For that reason, Britain continued to build most of them as coal burners with auxiliary oil-fired boilers, which were used to achieve maximum speed. The Admiralty also decided to build a division of fast, oil-only battleships with a flank speed of 26 knots. This decision effectively placed the battle cruiser program in stasis. The plan called for a minimum of four such ships that formed the van of the battle line. Another flight of four fast battleships would form the battle line's rear when the colonies fulfilled their promise to provide the ships. The navy designed its fleet of fast, light-armored cruisers for speeds of 30 to 31 knots. The cruisers required high speeds to move rapidly from one geographic area to another to deal with contingencies, patrol shipping lanes, and avoid combat against bigger gunned and heavily armored battleships. The building program included eight advanced-design cruisers.

When the Admiralty decided to use fuel oil in all the warships, it also committed Great Britain to procuring vast quantities of oil. When Churchill became First Sea Lord in 1911, his admirals told him that British oil reserves consisted of a four-month supply for oil-only ships and three months for coal-with-oil auxiliaries. The Admiralty obtained its oil in annual contracts and had agreed that year to purchase 200,000 tons. Not satisfied that planners had done their homework, Churchill directed them to calculate oil consumption for all ship types in peacetime and under wartime conditions, assuming that Britain would remain at war for a year. He also assumed that the nation's full command of the sea would suffice to permit adequate oil imports. He dismissed questions about risks to supplies, asking, "If we cannot bring oil, how can we get corn?" Running the figures for five consecutive years, including ships projected to enter the fleet, Admiralty planners determined that actual fleet requirements for fuel were much higher than contracted. The 200,000 tons proved adequate only for peacetime conditions for the ships in the fleet in 1911; this excluded new ship construction. Their calculations indicated that Britain should hold six months fuel-oil supply in reserve for wartime contingency. The Admiralty also needed to procure between 569,000 and 729,000 tons annually over the next five years to meet anticipated demand.

Great Britain could have continued to procure its oil in annual contracts, but a number of factors pushed the Admiralty into finding a long-term supply. To entice customers to invest their capital, the manufactures of oil engines found it necessary to guarantee the future availability of fuel. Manufacturers therefore began immediately to contract with oil companies for long-term supplies, in the process creating the oil futures market. Much of the oil production in future years was divided among various consumers who took steps to protect themselves against potential artificial market manipulation and shortfalls in supply.

Churchill noted that the United States had a stake in its national oil fields. Germany had contracted for Romanian oil, which it could receive via a secure land route. Arguing that oil and ammunition were equally important to the proper functioning of the Royal Navy, and therefore crucial to national security, Churchill recommended that Britain also contract for a secure long-term oil supply. London's options included several potential suppliers, all of which would supply some of the Admiralty's fuel requirement with some level of risk. Royal Dutch Shell was 60 percent Dutch owned, but under certain political conditions could rapidly convert to German control. Britain mitigated this by contracting with Shell under an independent subsidiary to provide oil from

Romanian fields. British-flagged ships transported this oil via the Black and Mediterranean Seas. Nevertheless, because of the origin and the route, the Shell option remained susceptible to Triple Alliance interdiction.

Union Oil of California, another source, relied on the Panama Canal's completion in 1914 so oil could transit from the Pacific Coast to Great Britain. The company planned to provide the tankers necessary for transport, but the company used foreign ships for transit and traversed a route over which Great Britain had no control. The Mexican Eagle Company offered oil of poorer quality than the other sources and therefore required additional refining. The company's chief advantages were lower cost, immediate availability, and ability to rapidly expand capacity to meet wartime needs. A home supply that could meet the Admiralty's needs for approximately 150 years existed in Scottish oil shale, but it remained untapped because extraction was more expensive than oil from other sources. A government subsidy could stimulate production, but it would take years before oil could be produced in the quantities and at prices useful to the Admiralty.

Churchill recommended that the Admiralty also establish a long-term contract with the Anglo-Persian Oil Company. This fulfilled some parameters that Britain felt helped protect oil supplies. First, it offered geographical separation from other sources so that local failure or emergency would not become crippling. Second, Anglo-Persian promised the capability to expand oil production to meet demand surges, which tended to stabilize a potentially volatile market. The outfit pumped 200,000 tons annually with capacity to expand production to 500,000 tons. Third, Anglo-Persian remained entirely under British financial control. The company required an infusion of capital, however, to forestall a bid from Shell to absorb it. This proved somewhat of an advantage for the Admiralty because it could garner more favorable rates on future oil production. Most important, oil extracted from Persia would transit to Britain in wartime around Africa, via the Cape route. The Royal Navy exercised sufficient control over this passage to make enemy interference with oil deliveries difficult.[41]

The Admiralty concluded an agreement with Anglo-Persian Oil in May 1914 requiring the company to provide 50,000 to 70,000 tons for the year July 1, 1914, through June 30, 1915. Each year thereafter, until 1918, the Admiralty required a larger delivery until reaching 300,000 to 350,000 tons. The contracted delivery would remain at this higher level for the duration of the agreement, which ran through 1934. With written notice, the Admiralty could retain the right to an additional 50,000 tons the first year. In out years, the Admiralty could call on Anglo-Persian to provide up to 450,000 to 500,000 tons.[42] This contract initially provided the Royal Navy with about 10 percent of its fuel needs in 1914, but with development by 1918 this important source had the potential to provide as much as 70 percent of the Admiralty's projected requirement.

The Admiralty had taken steps over time to radically improve its intelligence gathering and fusion. As far back as 1905, when Admiral John A. Fisher was First Sea Lord, the Admiralty viewed the navy's mission as threefold: defend the British Isles from invasion, safeguard overseas territories from attack, and preserve the global trading system by protecting oceanic trade routes.[43] Fears of attacks on trade cropped up during the Boer War; if a European power intervened on behalf of the Boers, trade would likely become a target. The plan to protect trade thus called for stationing cruisers at trade route focal points. No one, including Lloyd's of London, the maritime insurance broker, knew exactly where the focal points would be, or their number, or how many cruisers would suffice to protect them. At the time, the density of traffic of the various routes and seasonal flow were unknown.[44]

With Fisher as First Sea Lord, the Admiralty's approach to gathering and exploiting intelligence became systematic, with analysis centralized in London. Beginning in 1901, the Naval Intelligence Department (NID), through the Trade Division, collected data and compiled statistics on commerce and its usual routes from which it constructed trade charts showing where British merchant vessels congregated in the greatest numbers at different times of the year. The NID provided these to the various regional naval commanders so they could prepare to protect commerce in time of war.

In 1905, the trade and intelligence divisions began to pool their efforts and maintain a daily tracking record of every ship of war, foreign and British, worldwide. They also tracked some 100 liners and fast cargo ships thought to be candidates for conversion into auxiliary cruisers. The NID collected sighting reports from regional intelligence officers, customs, consular and diplomatic sources, and the Lloyd's signal stations along with other relevant data to plot daily. Moreover, analysts predicted likely movements by analyzing ships' logistics. For instance, merchant ships followed great circle routes to conserve fuel. This kept freight costs lower. Few places in the world maintained any significant reserve stock of coal, so coal supply largely governed a ship's destination and assisted forecasting the enemy's strategy. This is why the Admiralty also tracked colliers. Approximately 75 percent of the world's steam coal emanated from Welsh mines, leaving Great Britain from Cardiff's docks. The navy kept an office at Cardiff to track shipments.[45]

Difficulty obtaining coal would hamper the activities of commerce destroyers, although they might be able to rely on coal supplies taken from their prizes or otherwise obtained at sea for a time, with favorable weather and calm seas to aid in the transfer of bulk cargo. Eventually, however, the raiders would have to seek a port to replenish food and coal. When that occurred, the NID system could plot their positions and direct cruisers to their locations. With timely, accurate intelligence, the raiders' prospects of continuing to elude pursuit diminished.[46]

From 1904 to 1909, under Fisher's direction, NID continued to develop its intelligence system. At the outbreak of war, the Royal Navy would have to contend with potential commerce raiders whose positions would be known at least roughly, some specifically. The navy established regional centers in Colombo, Singapore, and Hong Kong. By 1909, the NID was providing intelligence officers at remote centers with timetables so they would know when to expect the arrival of certain German ships in their sector. The Admiralty, naturally, tracked German vessels likely to be used as auxiliary cruisers daily.[47]

In late 1911, the NID began work on a scheme to warn and reroute merchant ships away from enemy raiders' known locations.[48] Clearly, the Admiralty had changed its ideas about protecting commerce. No longer did only the Royal Navy focus on protecting trade routes. Instead, British merchants took advantage of navy-provided armaments to defend themselves and naval intelligence to avoid raiders. The navy concentrated on knowing threat locations and its own ability to direct naval forces to the scene.

Great Britain completely altered its grand strategy between 1900, when Germany announced its intention to double the size of its naval fleet, and 1912. It abandoned splendid isolation to form an alliance with Japan and used diplomacy to allay grudges with the United States, France, and Russia. The British cabinet no longer contemplated war against any of its traditional rivals. Rather, Germany and the Triple Alliance constituted the basis for all defense planning.

Britain championed international law as a means of preserving the peace and promoted the rights of nations to trade. To ensure that British trade prospered in time of war and that traders had the incentive necessary to complete voyages, the government organized a national guarantee insurance scheme. The Royal Navy remained superior in the quantity and quality of its ships. Moreover, the Admiralty concentrated the fleet in home waters and developed an intelligence system to track threats to commerce. Britain took all of these measures in response to the growing threat it perceived from Germany.

4 GREAT BRITAIN'S STRATEGIC OPTIONS IN THE COMING WAR

Britain's diplomacy leading up to the Great War and its subsequent entry into war as an Entente Cordiale power remain the subject of historical debate. Some claim, including David Lloyd George, then–chancellor of the exchequer, that more able statesmen could have prevented the war. Others have decried Britain's entry into the conflict because it turned an isolated continental war into a world war. Still others laud Britain's intervention to uphold the rule of law, and preserve the rights of Belgium, which represented small independent nations everywhere. When one considers Great Britain's interests and options, however, its actions appear pragmatic; preventing war best served Great Britain's interests. When war nevertheless came, the island kingdom's interests lay in preventing Germany from dominating the European continent. To achieve that end, Britain joined France and Russia in war against Germany.

Lloyd George believed that none of the combatants' diplomats, or heads of state, wanted war in July 1914. He viewed these statesmen as seamen, able enough to steer their respective ships in steady seas but incapable of handling a typhoon. He judged them as lacking passion, stubbornness, and aggression. Lloyd George asserted in his memoirs that military chiefs in Austria-Hungary, Germany, and Russia thrust their respective nations into a war that their bewildered and confused diplomats attempted to stop but could not.[1]

Lloyd George believed that the pact between France and Russia obligated both parties to an offensive and defensive alliance. In his postwar memoirs, he lamented the fact that France had chosen to support Russia and had not stood aside. Had the latter happened, he argued, Germany would have left France alone.[2] Lloyd George advocated husbanding Britain's army rather than immediately sending an expeditionary force to the continent. In the former case, when Great Britain then raised a large army, the belligerents would have been compelled to heed Britain's agenda. Instead, in order to quickly conquer France, Germany invaded Belgium, which ended all possibilities for peace.[3] Lloyd George blamed British foreign minister Edward Grey for not warning Germany sooner, and more boldly, that Britain would stand by its treaty obligation to Belgium, asserting that "it might have averted war altogether."[4]

Other sources paint a different picture. Richard Burdon Haldane, Britain's emissary to Germany for negotiating naval ratios in 1912, recorded in the diary of his mission that he had told German chancellor Theobald von Bethmann-Hollweg that if Berlin sought to crush France, creating a condition where the latter no longer had the capacity to defend itself, Great Britain's interests would be so affected that the island nation could not stand by and see it done.[5] The British had mobilized previously, in 1911, to support France during the second Moroccan crisis. In a speech to the London Banker's Association, delivered July 21, 1911, Lloyd George had warned Germany that before Britain would see its interests surrendered, it would come to France's aid in a war against Germany.[6]

Thus, Britain had unambiguously communicated its position on a Franco-German war to the German leadership twice within three years prior to the July 1914 crisis precipitated by the assassination of Austria-Hungary's Archduke Ferdinand while he was touring Sarajevo. Grey had also drafted a telegram to Edward Goschen, Britain's ambassador in Berlin, concerning a conversation he had had with Karl Max Lichnowsky, Germany's ambassador in London. The telegram pertained to Britain's position on the July 1914 developments in Europe. Grey indicated that as long as Germany and France did not become involved, Great Britain had no intention of intervening in the conflict. If, however, Germany entered the war and France followed, Grey reminded Lichnowsky that Great Britain's "interests required [it] to intervene, [Britain] must intervene at once, and the decision would have to be very rapid, just as the decisions of other Powers had to be."[7] Germany's march through Belgium was incidental to invading France. Irrespective of Britain's position on Belgian neutrality, Germany could hardly have mistaken Britain's desire to preserve France as an independent power.

The Treaty of London (1839) had established Belgium as a perpetually neutral state, which Europe's various powers, including Britain, France, and Prussia, pledged to guarantee. A similar treaty signed in 1867 guaranteed the neutrality of Luxemburg.[8] Whitehall's planners had contemplated Britain's position on the contingency of a German invasion of Belgium for decades prior to the events of July 1914. During the 1870–71 Franco-Prussian War, Britain drafted a supplement to the 1839 treaty asking Prussia and France to reaffirm their commitment to Belgian neutrality. Both nations agreed that they would. Britain clarified its own position, stipulating that if either party violated Belgium's territory, Britain would immediately aid the other party. Although treaties guaranteeing the neutrality of both Belgium and Luxemburg existed, Britain chose to emphasize its obligation to uphold Belgian neutrality. If the Belgian coast were occupied by a hostile continental power, the Royal Navy's control over the English Channel would be threatened. As Britain's ministers saw it, neutrality of the Belgian coast remained a British strategic imperative while upholding Luxemburg's sovereignty figured only as a secondary consideration. Britain's supplement to the 1839 treaty expired at the end of the Franco-Prussian War, leaving the original in effect.[9]

Meanwhile, Berlin's war planners sought to circumvent the treaties by interpreting neutrality in ways favorable to its military forces. For example, in 1897 corvette captain Schröder of the German naval staff proposed an audacious contingency to seize the Scheldt estuary and Antwerp, in the Netherlands and Belgium, respectively, as preliminary steps toward invading Great Britain. Schröder explained that considerations as to the neutrality of these two nations should not dissuade Germany from conquest when the nation's life was at stake. He rationalized that it was not a question of annexation, but only the temporary occupation of their territory to facilitate a military campaign. Full compensation to the landowners for damaged and destroyed property would be paid at war's end.[10]

Germany's loophole closed when the Fifth Hague Conventions of October 18, 1907, made the rights and responsibilities of neutral states explicit. The articles stated that a neutral's territory was inviolable and forbid belligerents from moving troops or supplies across it. Neutral powers could not allow belligerents to use their territory, and a neutral using force to resist an attempt by another to violate its neutrality did not constitute a hostile act against the belligerent.[11]

During the crisis preceding the Great War, First Lord of the Admiralty Winston Churchill reported that on Friday, July 24, 1914, he had dined with the director of the Hamburg-America Line, Albert Ballin, the friend of Ernest Cassel, a prominent London banker who had facilitated Haldane's mission to Berlin. Ballin asserted that the outcome of the crisis depended wholly on Tsar Nicholas II. If Russia attacked Austria-Hungary, Germany must march against Russia. He felt certain that France would then mobilize against Germany. Ballin desperately desired to know what Britain would do. Churchill replied that for Germany to presume Britain would stay out of the war would be a grave mistake. Ballin then offered that Germany could guarantee that if it defeated France, Kaiser Wilhelm II would take nothing in Europe; a few French colonies would satisfy Germany as an indemnity. He inquired as to whether that would alter Britain's attitude. Churchill reiterated that Britain's response would be to events as they developed and that Germany would be mistaken to assume Britain would remain neutral. Soon thereafter, Churchill reported his conversation to Grey and early in the following week to the cabinet as well.[12]

On Wednesday night, July 29, 1914, Chancellor Bethmann-Hollweg provided Goschen a formal proposal requesting British neutrality. Goschen telegraphed the proposal to Grey, who received it July 30. The chancellor indicated that should Russia attack Austria, Germany's alliance with Austria might render a general European war inevitable. Bethmann-Hollweg judged that Britain would never permit Germany to crush France, and he assured Goschen that Germany did not contemplate so severe a result. Provided that Great Britain remained neutral, Germany stood ready to provide every assurance that should France be defeated, Germany would annex no French territory. When Goschen questioned him about colonies, Bethmann-Hollweg stated that he could not give any assurance on the matter of colonies. The chancellor offered, however, that as long as the neutrality and integrity of the Netherlands was respected by Germany's adversaries, Germany would also respect it. He could not specify what operations might, because of French actions, be forced upon Germany. He could, however, state that if Belgium did not side against Germany, its integrity would be respected after the war concluded.[13] The proposal, identical in substance to Ballin's exchange with Churchill, reflected Schröder's rationale.

The British cabinet had already considered Germany's proposal when Ballin broached the idea informally to Churchill. Grey, therefore, did not need to contemplate before rejecting it. Marginal comments made on the telegram by Eyre Crowe, a deputy in the Foreign Office, demonstrate how poorly the British received the German overture. Crowe wrote, "The only comment that need be made on these astounding proposals is that they reflect discredit on the statesman who makes them." He also remarked that Germany tacitly admitted its intention to violate Belgian neutrality while intending to respect the Netherlands' neutrality. He assessed that Germany intended to maintain Dutch neutrality to continue trade through Rotterdam and up the Rhine River, while simultaneously violating Belgium's neutrality in order to quickly invade France. He concluded that Germany desired the war, and Britain's possible entry constituted the only real restraint on its actions.[14]

Historian Niall Ferguson has argued that when Britain rebuffed Germany's proposal, the island nation needlessly expanded what would have been a continental war of limited aims into a world war. Britain had chosen not to intervene in Prussia's victory over France in 1871 and Europe's balance of power had not come undone. Therefore, Britain had a precedent on which to fall back.[15] Ferguson also contends that Germany's modest aims, as proposed by Bethmann-Hollweg to Goschen, posed no direct threat to British interests. German goals, Ferguson postulates, would have been limited to drastically weakening Russia, stripping France of its colonies, and forming a Central European Customs Union run by Germany. Each of these actually complemented Britain's goals.[16]

If Britain's interests truly fell in line with Germany's plans, as Ferguson claims, then Britain squandered the opportunities presented in the first and second Moroccan crises to capitalize on Germany's efforts. British diplomats and planners, however, had to work within their understanding of potential outcomes. Moreover, British policy makers should be given credit for understanding their own interests. Germany simultaneously proposed to respect the neutrality of the Netherlands, which lacked a treaty sanction making it perpetually neutral, while violating the neutrality of Belgium (and Luxemburg), which did have treaty protection. Germany argued that it must wage war against France because of its treaty alliance with Austria-Hungary and thus consequently violate the treaties respecting Belgium and Luxemburg.

While Germany's ministers concocted these arguments, neither Austria-Hungary nor Russia had yet to declare war. In fact, Austria-Hungary's declaration of war on Russia followed Germany's declaration against Russia by five days. No principle of international law governed Berlin's actions. If Germany had to disregard a treaty obligation, why not the one preventing a major European conflagration? If Germany desired peace, it took the wrong approach. Even if Britain had stood aside and Germany remained true to its word, the latter would have defeated France and been able to demand an indemnity that likely would have included ceding control of Morocco. In an optimistic scenario, Germany would have required France to pay the costs of indemnifying Belgium for any damage caused by the German army. In a less optimistic case, France's indemnity would leave the nation so impoverished that it would take more than twenty years to recover militarily.

In short, for Britain's absolute pledge of neutrality, the kaiser promised to refrain from molesting nations not directly in the German army's path to France and to "look forward to a general neutrality agreement between the two countries [Britain and Germany]."[17] Berlin insisted that other nations permit its army free passage. Those that resisted would become belligerents. The kaiser hoped to force those invaded to pay for their own subjugation and expected other powers to endorse the practice. Whitehall simply could not work with Germany on the basis that Bethmann-Hollweg proposed.

One cannot credit the events that unfolded to amateurism on the part of German and British diplomats. As noted above, at least forty years earlier military planners in Germany had already raised the idea of violating Belgian neutrality. Germany had confronted France twice over Morocco and knew what the British reaction would be if Germany defeated France and stripped it of this crucial colony. Germany also knew Britain's position on a Franco-German war, so one must conclude that Germany expected Britain to join the entente. Thinking that London preferred mediation, as shown when Whitehall had used it to contain the Balkan wars, Berlin probably calculated that its diplomacy could buy time. Moreover, the British cabinet was consumed in early July 1914 with attempting to solve growing problems with home rule in Ireland. Germany therefore thought it could count on Whitehall adopting a wait-and-see position and stood to benefit if Britain entered the war later rather than sooner.

Grey countered Bethmann-Hollweg on August 1 by asking the Germans to refrain from attacking Russia and France. In return, Britain would guarantee that France remained neutral.[18] Grey's proposal quickly faded. To make it palatable, Berlin would have stipulated that to guarantee French neutrality, Paris allow Germany to occupy the fortresses at Toul and Verdun, the keys to France's main defensive line.[19] If Germany then elected to retain the fortifications, it could easily invade France at any time. How would France regain these crucial outposts, and who would assist France in recapturing them? If the German proposal were accepted, France would become a German satellite. France had no intention of prostrating itself or abandoning its Russian ally. Lloyd George and Niall Ferguson may have believed that Germany harbored no ill will toward France, but others in France and Britain had little reason to share this faith.

Britain had also reconsidered its response to a violation of Belgian neutrality by a continental power. During the first Moroccan crisis, in September 1905, Prime Minister Arthur Balfour had addressed three questions to the War Office General Staff: whether France or Germany had good reason to violate Belgium's neutrality; whether the Belgians could offer an effective resistance; and how long it would take to send two army corps from Britain to Belgium. The General Staff responded that the political consequences attendant to violating Belgian neutrality would likely deter both nations from taking that course in the initial stages of a war. As battle continued, however, wartime exigencies would render it imperative that one or the other, most likely Germany, disregard Belgium's neutrality. The Belgian army consisted of a garrison army that manned fortifications at Namur and Liege and a 92,000-man field army. The staff concluded that with the assistance of the field army, the garrisons could temporarily check an advance from the French or German army. Given twenty transports available by the tenth day of a war, the British could send two corps to Belgium in twenty-three days.

A German war plan against France, the General Staff believed, might have consisted of two advances—one through the Franco-German frontier and one through Belgium. Either one could form the main thrust. A push through Belgium made sense because France had heavily fortified its border along the German frontier. The countryside in Belgium made passage through the lowlands much more feasible than attempting to force the French defensive network. A disadvantage, however, was that the German army would have to move on foot unless Belgium cooperated by permitting the use of its railroads. Still, the Belgian rail network lacked the carrying capacity of the German railways in Alsace-Lorraine.

The General Staff judged that Germany could mobilize and place its army on the Belgian frontier in seven to eight days. If unopposed, the army might make the French border by the twelfth or thirteenth day. Any measures Germany took to protect its lines of communication added time to the General Staff's estimates, as did the possibility of stiff Belgian resistance. If operations went well for the German army, it could subdue the Belgian fortress at Liege in one day. The staff calculated, therefore, that Germany could reach France via Belgium in three weeks.

Two other alternatives presented themselves as means for Germany to invade France, and both violated the neutrality of other states. Germany could attempt a maritime expedition, landing in Belgium, followed by marching to France. This course of action carried enormous risk in 1905 because of French naval superiority. The balance of naval power between France and Germany, however, began to tilt in favor of Germany at that time. The General Staff calculated that the Germans would require a landing force of nearly a million men, and to adopt this course would leave Alsace-Lorraine virtually undefended. France could easily have retaken these provinces. The General Staff dismissed this course of action. The second alternative consisted of a movement through Switzerland that would consume more than three weeks and could be easily countered by French forces. The British judged that this alternative lacked military effectiveness. In summary, as early as 1905, the War Office General Staff judged Germany's best chance of defeating France occurred with a violation of Belgium's neutrality.

Conversely, the General Staff argued that the French enjoyed an advantage if the main theater of operations remained in Alsace-Lorraine. French defenses were strongest there and made a good base of operations for a drive into Germany. A French advance through Belgium would initially pass through lightly defended territory while alerting both the Belgians and Germans to the threat. By the time the French reached Liege at the end of a march through Belgium, fortifications would have been strengthened by that nation's field army. By that time, moreover, Germany would have placed its army at the Belgian frontier to oppose a French advance. Yet with Germany, the opposite situation presented itself. The German army could surprise the fortress at Liege, subdue it, and then march through the lightly defended and easily passable Belgian countryside. Germany could move through Belgium more quickly and with fewer losses than France.[20]

By August 1907, the British cabinet wanted to move beyond hypothetical scenarios and begin actually planning for the contingency of a major European power invading the Low Countries. British foreign policy held the independence of the Netherlands and Belgium as critical to maintaining the balance of power in Europe. When Britain pledged with the other European powers to guarantee Belgium's neutrality, it had done so to prevent wars. A line between Berlin and Paris passed directly through Belgium. Using a line of advance through Belgium would have allowed the French to bypass the German fortifications around Metz, but likewise it would have permitted Germany to turn the main line of France's eastern frontier defenses. Thus a pledge of Belgium's neutrality made each nation's ability to defend itself easier. Likewise, Britain's defensive capabilities improved if Belgium remained neutral because it would prevent a major power from possessing Antwerp, Belgium's major seaport. If a major power held Antwerp, that power could eventually stage enough naval power there to make control of the English Channel difficult and invading the home islands more likely.

An independent Netherlands mattered more to the British than did Belgian neutrality. The Rhine, Meuse, and Scheldt Rivers, each with navigable estuaries, all lay within the Netherlands. In the event of an invasion, these rivers would be the most likely points of origin. The Netherlands itself lacked sufficient power to pose an invasion threat to Britain and is why Britain desired that it remain a neutral power in its own right, separate from Belgium.[21]

While preparing contingency plans for a German attack on France, the General Staff examined the possibility of Britain responding by sending a military force to the continent to assist France versus relying on naval forces alone. The War Office preferred sending a ground force in the early stages of conflict. Noting that a German occupation of the Netherlands would be prejudicial to British interests, the staff concluded that it must plan for that contingency. The War Office requested permission from the cabinet to appoint a joint military and naval board to work out detailed plans.[22]

By late 1909, the War Office's General Staff had begun to consider the effects of a blockade on the Triple Alliance. Reliable data being difficult to obtain, the office addressed a memo directly to Winston Churchill, then-president of the Board of Trade, asking the board's opinion. The Board of Trade believed that Austria-Hungary would be least affected by blockade because it did not rely on imports and exports for its industries; for food it was nearly self-sufficient. Germany would likely obtain adequate supplies through the Netherlands and Belgium, provided these two countries remained neutral. Germany could also rely on Norway and Sweden for imports via the Baltic Sea. The Balkan states and Turkey would be capable of supplying German needs overland. Interference by British naval forces would raise the freight rates Germany had to pay and impose time delays. The effect of these factors would be to generally increase prices in Germany. Nevertheless, the board concluded that Germany could meet its needs. Italy, however, was largely dependent on foreign meat and grain and imported it by sea, making it the most affected. Thus, British naval power rendered Italy vulnerable.[23]

Brigadier General Sir Henry Wilson, director of Military Operations for the War Office, sent a memorandum to the chief of the Imperial General Staff in August 1911 during the height of the second Moroccan crisis. Wilson's memorandum pondered the question of British policy in the event of a German attack on France. The memorandum began with the axiom that Great Britain must "prevent any continental power from attaining a position of superiority that would allow it to dominate, and dictate, to the rest of Europe."[24] The problem Britain faced historically was French domination of the continent, but the axiom applied equally well to Germany. British policy options included remaining neutral or becoming the active ally of France. On land, the combined armies of Germany and Austria-Hungary would suffice to meet the Russian threat with no discernible relief on the French frontier. If Britain remained neutral, France would fight alone against Germany. The German army and fleet overmatched those of France, and Russia provided no naval assistance to France, so the outcome of a war would scarcely be in doubt.[25] German seaports would have remained open while French ports, at least on the north coast, would have been subjected to blockade. The resulting financial dislocation for Germany would be minimal, while for France it would be acute.

In Wilson's thinking, Great Britain's remaining neutral in a war between Germany and France would result in Germany attaining the dominant position that London's declared policy was to prevent. Moreover, if Britain waited and permitted Germany to defeat France, it would render the British Expeditionary Force useless because its small size in relation to continental armies left it unable to act alone. Germany would likely annex Belgium and the Netherlands. The power concentrated in continental Europe's combined navies, along with their dominant geography, would in a matter of some years defeat the Royal Navy.

If Britain became France's active ally, however, the British and French fleets could command the sea. French ports could remain open while those in Germany closed, maximizing the fiscal and economic harm to the Germans. Moreover, the combined French and British militaries would be able to reach near parity in numbers with the German army at decisive points on the continent. The Allies might attain some early victories, boosting their morale while German morale declined. Wilson concluded that British neutrality in such a war was impossible. Britain must obviously aid France.[26]

General Wilson's memorandum presented a coherent analysis of a Franco-German war's effect on British interests.[27] On August 23, 1911, during the height of the second Moroccan crisis, Prime Minister H. H. Asquith convened a special meeting of the Committee of Imperial Defence (CID). In addition to most of the committee's regular members, the meeting also included the principal officers of the army and navy, the chancellor of the Exchequer Lloyd George, and Churchill, now the home secretary. Wilson briefed them on the General Staff's assessment of potential German plans to attack France and its belief that Berlin intended to invade by way of Belgium. To make the staff's case, Wilson presented overwhelming evidence of German preparations. Looking back, Churchill noted that Wilson laid out with uncanny accuracy nearly the whole of Germany's plan for attacking France.[28]

Maurice Hankey, CID secretary, recalled that Wilson presented an assessment and plan to immediately send an expeditionary force to the continent for the aid of France in the event of war with Germany. Most of the CID found General Wilson's presentation compelling, although Hankey admitted he did not. After lunch, Admiral Arthur Wilson, the First Sea Lord, gave a presentation with a dismal performance that it sounded to Hankey as if it had been invented during the meal. The meeting produced several results. From that day forward, according to Hankey, there was never a doubt about London's strategy to support France in the event of being drawn into a continental war. Britain would send its expeditionary force to France.[29]

In September 1911, General Wilson elaborated on his views in a subsequent document to the chief of the Imperial General Staff. In this document, Wilson recommended that the chief circulate the paper to the Foreign Office and to members of the CID, and the chief did as Wilson had asked. Wilson assessed that as with Britain and France, the interests of Belgium, the Netherlands, and Denmark lay in opposing German dominance of the continent. If these three countries remained neutral, and Germany emerged victorious over France, then each of them would be compelled to rely on Germany's grace to remain independent. The Rhine, Meuse, and Scheldt Rivers provided outlets for German trade, while Denmark's territory granted access to the North Sea. Belgium had a robust port at Antwerp and a direct line of advance into Germany. If Germany tolerated these nations remaining independent, they could interfere with German trade and possibly provide bases for future military operations against it. Germany would have no strategic reason to permit their continued independence.[30]

These countries were on the fence. None of them had the power to enforce its own neutrality against an aggressor. Wilson judged that without British and French resolve, these countries likely would feign neutrality while in reality cooperating with Germany. Such political posturing might help them retain their independence for a time, but their inevitable fate would be decided by German power. Their common interest lay with Britain and France, but fear of Germany could make them pliable and susceptible to persuasion and threat. Wilson also calculated that Austria-Hungary and Italy shared a mutual distrust and were both only lukewarm in their support for German aggrandizement. Neither power had much to gain by supporting Germany in a war, but both stood to lose vast sums of money with little prospect for compensation. Italy stood to lose from a more powerful Germany and was vulnerable to British naval power. The general wrote that he would not be surprised if Italy remained neutral in a war started by Germany.[31]

Wilson summarized that if France were defeated, then as a matter of course Belgium, Denmark, Luxemburg, and the Netherlands would all succumb to German domination or possibly outright annexation into the German empire. Italy would likely become the first among vassal states. Britain might for a period trade with Portugal and Spain, but trade in the Mediterranean would become dominated by Germany, Austria-Hungary, Italy, and France. Morocco would fall into German hands. The fleet that this combination of nations could muster and the dominating terrain it would command would be stronger than anything Britain could manage. Even if this chain of events did not lead to war with Great Britain, Germany would take British markets. Most of the Baltic and Mediterranean markets would be closed to British trade, as would all commerce with Belgium, Denmark, France, Luxemburg, and the Netherlands.[32] Based on British trade data, presented earlier, German domination of continental Europe could have eventually eclipsed between one-third and one-half of Britain's trade.

The general principles that governed British interest in Belgian neutrality pertained to all of the countries along the coast opposite Britain. To be prepared, the War Office also generated plans to support the independence of the Netherlands, and Denmark, in the event of German aggression.[33] Wilson did not discuss the interest of landlocked Luxemburg nor did the War Office consider plans to support the tiny nation's independence despite Britain's treaty obligation guaranteeing its perpetual neutrality.

Britain's cabinet ministers intensely felt the threat posed by German domination. Whitehall believed that German possession of Morocco would create a threat to France just as serious as German occupation of the Low Countries or France posed to Great Britain. Germans in Morocco became a potential stepping-stone to France's southern coast, similar to the way Belgium's coast offered a staging area for an invasion of the British Isles. Britons mobilized for war in 1911 to prevent the Teutons from attaining Morocco. Lewis Harcourt, secretary of state for the colonies, wrote to Herbert Gladstone, governor general of South Africa, about the great anxiety the second Moroccan crisis caused him. Harcourt believed that diplomacy eventually would preserve the peace. "The idea of war," he wrote, "[was] monstrous and inconceivable—if it took place it would involve the whole of Europe."[34] A German invasion of Belgium certainly constituted a greater and more direct threat to Britain than did German control of Morocco.

General Wilson's arguments persuaded Prime Minister Asquith that he must implement drastic changes to improve the Royal Navy's readiness. In October 1911, Asquith replaced Reginald McKenna, the First Lord of the Admiralty, with Churchill. McKenna assumed Churchill's old job as home secretary. Churchill sacked Admiral Wilson and replaced him with Admiral Francis Bridgeman. The Admiralty, in coordination with the War Department, began in earnest creating deliberate plans for war.[35]

Whitehall created a War Book in 1912 to coordinate the various activities of government departments in wartime. Britain's planning effort ramped up significantly from this point in time. By 1914, planning had developed apace such that the plan Britain entered the war with was larger than the two previous editions of the War Book combined. It encompassed actions by the Foreign Office, the Admiralty, the War Office, the Colonial Office, the India Office, the Home Office, Privy Council, Treasury, Board of Trade, the Board of Customs and Excise, and the Post Office. Each chapter in the War Book listed actions to be taken by a department in support of such activities as issuing warning telegrams, treatment of enemy merchant vessels, mobilizing reserves, naval intelligence, and blockade. In July 1914, Great Britain was more prepared for war against a great power than it had ever been.[36]

On August 2, 1914, Prime Minister Asquith wrote in his journal about the bleak situation, information he would later include in his memoir. Germany had declared war on Russia the day before. Moreover, the Germans had violated Luxemburg's neutrality earlier on August 2. Asquith waited to see if Germany treated Belgium similarly. That morning he had breakfast with Ambassador Lichnowsky, who pleaded with Asquith that Britain not side with France and Russia. Lichnowsky argued that if Germany's army were split between two fronts, it was more likely to suffer a crushing defeat. Asquith maintained that Britain had no desire to intervene, but he told Lichnowsky that Germany must make that option possible by guaranteeing that Germany would not invade Belgium and that the German fleet would not use the English Channel to attack the French coast.[37]

Later Asquith collected his thoughts to clarify, in his own mind, right and wrong, facts, and assumptions. First, he ascertained that Britain had no obligation of any kind to France, or Russia, to provide military or naval assistance. Second, the dispatch of the expeditionary force to France at this early stage would serve no purpose. Third, Britain must not forget its ties of friendship with France. Fourth, British interest opposed eliminating France as a great power. Fifth, Germany must not use the channel as a hostile base of operations. Sixth, Britain had an obligation to Belgium to prevent its use and annexation by Germany. Asquith's scribbling, however, did not help him determine a course of action. In his mind, everything turned on the issue of Belgian neutrality, a position he had maintained for several days.[38]

That day, Asquith penned a letter to Andrew Bonar Law, the leader of the opposition Unionist Party, to explain his policy regarding aid to France and Russia. In the letter, Asquith produced essentially an identical list to that above. He pointed out that France had concentrated its naval forces in the Mediterranean, and British interest required it to prevent Germany from using the North Sea and the English Channel for hostile naval operations against France. He also stressed Britain's treaty obligation regarding the neutrality and independence of Belgium.[39]

Asquith, and his cabinet, decided to dispatch a telegram to Germany requiring that Kaiser Wilhelm assure Great Britain that he would respect Belgium's neutrality. The cabinet also permitted Grey to reassure France that the Royal Navy would check any attempt by the German High Seas Fleet to use the English Channel. Beyond this, Asquith struggled to hold his cabinet together. According to historian David French, Britain realized that without its assistance, Russia and France would lose.[40] This may have been true for those directly involved in developing Britain's foreign policy and war plans, but many in the cabinet held different views. Lloyd George favored neutrality. Grey declared his intention to resign if Britain declared that it would not intervene. Churchill saw extreme danger in the situation, and fully intent on supporting France, demanded immediate mobilization. Equally adamant that Britain should stand aside, First Commissioner of Works William Beauchamp, Attorney General John Simon, President of the Council John Morley, and John Burns, president of the Board of Trade, all resigned. Asquith persuaded Beauchamp and Simon to stay on, but Morley and Burns held their ground. Filling the gaps left by the resignations, Beauchamp succeeded Morley, and Alfred Emmott accepted the position to the Board of Works to replace Beauchamp, Walter Runciman moved from his position as head of the Board of Agriculture to replace Burns, and Auberon Herbert Lucas became head of the Board of Agriculture.

On August 3, Bonar Law and Henry Lansdowne, the opposition Union Party leader in the House of Lords, visited Asquith. They agreed with the prime minister's course and stressed the importance of Belgian neutrality. They understood that Germany had delivered an ultimatum to Belgium and invaded. Belgium's King Albert I had appealed to King George for assistance. Later that day, Grey made his eloquent speech to the House of Commons stressing the need for Britain's intervention in the looming war.[41] Asquith had the Unionist Party's cooperation. For the sake of presenting a unified front to continental Europe, the parties agreed to table the issue of Irish home rule. That evening, Germany declared war on France.

London recognized Berlin's duplicity by this point. Germany presented its case to London as fulfilling an obligation to support its ally, Austria-Hungary. By this time, however, Germany had declared war on Russia and France and had violated the neutrality of Luxemburg and Belgium. With the exception of Austria-Hungary initiating war with Serbia on July 28, none of the other great powers involved in the crisis had taken the drastic step of declaring war. Austria-Hungary would declare war against Russia on August 6, and then only because of pressure from Germany. Britain's attempts to avert war had come to nothing. Germany had wanted war. Opposition to war within Britain evaporated after Germany invaded Belgium.

The secret alliances in no way caused any of Europe's powers to go to war. Italy recognized this and chose to remain neutral. Rome had mulled the possibility that London would enter the war allied with France and Russia. Britain was Italy's major trading partner, and the peninsula was vulnerable to British naval power. After conferring with Foreign Secretary Grey around July 31, the Italians elected neutrality.[42] Germany chose to honor an alliance with Austria-Hungary while reneging on treaty obligations with respect to Belgium.

Britain's treaty obligation with respect to guaranteeing Luxemburg's neutrality, however, was the same as the obligation it had toward Belgium. Despite this, Asquith refused to push Britain to aid landlocked Luxemburg the way he did for coastal Belgium. No one in his cabinet argued for the plight of beleaguered Luxemburg either. The General Staff also did not consider how Britain would aid Luxemburg's defense. Ultimately, none of the nations that had signed the 1867 treaty lent Luxemburg assistance, and it elected not to resist the German advance. Belgium's neutrality mattered, but not because of the treaty obligation. Rather it was the other way around: The treaty mattered because the neutral status of Belgium's territory held such significance for European security. If treaties, the rule of law, or the virtue of defending small independent countries were key issues, Luxemburg's defense would have been just as powerful a motivation for intervening on the continent.

So why did Britain go to war? Whitehall maintained as a cornerstone of policy preventing any great power from achieving a dominant position on the continent. Position in this sense refers to commanding geography that controls trade routes to the British home islands and the capability to control the English Channel. This interest animated British policy during the Napoleonic Wars.

The policy remained in effect in 1839 and constituted the primary reason for creating perpetually neutral, small states along the English Channel's continental coast. In 1867, the policy served to extend the provision of perpetual neutrality to Luxemburg. In the 1870 Franco-Prussian War, the policy led Britain to reassert Belgium's neutrality. London also believed that if Berlin gained control over Morocco, Germany would dominate France. Britain, therefore, opposed Germany's acquisition of the colony in 1905 and again in 1911. The same policy had guided British actions for more than a century, and once again did so in 1914 when Germany threatened Belgium and France. On that fateful day in August 1914, when Foreign Secretary Grey addressed Parliament on the eve of the Great War, he understood the situation as he had learned it from Wilson and from the perspective of his own experience. Britain would suffer whether it stood aside or supported France. He knew that if Britain elected neutrality, all of Europe, including Britain would succumb to German domination.

5 AVOIDING DEFEAT: THE FIRST STEP TOWARD VICTORY

At 2:00 p.m. on August 4, 1914, British foreign secretary Edward Grey, having learned that German armies were violating Belgium's border, transmitted a message to Berlin via Britain's embassy demanding immediate withdrawal. Whitehall's ultimatum to Germany expired at midnight August 4 thrusting the two nations into war. Germany and its Austrian ally constituted formidable foes. That alliance, known as the Central Powers, had several methods with which it could defeat its island adversary. Britain's Grand Fleet constituted the bulwark of its defense. If Germany's High Seas Fleet defeated the Grand Fleet, it would leave Britain vulnerable to bombardment, blockade, and invasion. After Turkey became a German ally, the Royal Navy's oil supply, the Abadan oil fields of Persia, became vulnerable to capture by the Turkish army. If the Central Powers were able to deprive the Royal Navy of fuel, they could confidently seek a decisive sea battle. German commerce raiders could also attack British trade, deterring British merchant vessels from sailing, driving up prices in Britain, and creating a credit crisis. With Britain's economy in shambles, the island nation would seek peace under terms favorable to Germany. Whitehall, particularly the Admiralty, had to rapidly emplace effective counters against each of these potential threats.

H. H. Asquith's Liberal government had for more than three years studied the strategic problem that Germany's increasing power presented to Great Britain's security. The government concluded that command of the sea would secure British territory worldwide against invasion and protect commerce. Moreover, British dominance on the seas would bring unbearable economic pressure against Germany.[1] Such pronouncements coming from the government compelled the Admiralty to clearly define "command of the sea." Moreover, the Admiralty needed to educate the cabinet to avoid creating an unrealistic expectation of what the Royal Navy could achieve in war.

Large ships haul cargo in greater quantity and more cheaply than any other means of conveyance. Because of this fact, nations value navigable rivers, ports, and the ocean for trade. In essence, the right to travel on the ocean constitutes its value for trade. When fighting wars or maintaining empires, nations move armies by sea. One reason a nation invests in a navy is to protect its right to transit the ocean; another reason is to deny an enemy this same right. Thus "command of the sea" refers to the condition between nations whereby the one in command moves on the ocean freely while its enemy is prevented from using the seas altogether.

In practice, however, even a nation with a powerful navy rarely achieved such dominance over its adversary. Only after an enemy fleet's destruction could a nation freely use the oceans without fear of interference. Until that battle occurred, no fleet could dominate the seas. Moreover, the result of an engagement might remain inconclusive while weakening both powers proportionally, such that neither achieved the dominating superiority it sought. The normal state of affairs between naval powers was that neither commanded the sea. This allowed each nation the power to execute some naval operations successfully wherever it could gather superior forces.[2] The Royal Navy could not eradicate the threat that the navy of Kaiser Wilhelm II posed. Command of the sea, although sound theory, remained a chimera. Whitehall had to determine where it wished the Admiralty to maintain its strength and where to accept risk.

At a Committee of Imperial Defence (CID) meeting held May 14, 1914, the Overseas Defence Committee fielded questions concerning the risk of invasion Britain's overseas possessions faced. The committee's replies concerned British territories most at risk in the Americas and in the Mediterranean.

Regarding Bermuda, Jamaica, and the West Indies, the committee expressed the opinion that none of these islands could hold against the scale of attack that the United States could mount. The members agreed that the size of the garrisons should prevent the colonies from becoming easy prey for a hostile

European power. Bermuda's garrison, for example, consisted of such a light force that one German cruiser could subdue it. The committee recommended that the garrison's size be increased so that a hostile European nation would require a combined naval and military force to seize the island.

In the Mediterranean, Britain possessed the key ports at the Suez Canal, Malta, and Gibraltar. If the island nation found itself at war alone against the Triple Alliance, Britain had to consider whether it should evacuate its fleet from the Mediterranean. To retain these outposts, the Royal Navy would require a Mediterranean fleet sufficiently strong to balance the combined Austrian and Italian navies should the Italians decide to join the alliance in war. This would weaken the Grand Fleet against Germany's High Seas Fleet in home waters. Should this scenario arise, Winston Churchill, First Lord of the Admiralty, recommended that Britain temporarily evacuate Egypt and Malta to permit combining the British fleets in home waters.[3] The cabinet would commit enough military and naval forces to hold Gibraltar in order to prevent the Austrian and Italian navies from joining with Germany's fleet in British home waters. If France assisted Britain, those two nation's combined Mediterranean naval forces could generate a margin of safety over the Triple Alliance fleets. In that case, the cabinet would attempt to hold Britain's Mediterranean territories.[4] Churchill's advice revealed the magnitude of the threat the Central Powers posed. He was convinced that the Royal Navy could not simultaneously protect the empire's remote outposts and prevent invasion.

Germany's capability to raid or invade the home islands posed a more serious threat than did similar operations France might have attempted fifteen years earlier. Britain had developed a substantial buffer of naval and military strength to deter a possible French threat. Warships stationed at Berehaven, Queenstown, Pembroke, Falmouth, Plymouth, Portland, Portsmouth, Shoreham, Newhaven, Dover, Sheerness, and Chatham covered all points of strategic significance. Each naval base offered excellent logistical support over a short distance to sustain a British blockade of French ports. Strong military installations at Aldershot, Salisbury, and Curragh buttressed the naval bases along the coast. As late as early 1913, however, the North Sea coast opposite Germany lacked anything resembling the defensive infrastructure that existed in the south. The northern ports did not even posses the dry docks necessary to service dreadnoughts. The major northern cities—Edinburgh, Glasgow, Hull, Newcastle,

Map 3. *The British Isles and North Sea*

and Norwich—were all essentially undefended. The Shetland Islands and the Orkneys lay equally open to attack.[5] The Admiralty began immediately to build up defenses to protect the area, hurriedly completing them in December 1914.[6]

Churchill understood that Britain's security rested on maintaining a battle fleet in a secure position and capable at all times of defeating the German High Seas Fleet in battle. This remained the Grand Fleet's highest priority.[7] Before the war, the Admiralty had investigated the prospects of seeking out and destroying the German High Seas Fleet, but rejected the idea. Germany enjoyed an advantage near its own shores. Its fleet could enter the North Sea from the Baltic Sea via the Kiel Canal, to Denmark's south, or via the Skagerrak Strait, north of Denmark. Germany heavily fortified these areas, rendering any British attempt to conduct battle there extremely risky. German torpedoes would inflict heavy damage on the Grand Fleet, and Germany's battle line would receive support from shore batteries that ship-mounted guns could not match.

If the Admiralty attempted a close blockade, the blockading forces would be subject to attrition from the same dangers. Moreover, the blockade would have to split to guard both entrances to the North Sea from the Baltic. Maintaining a fleet split between the two entrances increased the Royal Navy's vulnerability to defeat in detail because the bulk of the kaiser's navy could be brought against a smaller British force in succession. The Royal Navy could not have prevailed by maintaining a close blockade or by seeking a battle decision near the German coast. The Admiralty argued that deciding command of the sea might be prolonged indefinitely because Britain would have to wait for the German fleet to sortie into the North Sea.[8]

Most senior officers of the German navy believed that the Royal Navy possessed such an offensive spirit that it would seek out the German High Seas Fleet and attack. For years prior to the war, Germany's naval staff feared the possibility of a British attack to destroy the High Seas Fleet before the latter could become a serious threat. Hence, Germany had procured mines, submarines, and torpedo boats to protect its battle fleet. The Germans also constructed shore fortifications to guard the approaches to their bases. The design produced conditions adverse to any naval actions by a foreign power in the Helgoland Bight, the area of the North Sea next to Germany's shores south and east of the island Helgoland.[9]

Vice Admiral Wolfgang Wegener, noted in the German navy for his intellect, eventually became first Admiralty Staff officer to Vice Admiral Wilhelm von Lans, commander of the High Seas Fleet's 1st Squadron of battleships. Wegener strongly repudiated the German naval staff's belief that Britain would attack. His view of naval warfare posited that the main objective of sea control and its execution was the interdiction of trade.[10] He argued that the Royal Navy had no need for a Trafalgar-like battle because it already possessed the geographic position required to strangle German commerce. Germany's High Seas Fleet, cornered as it was in the Helgoland Bight, was incapable of interdicting British trade or protecting German trade.[11] The position of the British Isles, astride the entrance to the North Sea from the Atlantic, enabled the Royal Navy to simultaneously interrupt German trade and protect its own trade from the ravages of the German High Seas Fleet. Germany, he insisted, must fight for access to the trade routes. Germany had to therefore attack the British fleet.[12]

Meanwhile at Whitehall, the Admiralty feared a German surprise attack on its fleet. As tensions mounted toward the end of July, the First Sea Lord, Admiral Prince Louis of Battenberg (later Louis Alexander Mountbatten), kept the fleet assembled following summer exercises, which consisted of gathering the fleet for a test mobilization at Portsmouth, a grand review by King George V, followed by maneuvers at sea. Churchill ordered the fleet to proceed north to Scapa Flow on July 29, 1914. The ships moved under cover of darkness and without lights.[13] On August 2, the British government notified the German and French ambassadors that Britain would not allow German ships to pass from the North Sea though the English Channel to attack French coasts or shipping. The Admiralty warned its fleet commanders to "be prepared to meet surprise attacks."[14] On August 4, all British ships received official word that London's ultimatum to Germany had expired at midnight and that the Admiralty expected to issue the war telegram promptly authorizing hostilities against Germany. The Admiralty further cautioned all ships to remain ready for battle because Germany might decide to initiate hostilities by opening fire before that time.[15]

The Admiralty considered its options to counter the trap set by Tirpitz in the Helgoland Bight. The Royal Navy desired to avoid attrition warfare close to German shores, where over time, with the Royal Navy forced to split its fleet guarding each entrance to the North Sea from the Baltic, the German fleet could reach parity with one or the other blockading squadrons and invite a major battle on its terms. War orders prepared for the Grand Fleet in December 1913 called for a distant blockade, rather than imposing a traditional close blockade, and seeking out the German High Seas Fleet.[16] Some background in naval theory is necessary to understand the distinction.

In *Some Principles of Maritime Strategy*, Julian Corbett categorizes various types of blockades based on the intended objective. The first distinction is between a close blockade and an open blockade. The close blockade is maintained by smaller, fast-moving destroyers and cruisers often within view of the port being blocked. These ships' close proximity to the harbor enhances their ability to identify and intercept vessels attempting to flee the port, thus making the blockade effective. On the other hand, their position also entails providing difficult logistic support to maintain the blocking force as the ships operate typically far from their home ports. Moreover, imposing a close blockade tends to expose the blockading ships to more danger from enemy shore artillery, submarine attack, and sinking by mines. An open blockade is one in which the naval force assumes a position somewhat over the horizon from the port to mask the fleet from the enemy's view. The blockading force allows the sortie, usually of an enemy naval force, for the purpose of engaging and destroying the enemy in battle. The open blockade lessens the danger to the fleet posed by such coastal threats as fortifications and mines, but does little to alleviate the logistical strain.

The second distinction is whether the blockade's intended target is naval forces or commerce. Often, the blockade has the dual purpose of restricting a belligerent's commerce in the expectation that the enemy's fleet will sortie in an effort to reopen the blocked port or ports. Such a scenario typically leads to a major naval battle in which the blockading force intends to destroy the enemy fleet. To accomplish such a maneuver, a fleet would use a combination of a close blockade and an open blockade. The close blockade maintained by small, fast ships is directed against enemy commercial interests, while a stronger covering force maintains an open blockade in position to intercept an enemy fleet seeking to disperse the close blockading force.[17]

The distant blockade imposed by the Royal Navy on Germany followed a similar logic to that just described except that the blockading forces were far from the German ports the Royal Navy targeted. The general plan for the distant blockade remained vague but consisted of exerting economic pressure on

Germany by cutting off its shipping. Cruisers patrolled the Atlantic approaches to the North Sea to interdict Germany's trade. Two battle fleets stood by in supporting distance with the assignment of bringing the German High Seas Fleet into action in the event it put to sea to drive off the cruisers. The 1913 war order also assigned the Grand Fleet the task of frustrating any German attempt to land an invading force in Britain or conduct raids.[18] The strength of the distant blockade lay in its ability to curtail Germany's overseas commerce, as Wegener feared, while completely avoiding the danger Tirpitz had created in the Helgoland Bight. The distant blockade also had the significant advantage of solving the logistical problem of maintaining the cruisers on station and providing a covering force because of its proximity to bases in Great Britain. That German coastal traffic and trade with the Scandinavian states remained open, constituted the distant blockading force's chief disadvantage.

Revised orders, issued in April 1914, laid out specific tasks for the commander in chief, Home Fleets, in the opening phase of the war. The order required the Home Fleets to provide for the destruction of Germany's naval forces and gain command of the North Sea and English Channel. The objective was to prevent Germany from making serious attacks on Britain's territory and trade. The Royal Navy's fleets were organized with a Grand Fleet based on the Scottish Islands and coast in northern waters consisting of four battleship squadrons and two battle cruiser squadrons. A second Channel Fleet of one battleship squadron supported by four more reserve battleship squadrons occupied the traditional naval ports along Great Britain's southern coast. The commander of Home Fleets exercised overall control of the Grand Fleet and Channel Fleet in this scheme. The order also required the Grand Fleet to prevent the enemy interfering with transporting the British Expeditionary Force (BEF) to France. Until the enemy fleet's destruction, the commander remained responsible for ensuring that the Grand Fleet maintained superior numbers in all classes of vessels to those of the German Navy. Moreover, the Royal Navy was to interdict all overseas German trade to inflict serious injury to German interests and credit. Whitehall expected the blockade to produce serious social and economic disruption in Germany.

The Admiralty created two cruiser squadrons, independent from the Grand Fleet, and assigned them the specific duty of maintaining the blockade. Cruiser Force B held the line between the Scottish coast, the Shetland Islands, and the Norwegian coast. In the western approach to the English Channel, the Admiralty posted Cruiser Force G. In addition, torpedo craft and light cruisers patrolled the Straits of Dover. The order anticipated Germany sending a force into the North Sea, to counter the long-distance blockade, that might be of sufficient size to warrant a general naval action. The German navy could also dispatch smaller forces for coastal bombardment or land forces for quick raids. From the Grand Fleet's location based on the Scottish Islands and coast, the fleet could swing to protect the blockading cruisers along the Scottish-Norwegian line, or it could move south to assist the Channel Fleet with protecting channel ports and transports moving the BEF to France. Beyond these tasks, given the impossibility of maintaining a close watch on German ports, the fleet made periodic sweeps close to enemy shores to create the impression of overwhelming force in the North Sea. The Admiralty hoped these demonstrations would hold the enemy fleet close to his own shores. The commander of Home Fleets conferred with the Admiralty around the first of each month to consider revisions to the general plan.[19]

Admiral John A. Fisher returned to the Admiralty as First Sea Lord for a second time, in October 1914, following a succession of short-term leaders. Churchill had appointed Admiral Francis Bridgeman to replace Admiral Arthur Wilson in the position in 1911. Admiral Prince Louis of Battenberg then relieved Bridgeman in December 1912, when the latter retired due to failing health. Public uneasiness over Battenberg's German birth, relationship to German royalty, and possibly that the cabinet considered him too passive in his approach to the First Sea Lord induced Battenberg to tender his resignation.[20] Later in the war, approximately July 1917, Battenberg changed his surname to Mountbatten and renounced all claim to German royalty to mollify those who continued to question his loyalty.[21] Fisher became First Sea Lord upon Battenberg's resignation.

Fisher believed it worth considering a scheme Admiral Wilson had proposed for taking Helgoland as an advance base for naval operations against the German coast. He asked Vice Admiral Cecil Burney, the commander of Channel Fleet and second in command of the Home Fleets, to examine the plan with an eye toward revising the instructions for the Home Fleet. Burney judged the scheme too risky. Germany had fortified the island with 16-inch gun emplacements, which outmatched those on Britain's newest dreadnoughts.

Burney concluded that even if the island were taken, Britain could not hold it long enough for it to serve as an advance base. Moreover, if not taken, the loss in warships Britain would certainly suffer from mines, torpedoes, and bombardment from the shore fortifications would create a moral victory for Germany. The German fleet retained an advantage if a major battle for command of the North Sea were fought at that location.

Having sought the opinion of the fleet's other admirals, who unanimously agreed, Burney concluded that the scheme was unwise; it represented poor strategy that if attempted would result in a national disaster. The current policy of distant blockade, Burney and the other admirals believed, was the correct approach. Britain's preponderance in capital ships was not so overwhelming that any could be sacrificed prior to a great fleet battle. The Royal Navy could not risk its best ships to capture an advance base and still retain the required superiority over Germany's High Seas Fleet. Burney remained convinced that Germany hoped Britain would adopt some operation such as the Helgoland invasion so that the former could attrite Britain's superiority in battleships without risking its own. Germany prepared for this course because German intelligence had predicted a British naval offensive. Burney advised Fisher to stay the course and keep hunting down German submarines, small craft, and mine layers. Hold the blockade, he cautioned, and this will "undoubtedly, in time, bring their fleet out."[22]

The British government desired to add dreadnoughts to the fleet quickly to ensure that the Grand Fleet had more first-line battleships than the German fleet. Whitehall turned to the expedient of requisitioning two dreadnought battleships under construction in British shipyards that had been ordered by Turkey. British law and the contracts to build the ships permitted the Admiralty to purchase the vessels, thus augmenting the fleet in time of emergency. Churchill issued the necessary requisition on July 29.[23] Unknown to Britain's government, Turkey had secretly proposed an alliance with Germany. Negotiations between Germany and Turkey had begun on July 27 and concluded with an alliance signed on August 2.[24] Austria-Hungary accepted the pact with Turkey three days later. Turkey's leader, Enver Pasha, planned to use one of the dreadnoughts in the Black Sea, where Russia no longer possessed any significant naval strength. It was assumed that if Turkey entered the war, its anticipated naval dominance would help it to capture territory in the Black Sea region from

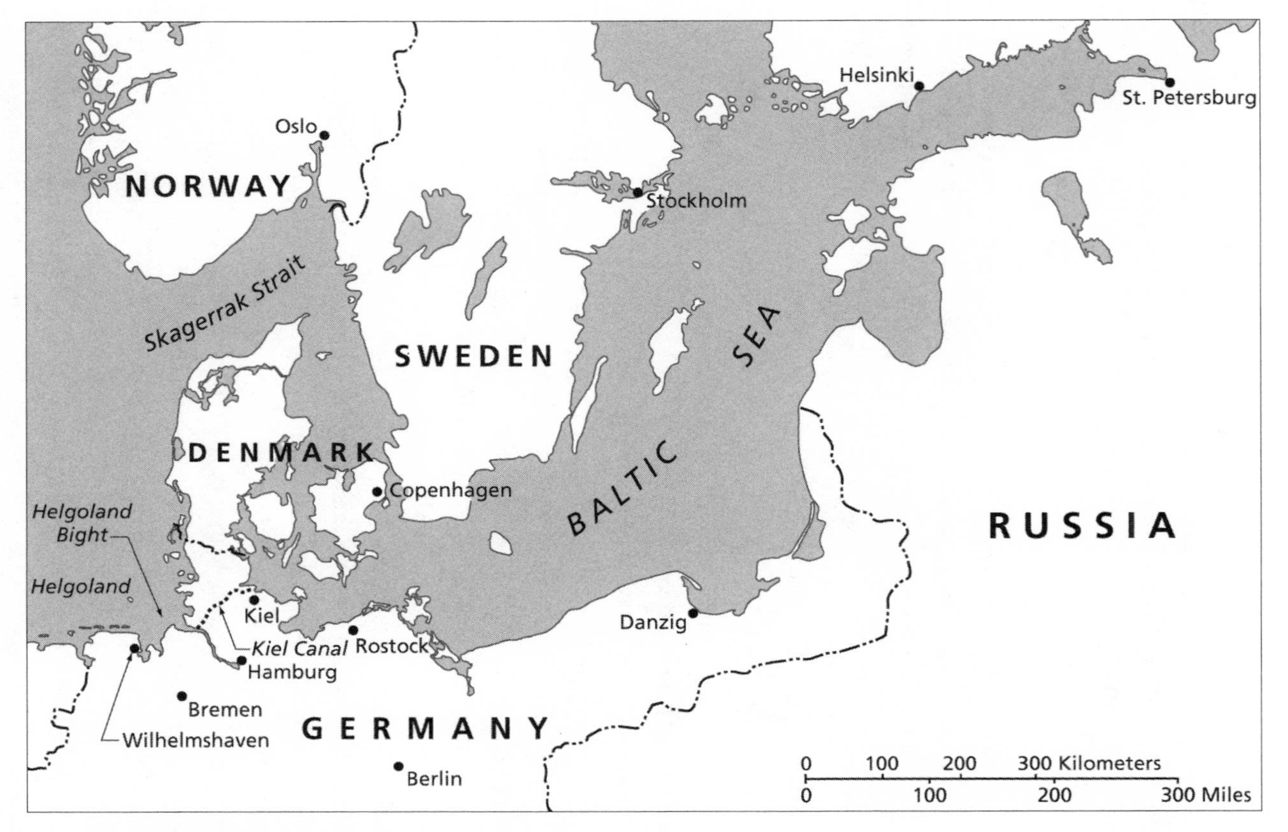

Map 4. *The Baltic Sea and German Coast*

Russia. Enver offered the second battleship to Germany as a gesture of goodwill. Had Churchill not commandeered the two warships, Turkey's gift would have tilted the balance of naval power in the North Sea more favorably toward Germany. Denied the new dreadnoughts, and stunned by Great Britain's entry into the war, Enver reconsidered Turkey's participation and decided to act as a benevolent neutral toward Germany.[25]

Enver's decision, however, was not the end of the matter. The Wilhelmstrasse seized the opportunity presented when Britain requisitioned the two battleships to push Turkey from neutrality toward war. SMS *Goeben,* a battle cruiser, and SMS *Breslau,* a light cruiser proceeded under orders toward the Dardanelles. Berlin offered the warships to Turkey as substitutes for the two commandeered by London. The German warships successfully evaded the Royal Navy and arrived off the Turkish coast on August 10. After some haggling with Germany, Enver permitted the vessels to enter the Dardanelles. Tsar Nicholas II had nothing in the Black Sea that could match the powerful *Goeben.*[26] With Turkey's purchase of the German warships and a substantial loan from Berlin, Enver's original war plan could unfold.[27]

London hoped to avoid provoking Turkey so the latter would remain neutral in the war. Messages between Germany and Turkey intercepted by British intelligence, however, increasingly revealed that Turkey's overt diplomacy was a sham.[28] In late August, Churchill ordered his Mediterranean squadron to sink *Goeben* and *Breslau* if they returned to the Mediterranean, irrespective of the flag under which they sailed.[29] On September 26, Turkey closed the Dardanelles to foreign shipping. To guard against a sortie by *Goeben* and *Breslau,* on October 2 the Admiralty directed the Mediterranean squadron to blockade the Dardanelles. On September 25, one day prior to Turkey's declaration, Edward Barrow, the India Office's military secretary, had suggested sending the 6th Poona Division from India to the Shatt al-Arab at the head of the Persian Gulf. Whitehall acted on the suggestion.

Anglo-Persian Oil, which supplied a portion of the Royal Navy's fuel oil, used the port on Abadan Island adjacent to the Shatt al-Arab to export oil to Great Britain and the Admiralty. On October 6, Turkey announced that it considered the Shatt al-Arab territorial waters. Constantinople's pronouncement compelled London to protect its interests. So as not to push Turkey over the brink, however, on October 23, London diverted the 6th Poona Division to the

British colony at Bahrain. There the force, which became India Expeditionary Force D (IEF D), waited in readiness to defend the Admiralty's fuel source should Turkey declare war.[30]

The prospect of Turkey entering the war gravely concerned the British government. General Helmuth von Moltke the Younger, of the German General Staff, hoped Turkey's presence in the war would spark a general Muslim uprising against Britain, Russia, and France. A pan-Islamic jihad would tie down Russian troops in the Caucasus, British forces in India and Egypt, and the French army in Morocco. Enver declared jihad, holy war, and sent the declaration throughout the Islamic world attempting to create revolt. Germany went so far as to recruit Muslim students in Germany and send them home to foment rebellion. The notion of revolution, however, tended to create ideas of independence in the minds of the Muslims. The citizens of Egypt, and Sudan, for example, viewed overthrowing British rule as simply creating the opportunity for increased subjugation by the Turks. With Turkey as an enemy, however, Britain and France were diplomatically better positioned than was Turkey's ally Germany to offer guarantees of independence to local Arabs. Moreover, given the long overland logistics routes, Germany had little success sending weapons to remote areas of India and Persia to support local uprisings. Thus Germany's hoped for pan-Islamic jihad never materialized.[31]

Turkey held the potential to interfere with and cut several critical trade routes. Because the French navy easily matched Austria-Hungary's navy, Britain's Admiralty would have preferred to reposition the Mediterranean squadron's battle cruisers with those of the Grand Fleet in home waters. It nevertheless retained them in the Mediterranean because of the threat Turkey posed. The Admiralty's cruisers, which could have assisted in tracking down commerce raiders, remained in the Mediterranean to protect the Suez Canal. Lord Kitchener, Britain's secretary for war, desired to convoy two Indian divisions through the canal to bolster the army in Europe prior to open war with Turkey. He expedited the troop movement because he wanted to avoid any possible time delay caused by diverting the convoy around Africa via the Cape route. The early arrival of these two divisions in France could spell the difference between victory and defeat on the continent.[32]

Not only did the prospect of Turkish intervention in the war stretch Britain's naval resources, it also threatened to interrupt the Royal Navy's fuel supplies.

One potential fuel source for the Royal Navy came from a British-owned subsidiary of Royal Dutch Shell in Romania. When Turkey closed the Dardanelles to foreign shipping, however, this option evaporated.[33] Turkey also threatened to occupy the Shatt al-Arab, which would cut off the Admiralty's fuel oil supply provided by the Anglo-Persian Oil Company.[34] Turkey planned, and ultimately made several attempts, to sabotage the Anglo-Persian installations at Abadan. If the Turks had succeeded, the German army high command hoped to seize the oil fields. Britain, however, strengthened the position with additional Indian troops and pushed the Turkish forces north. Subsequent fighting took place nearer to Baghdad, and retaining that city became Turkey's military object.[35]

Union Oil and Standard Oil in the United States had plenty of petroleum to sell, but the Admiralty's purchase of the fuel would have rendered it contraband of war under the Declaration of London rules for conditional contraband. The United States had been the only nation to ratify the Declaration of London, and selling oil to Britain for the Royal Navy but not to other belligerents broke the provisions of neutral behavior.[36] Therefore, American oil companies might choose not to sell to Great Britain. The Admiralty thus considered it crucial to protect the port at Abadan. The Royal Navy relied on fuel oil for propulsion in the line of cruisers blockading the North Sea and its first line of battleships. Without a secure source of fuel, the North Sea blockade would fail. Without fuel oil, Britain's modern battleships could not reach top speed, which made them inferior in battle.[37] If fuel sources were cut, one squadron of dreadnoughts fueled by oil only, the Queen Elizabeth class, could not remain at sea and contribute to the strength of Britain's main battle fleet. Britain's safety depended on the Royal Navy operating at full capacity.

Turkey's entry into the war indicates that Germany's military planners had not counted on Britain remaining neutral. By the bold strategic move of ordering SMS *Goeben* and *Breslau* to proceed to Turkey before Britain declared war, Germany offered one battle cruiser and one light cruiser, both of which likely would have been lost to the British anyway, to secure an ally. Moltke's enthusiasm for a Turkish alliance stemmed from its ability to disrupt Russia's and Britain's military and naval potential against Germany.[38] The alliance forced Russia to divert portions of its army southward and caused Britain to invest both naval and military forces to protect its interests in Southwest Asia. War erupted between Russia and Turkey on October 29. The Turkish fleet, newly augmented by *Goeben* and *Breslau*, attacked various Russian ports on the Black Sea.[39] On November 5, Britain and Turkey were also at war.[40]

Turkey set aside its 2nd Army in Syria and its VIII Army Corps for an offensive against the Suez Canal. Germany hoped that this attack would strike a mortal blow to the British position in the Middle East. A raid against the canal, if successful, stood to spark the general Islamic uprising against the British in Egypt and the Sudan.[41] France sent *Requin* and Russia *Askold* to assist Britain in the defense of the Suez Canal. They entered the canal and acted as floating batteries in Egypt's defense. Turkish forces made several feeble attempts against the forces at Suez, but when confronted with several ships and a substantial number of imperial troops, they fell back to gather strength. On December 1, Kitchener halted transports at Suez filled with the Australian and New Zealand Army Corps bound for Europe and directed that the troops remain in Egypt as part of the canal's defense. The soldiers also used the stop to complete training that they would later need on Europe's battlefields.[42]

Meanwhile, the Royal Navy transported troops and supplies to France ceaselessly. After the Allied armies turned back the Germany army's attempt to encircle Paris at the Battle of the Marne, the latter began to move in a direction that brought it increasingly closer to the Atlantic coast. Most historians have discussed this operation as a race to outflank the French and British armies that reached a stalemate when the opposing armies arrived at the sea. From the naval perspective, the German offensive threatened to capture the key ports of Boulogne, Calais, and Dunkirk, which were vital to resupplying the Allied armies. Moreover, if Germany gained control of the ports along the Belgian and French coasts, it would diminish the Royal Navy's ability to keep the English Channel open. Germany would have fortified the ports and converted them into bases for torpedo craft, destroyers, mine layers, and submarines. Operating in the English Channel would have become the same nightmarish scenario that existed in the Helgoland Bight along the German coast. As the German offensive culminated in the first battle at Ypres and the Yser River in late October, the Allied line held. Britain retained the ports. The Royal Navy actively supported the army by preventing enemy cruisers from venturing south in support of the German army.[43]

Trade constituted the third area where Great Britain was vulnerable. One way to compel a British surrender would be to impose a tight blockade around the island. Another involved flooding the trade routes with enough raiders to choke British trade by capturing and sinking that nation's merchant vessels. At the beginning of the Great War, few in the cabinet or at the Admiralty considered Germany capable of interdicting enough trade to challenge Britain's survival. Admiral Fisher, however, believed Germany could strangle Britain's maritime commerce, though not through traditional methods of cruiser warfare. He argued that Germany would use submarines to sink merchant ships without warning and without regard for crew safety.[44] Churchill disagreed with Fisher, emphatically stating that sinking merchant ships with submarines would never "be done by a civilized power."[45] Submarines posed a considerable threat, especially to warships, but heretofore their short cruising range limited the danger they posed to the approaches to Great Britain and the North Sea. Until German submarines began operating from bases overseas, they posed nowhere near the threat that Germany's cruisers and converted merchant auxiliaries represented to the major trade routes.

Whitehall worried that if captures of merchant ships became frequent, insurance rates and freight rates would skyrocket. High inflation would drastically affect the average worker's ability to purchase sufficient food, possibly leading to unrest severe enough at home to force the government to sue for peace. In 1908, the number of potential German commerce raiders available on trade routes did not warrant government intervention. A shipmaster's decision to continue a voyage already in progress at war's outbreak, or to start a new voyage after the beginning of war, constituted a financial decision. The merchant vessels' crews understood that what they risked in war was money and time, not their lives. If their vessels were stopped, the rules of maritime war stated that the belligerent must provide for the crew's safety.[46]

Historical evidence indicates that German naval officers understood the effect of war on trade to be shortages caused by shipping losses, with the attendant inflated prices.[47] Within the British financial and commercial system, however, the effect would be exacerbated and dangerous. A 1913 special report prepared by the Standing Committee for the CID on maintenance of commerce during war indicated that the risk presented by German commerce raiders was much higher than that posed five years earlier. The crux of the problem was that the private insurance market refused to cover the risk. Without insurance, nothing but exorbitant prices could entice a merchant captain to sail. The merchant marine responded to the dearth of private insurance by organizing into mutual insurance clubs; the club charters, however, called for vessels to lay up in safe harbors to wait out the war. Such an action boded far worse for food prices at home than the losses likely to occur from enemy capture or sinking of the merchant vessels. The report recommended the government prepare to issue national guarantee insurance for its merchant vessels to induce them to sail. Without government insurance, the majority of Britain's merchant marine would stop trading for the duration of the war.[48]

The majority of the cabinet agreed with the necessity of national guarantee insurance. Prime Minister Asquith and Chancellor of the Exchequer David Lloyd George had little trouble convincing Parliament to pass the appropriate legislation.[49] With the insurance in effect, the government assumed 80 percent liability for the ships, and the clubs retained 20 percent liability. Moreover, the government also offered cargo insurance to promote stability in the private market. As long as the private market offered reasonable and competitive rates, the traders purchased insurance there. When the private market lost confidence in certain routes, or the rates simply rose rapidly, traders switched to the government-offered insurance. This scheme retained most of the liability for loss in the private sector and kept the price of premiums modest and stable. The government assumed liability only for the cargoes covered by its policies.[50]

The Royal Navy, however, became the ultimate guarantor for all British vessels and cargoes. Each vessel lost to the enemy generated a payout from the government to the ship's owner. The private insurance market paid for the lost cargo, but if significant losses occurred, private insurance rates increased to cover the risk. When private sector premiums rose to the government insurance rate, those seeking insurance would increasingly turn to the government for a policy. Ultimately, if the Royal Navy allowed too many captures, the government had to underwrite ships and all cargoes.[51]

In order to maintain the normal transfer of cargo under the terms of the bills of exchange, insurance policies covered all cargo conveyed in British ships. The British government, concerned that it must have adequate cash on hand to financially cover potential losses, considered prohibiting gold bullion exports. The Trading Subcommittee for the CID strongly opposed the idea and pointed out that crown prerogative could create a basis for prohibiting the export of gold, but that that had not been done since 1793. A letter to Prime Minister Asquith from Maurice Hankey, secretary of the CID, and Attorney General John Simon, stresses that the government's contemplated action, according to the Trading Subcommittee might "shatter our credit and jeopardize our pre-eminent position as the principal bankers of the world."[52] If the world lost confidence in British banking, extensions of credit, the essential lubricant for trade, would cease.

Credit made possible the transactions for purchasing cargo under the terms of the bills of exchange. Few investors had the capital to purchase an entire cargo. Without credit, trade would slow to a crawl and prices would rise, resulting in suffering throughout Britain. If Britain's credit failed, it would be the same as a failure in the insurance market or serious attrition of ships.[53] The supply of food and raw materials, the solvency of the insurance market, and the credit market all rested on the success or failure of the Royal Navy to protect trade. The Royal Navy thus drew the responsibility to keep losses to a minimum; otherwise government liability would create a deficit, necessitate borrowing in a system where it held poor credit, and harm the overall war effort. If the Royal Navy failed in its task, Britain would lose the war. Thus Churchill's second great responsibility lay in organizing the Royal Navy to adequately protect trade.

Despite such important consequences, the Admiralty's initial plan to protect trade demonstrated how poorly it understood the threat and the challenges it faced. The Admiralty had made tremendous strides in improving its plans and in coordinating with the British Army on the threat posed in home waters and continental Europe, but the same was not true of protecting trade. In April 1914, Churchill signed a memorandum spelling out the plan for protecting commerce. It called for creating a trade defense section inside the Admiralty's Operations Division to begin seriously considering how best to proceed. Churchill's initial plan ordered the navy's cruisers to hunt down enemy warships and eliminate that threat, rather than sparsely scattering British fleet units along trade routes in "defensive expectancy." Churchill reasoned that enemy raiders could not remain on the ocean lying in wait for merchants. German cruisers must steam to take prizes, and British ships with wireless radio sets would constantly report their locations. Because British cruisers were faster than their German counterparts, the enemy would eventually be brought to battle and destroyed. Churchill also explained that Germany only had a few cruisers stationed overseas, so to augment that force, cruisers would have to break through Britain's North

Sea blockade. When that occurred, the Royal Navy could release more cruisers from blockade duty to hunt German commerce destroyers. Moreover, the First Lord rationalized that Germany could not detach many cruisers without stripping the High Seas Fleet of its forward pickets. Without these assets, he reasoned, the High Seas Fleet would be crippled.[54]

Several aspects of the Admiralty's attempt to manage the cruiser threat readily present themselves to criticism. The Admiralty assumed that German cruisers had enough information on Royal Navy dispositions to run the blockade and evade cruisers placed along the trade routes, yet insufficient information to avoid combat with a British cruiser in pursuit, actively seeking its destruction. The plan also did not acknowledge that the Royal Navy might actually lose battles between individual cruisers hunting their lone German counterpart. Britain needed superior numbers at each engagement to ensure victory, thus several British cruisers would need to come together prior to engaging the enemy. This afforded an enemy more time and opportunity to escape. By dispatching cruisers to chase German raiders that broke out of the North Sea, Britain would continually weaken its own blockade, and eventually it would become ineffective. Not only that, but also if the High Seas Fleet remained defensively postured in the Baltic Sea, or behind the secure defenses surrounding Helgoland, it would not require an additional defensive screen of cruisers. Shore fortifications, destroyers, submarines, and torpedo boats would suffice to warn of an attack by the Grand Fleet. Thus Germany could afford to send more cruisers after trade than Britain could spare from blockading duty.

Churchill's plan also attempted to address the auxiliary cruiser threat. At the 122nd CID meeting in February 1913, Churchill stated that he could not say with specificity which German merchant ships carried armaments, but evidence suggested that a considerable number carried guns ready for mounting.[55] In the April 1914 plan, Churchill admitted, "the whole threat [was] very shadowy" and doubted whether German merchant vessels had any armaments on board, noting "not a scrap of evidence has been forthcoming during the last year and a half in spite of every effort to procure it."[56] He filled the document with a series of unanswered questions, which unintentionally rendered his proposal absurd. He asked how the merchants would convert on the high seas, and where they would let off passengers. He could not comprehend how Germany could possibly take hundreds of civilians with them to raid commerce. He also had no idea how the Germans intended to coal their auxiliary cruisers. Without answers to any of these questions, Churchill wrote, "To say that [Britain] had to maintain a large cruiser fleet to deal with this danger appears extravagant in the highest degree." Of course, the Royal Navy did not have the cruisers necessary to confront this particular threat, so Churchill postulated that providing a similar number of armed British merchants to ply the trade routes would furnish a constant and immediate counter to deter the Germans from any "injurious action."[57]

Churchill's proposal nearly repeated the line of reasoning he and Lord President of the Council Robert Crewe had sketched out over a year earlier at the 122nd CID meeting. The Royal Navy, however, only had one hundred fifty un-mounted guns available to arm British merchant vessels, while Britain's oceangoing merchants numbered almost four thousand ships.[58] Churchill set the priority as providing guns strictly as self-defensive armament for ships carrying food to the United Kingdom. He elaborated that the Royal Navy could not use these ships for any other purpose unless they were taken over by the Admiralty. Suitable liners, commissioned by the Admiralty for wartime use as auxiliary cruisers, would conduct offensive operations to hunt enemy armed merchants.[59] Here again, Churchill's plan showed inconsistency. Churchill expected the defensively armed merchants moving along the trade routes to deter Germany from attacking trade, yet he derided this practice for the Royal Navy's cruisers because protecting trade required hunting the commerce raiders rather than sparsely scattering the cruisers along the trade routes in defensive expectancy. A single armed British merchant ship would be no match for a German cruiser, and if Germany used its auxiliary cruisers in small squadrons, a singular armed opponent remained easy prey.

Moreover, the plan to arm merchants engaged strictly in bringing food to the home islands was unworkable. Merchant vessels often operated in circuits, not just back and forth between a food exporting nation and Great Britain. For example, on a typical circuit a vessel might have transported hardwoods from the South Pacific to a port on the west coast of the United States, food from the United States to the United Kingdom, and manufactured goods from there to destinations in the South Pacific. The vessel engaged in this circuit would carry food along only one of the voyage's three legs. To place the policy in effect, the limited guns would have to be moved from that ship to another in mid-circuit. Because conversion of vessels into armed merchants within a neutral state's territory violated its neutrality, all gun transfers between British merchant ships would have to be effected within the empire or Allied territory. This would force shipmasters to add legs to their voyage and impose delays injurious to rapid trade to obtain a suitable gun. Moreover, an armed British merchant sailing into a neutral port ran the risk of being treated as a warship. The neutral state might force the merchant vessel to leave within twenty-four hours with only enough fuel to reach the nearest British port.

The revised orders, issued in July 1914, corrected many of the previous plan's shortcomings. The principle that a prompt attack on the enemy's fighting ships served as the best method for gaining command of the seas still held; the Admiralty believed that destroying commerce raiders would guarantee British ships continuing to bring food and supplies home. British cruisers would attempt to intercept enemy merchant shipping only as a secondary operation. Any German ship that evaded the Royal Navy on the open ocean still had to make it past the blockading cruisers at the entrance to the North Sea.

The new orders acknowledged an important point: ships evaded their hunters more often than not. The Royal Navy intended to assist Britain's merchant ships to evade enemy commerce destroyers by exploiting Britain's superior communication and intelligence network. Once an enemy raider's location became known, naval intelligence could project its possible position for several days into the future. British shore posts and naval vessels would direct British commerce away from known and suspected enemy positions. Meanwhile, Royal Navy cruisers would relentlessly close in on the enemy. The navy still theorized that patrolling trade routes remained a fruitless endeavor. Cruisers, however, could profitably remain at areas of known trade convergence, such as straits and capes. Eventually raiders would also have to converge in these areas. The Admiralty directed cruisers to use intelligence to anticipate enemy movements into these traffic points.

Ships worked in squadrons of three or four vessels so that engagements would have a better prospect of success. Armed merchants taken up by the Admiralty and converted into warships were staffed with additional manpower to provide prize crews. These ships also worked with a squadron, never alone. The orders also encouraged the navy to use armed merchants to form convoys of convenience, but cautioned against overusing them so as not to divert them from their intended track.

The plan provided guidance to maintain fuel above 20 percent and to economize consumption to maximize the time spent scouting for the enemy.

This restriction permitted the navy some flexibility in refueling. Entering a neutral port already occupied by an enemy ship would prove problematic. A neutral state that executed its duty properly would forbid the cruiser's departure for twenty-four hours so it could not directly follow the other belligerent out of the harbor. The Royal Navy, by policy, scrupulously followed the rules with respect to visit and search, which were prohibited in neutral waters. To take advantage of that rule, British merchant vessels remained in territorial waters for as much of their voyage as possible to avoid being stopped and boarded. When British cruisers detected an enemy using neutral ports as bases of operations, they were to exhaust all diplomatic means to stop the abuse of neutral rights. If that failed, the orders permitted the cruisers to use force inside neutral waters. The Admiralty also made arrangements to divert merchant ships from the usual tracks to thwart enemy searches.[60]

Even with these standing orders in place, the Admiralty received a message on November 4 that Rear Admiral Christopher Cradock's squadron had engaged Admiral Maximilian Graf von Spee's squadron off of Coronel at a numerical disadvantage and had been soundly defeated. With the loss of the armored cruisers HMS *Good Hope* and *Monmouth,* and the other ships of Cradock's squadron badly damaged, the Royal Navy lost control of the South America trade route.[61] Fisher sent the battle cruisers, HMS *Indomitable, Inflexible,* and *Tiger* plus several cruisers from the Grand Fleet to join the battleship HMS *Canopus* in the South Atlantic to cut off von Spee's squadron and reclaim control of the route.[62]

Even before the loss at Coronel, the demands on the Royal Navy's resources necessitated replacing first-tier ships in the Mediterranean and some other overseas locations with older vessels. The strain on the Admiralty grew in September and October. By November the stress was acute, the Grand Fleet held only the thinnest margin of superiority over its German foe. The intensity of naval operations at the time could not have been increased or sustained for long. More than once the Admiralty discussed its priorities and whether it had to reduce operations.[63] With a plethora of key tasks to perform, the Royal Navy only just held its own through November 1914. Great Britain needed to do more than maintain a superior fleet, sustain a blockade in the North Sea, and hunt commerce raiders with its remaining available cruisers to ensure it did not lose the war.

6 A STRATEGY EMERGES: THE KEY IS IN THE COLONIES

Strategic necessity drove Whitehall to expand the Great War from continental Europe to the colonies. The Royal Navy had a force in the North Sea superior to its German counterpart, but insufficient for seeking out and destroying the High Seas Fleet wherever it might be found. Thus some in the British cabinet feared possible invasion. To retain its dominance in home waters, the Royal Navy thinned its presence elsewhere in the world. At the same time, global demands on the navy stretched its resources to the breaking point. German commerce raiders threatened British trade to such an extent that the cabinet realized the Royal Navy required assistance to maintain open trade routes. London expanded the war into the German colonies to sap commerce raiders' logistic support and aid the navy in protecting the vital arteries that brought in Britain's food and raw materials.

The key to Great Britain's safety and survival consisted of retaining use of the seas for its own trade while simultaneously preventing Germany from making any effective use of the oceans for economic purposes or for an invasion of the British Isles. At the same time, the presence of the German High Seas Fleet rendered any British Admiralty ideas about attempting amphibious landings on German shores unthinkable. Likewise, the Royal Navy's Grand Fleet deterred German plans to invade Great Britain. The fleets' proximity to each other prevented both nations from fully exercising their will in the North Sea. This is what British naval historian Julian Corbett and American naval officer and theorist Alfred Thayer Mahan defined as the "fleet in being."[1] Each fleet remained powerful enough to sortie for limited operations against the enemy. When concentrated, each could affect local temporary control of the sea to cover a specific operation. Moreover, each fleet could remain dominant in its home waters, exercising superiority and local control there. Neither fleet, however, could command the North Sea in such a way that prevented the enemy's general use of it for any extended period of time. Each navy's unwillingness to risk all to seize control of the North Sea resulted in a situation where control remained in dispute, or what Corbett and Mahan called an uncontrolled sea.[2]

Was control of the North Sea worth risking the fleet? Had the Royal Navy's Grand Fleet swept Germany's High Seas Fleet from the surface of the oceans, Whitehall could have more easily provided material aid to Russia through the Baltic Sea. Without a navy to protect the German army's rear, Berlin would have had to detach some divisions to guard the homeland's coasts against possible British and Russian incursions. With adequate intelligence, however, Germany could detect any British or Russian troop redeployment from the lines. Other things being equal, defense remained the superior form of war, and Germany's possession of interior lines permitted it to move forces more rapidly than its enemies to counter an amphibious threat.[3] Yet, if Kaiser Wilhelm II's naval forces were annihilated, the Royal Navy would have a freer hand to conduct operations elsewhere. Of course, Britain's naval edge might have been less than desired if defeating the Germans entailed taking heavy casualties.

If the Royal Navy lost a duel for rule over the North Sea, Royal Navy cruisers from overseas stations would have had to return home to prevent German raids against the British coast and possible invasion. Allied forces would likely have lost control of the European coast from Denmark to northern France. Whitehall's ability to supply its Slavic ally would remain impaired, and its ability to support its Gallic ally across the English Channel would have been seriously curtailed. That eventuality would possibly give the kaiser's armies a decisive advantage on the continent. Moreover, without a blockading force guarding the entrances to the North Sea, German trade could continue. Ultimately, a fleetless Britain unable to dispute Germany's use of the North Sea lay open to invasion.[4]

On the other hand, if the Royal Navy remained in a defensive posture, German trade suffered. The blockading force also served as an important barrier to neutral trade with Germany, including trade that passed through neutral

Dutch ports. With Britain's fleet guarding the English Channel, France remained supplied, and Great Britain protected itself from invasion. If Germany felt compelled to alter that situation, it had to sortie the High Seas Fleet and fight under conditions that favored the Royal Navy. In summation, London risked much and gained little by pressing for a decision in the North Sea.

The Wilhelmstrasse viewed the problem much the same as Whitehall did. Naval forces and merchant marine operate alongside each other. In naval warfare, consequently, the defensive actions one force takes also tend to inflict harm on the enemy, and the offensive actions one pursues tend to defend one's own commerce. The German fleet did pin down the bulk of the Royal Navy in home waters. The blockade interrupted German trade, but it also kept British cruisers occupied that would otherwise be available to hunt commerce raiders in the open ocean. Fewer Royal Navy cruisers available in the colonies presented Germany with a more favorable balance of forces. The threat to Britain was in the open ocean, where a comingling of naval forces and commerce created opportunities for Germany. Berlin's best option for striking a lethal blow against Great Britain resided in the shipping lanes.

The British Empire still held a considerable advantage in logistics and intelligence because of its many overseas territories and robust wireless and telegraphic cable networks. While German merchant vessels could no longer transit the North Sea with Britain's distant blockade in effect, this posed less of a problem for Germany than Whitehall might have supposed. Germany's naval plans relied on converting the bulk of the nation's merchant vessels into either commerce raiders or support vessels for those raiders. Yet when Germany used its merchant ships as naval auxiliaries, they could not conduct regular trade. German imports and exports could be carried by neutral vessels, likely through neutral ports, then transshipped via rail into the heartland. Thus Berlin thought it could ignore the British blockade without incurring additional economic hardship. Until this plan failed, the German fleet had no reason to challenge the Royal Navy's distant blockade. The Battle of Jutland, Germany's attempt to break British control of the entrances to the North Sea, would not take place until May 31, 1916, after the blockade had been in force for twenty-two months.

Britain's strategic position remained strong, but the cabinet perceived weaknesses, particularly in the trade routes. The Royal Navy existed to provide two vital functions. Dominating the German High Seas Fleet and protecting the British Isles remained the navy's first priority. The navy's second vital function was to protect trade and control sea communications. Some in the cabinet wavered in their confidence that the Royal Navy could successfully execute all that the nation required of it.[5] Former prime minister Arthur Balfour's August 4 and 5, 1914, exchange with Lord Chancellor Richard Haldane illuminates the latter's misgiving. Haldane proposed hedging Britain's bets by keeping the British Expeditionary Force (BEF) at home because it could then form the nucleus of a more substantial and formidable force. The larger force, he argued, could be used against the enemy lines of communication should Germany penetrate into France. Haldane continued his discourse, explaining that the small land force Britain could send immediately might be lost entirely rendering the kingdom weaker rather than stronger at the decisive moment in the war. Haldane's second argument revealed his nervousness with respect to the Royal Navy. He insisted that sending the BEF to the continent deprived the home islands of sufficient regular troops to secure the country from raids, and this would hamper the free action of the fleet.[6] Haldane's reasoning focused on more direct threats to Great Britain, invasion and loss of trade, than the more distant threat that loomed if France fell to the kaiser's legions. If the fleet remained in home waters to prevent invasion and raids, then it could not track down commerce raiders. Alternatively, he proposed that the British Army hold a large force at home to deal with possible invaders so portions of the fleet would be free to protect trade.

Disappointed by Haldane's arguments, Balfour reminded his colleague that they had both sat on the Committee of Imperial Defence (CID) when British strategy had been formulated.[7] In fact, Haldane, who had served as secretary for war in 1911, had presided over the War Department when its generals developed the basic plan. Balfour recalled for Haldane that as of February 1914, the CID had agreed that a mobile force of two effective divisions working in conjunction with the rest of the forces in Britain were adequate to secure the island against raids, while an expeditionary force of up to 100,000 men could aid France. Balfour doubted that waiting to send the army could be justified on military grounds because so much of the War Department's planning hinged on the immediate dispatch of the expeditionary force. Training the army Haldane proposed required a minimum of six months of drilling reserves to match the caliber of the German force. The following day, Balfour recorded that Haldane seemed "rather depressed by a certain wooliness of thought and indecision of purpose."[8]

The British needed to keep the fleet at home, thus the trade routes remained exposed to danger. In overseas locations Germany maintained numerous liners capable of becoming auxiliary cruisers. The kaiser also stationed several modern cruisers, among them the SMS *Emden, Dresden, Karlsruhe,* and *Königsberg,* overseas and maintained two armored cruisers, SMS *Scharnhorst* and *Gneisenau,* in his East Asia squadron. In total, forty-nine potential German commerce raiders roamed the oceans. If the raiders succeeded only marginally, taking two to three prizes each, they could capture some ninety to a hundred thirty ships. Recall that in the U.S. Civil War, CSS *Alabama* took sixty-nine prizes. Germany's forty-nine commerce raiders operating worldwide could seriously affect Britain's insurance rates and delivery schedules and induce hoarding and panic in markets without approaching *Alabama*'s extraordinary success.

Whitehall's ministers strongly perceived the threat to British commerce. They had heard reports of Admiral Alfred von Tirpitz's proclamations to the Reichstag explaining his intentions for the risk fleet in the bills used to introduce naval funding. The rationale behind Germany's fleet had been the subject of numerous debates and newspaper articles. Moreover, it had been the object of British-German diplomacy for more than a decade. Tirpitz's risk fleet created freedom of action for Germany in the colonies. The key was whether Germany could effectively exploit its opportunity. The kaiser's overseas cruisers constituted a known threat, and Germany's fast liners created a potential threat. Berlin had stonewalled all international efforts to regulate conversion of merchants to armed cruisers, insisting on the right to make conversion on the high seas. This and unresolved issues over determining ownership of cargoes rendered creating an international prize court moot. Britain could not count on support from the body of international law to help protect its shipping. Many nations might agree with Britain's claims against the unauthorized taking of prizes, but without a court, none of the claims would be adjudicated. Moreover, no one in the British cabinet doubted the thoroughness of the kaiser's military planners. Storage facilities stocked with guns and ammunition at Germany's naval ports had the names of liners emblazoned on the sides, indicating that the government had plans to create a number of auxiliary cruisers.[9] Since Germany had gone to the trouble of maintaining squadrons overseas, and insisted on the right to convert merchants to men-of-war on the high seas, then the Admiralty presumed Germany had a plan to bring the threat to fruition.

Churchill had a rule of thumb that held the Royal Navy needed five cruisers to hunt down each commerce raider. He claimed, however, that the threat was overblown and that to catch them all would require hundreds of cruisers. The stark reality was that the Royal Navy simply did not have that many cruisers available, and it would take years to build them. If the Admiralty sent the cruisers Britain did have to chase all the potential commerce raiders, it would impair the blockade of the North Sea and weaken the Grand Fleet. Churchill believed stripping cruisers from the North Sea blockade remained unacceptable. Britain converted some of its own merchant liners into auxiliary cruisers, but every conversion was one merchant lost to trade. Each lost merchant reduced the world's cargo-carrying capacity, which in turn caused market forces to react by increasing freight rates.

Britain planned to drive Germany's merchant marine from the seas, an act that Whitehall calculated would increase freight charges but not to unaffordable levels. Diverting too much British shipping from its regular carrying traffic would stress transportation costs even more. For these reasons, Churchill still favored providing guns to arm British merchant vessels. Merchant ships so armed would continue to trade along regular routes and, he argued, could defend themselves. He had at his disposal, however, too few guns. More than four thousand merchant vessels flew a British flag.[10] The tramp steamer made up the vast majority of Britain's merchant fleet. These slower ships could neither flee their speedier pursuers nor could the Admiralty immediately supply the guns they needed to protect themselves.

Corbett and Mahan provide strategic insights in their writing, on which the British cabinet apparently drew to find a strategy to protect commerce. Corbett explains that the number of cruisers needed to protect commerce did not vary with the volume of trade, but that only a fixed number of warships was required to cover the ports and areas where trade routes converged. The locations with the greatest concentration of merchants, and hence the most profitable hunting for a commerce destroyer, consisted of the largest ports for trade and areas where land mass constrained merchant traffic. Cruisers should therefore concentrate their defense on those areas, rather than attempt to sweep the entire ocean.[11]

Mahan observes, and Corbett agrees, that commerce raiders were most successful when operating close to their bases of supply. Modern steamships had become the weapon of choice because of their superior speed. These ships required frequent replenishment of coal, so they were more dependent on logistics than their wind-propelled predecessors.[12] The commerce raiders' logistics offered appropriate targets. To carry out oceanic trade, one has to have access to the ocean; likewise those that would prevent the passage of trade must also have entry points. All connections to the seas begin and end at ports. As a consequence, Great Britain decided to attack the German Empire's overseas ports. Seizing Germany's overseas harbors would strip German cruisers of their most obvious bases of supply. If German commerce raiders continued to operate, they would have to do so using whatever German merchants, or cooperative neutrals, could bring from the homeland. In the North Sea, the British blockade made merchants that supplied raiders subject to capture.

British trade secured an additional measure of safety if by attacking German colonies, the invading forces degraded commerce raiders' intelligence and command and control. If German wireless stations and submerged telegraph cables fell into British hands, German cruisers would lose information on British merchants and the location of enemy naval forces. German raiders would also suffer reduced ability to coordinate with merchant supply ships to replenish coal. The British strategy would eventually drive German commerce raiders to try operating out of neutral ports, where British diplomats could exert soft power on the neutral governments to curtail those raiders' activities. Whitehall also believed that many German vessels would seek a neutral port to become interned for the duration of the war. The raiders' other alternative remained to return to home port in Germany. That meant a dangerous attempt to run the British North Sea blockade with a ship low on coal and ammunition.

The fact that Germany had colonies on Africa's east and west coasts, as well as in the Pacific, compounded the problem for the British. To curtail German commerce raiders' logistical support, the Royal Navy needed to subdue all potential German supply bases. Designing operations to attack each port required substantial military and naval resources, which Britain desperately needed in Europe. The cabinet had to find solutions that would not undermine naval operations in home waters or support for the BEF on the continent.

On August 5, 1914, Prime Minister H. H. Asquith appointed a joint naval and military committee, which included members from the Foreign Office and the Colonial Office, to consider combined operations in foreign territory. This committee, the Offensive Sub-Committee of the Committee of Imperial Defence, met that same day to produce a strategy within specific constraints imposed by the cabinet. The key point was that any offensive operation overseas had to enhance the war effort; it could not be of marginal value. First, any contemplated operation could not degrade the effort to concentrate troops and naval vessels in Europe. Second, these operations, if to be of value at all, had to improve the safety of the trade routes.[13]

In order to retain British forces in Europe, the Offensive Sub-Committee decided that overseas operations would rely for resources on those that were available locally in the colonies, dominions, or allies.[14] Germany had few regular military forces stationed abroad. Native troops led by German officers constituted the only defenses throughout most of the German Empire. Thus, the Offensive Sub-Committee judged that local British forces would suffice to execute several nearly simultaneous operations against Germany's colonies. This would be especially true if Whitehall limited the scope of proposed operations to seizing the ports, submerged telegraph cables, and high-frequency wireless stations. The British attackers would have to refrain from annexing territory or governing territory since that would require additional manpower and antagonize allies. To the maximum extent possible, Britain's field commanders would keep German colonial officials in their administrative responsibilities.

The Offensive Sub-Committee proposed dispatching an expedition from India to attack the German East African port of Dar es Salaam. This objective would deprive German naval forces of a logistics base and assist the Admiralty in protecting commerce. The capture of Dar es Salaam would produce the dual effect of protecting British possessions in East Africa from German attack. Whitehall could also strengthen Britain's strategic posture if the wireless telegraph stations in Luderitzbucht and Swakopmund, German Southwest Africa, were destroyed. The Offensive Sub-Committee recommended inviting the government of South Africa to undertake the operation if subsequent military study demonstrated the plan's feasibility. The committee also desired that British forces in the Gold Coast, reinforced by those from Sierra Leone, destroy German wireless stations in Togoland. The wireless station in the Cameroons would present a more difficult challenge. The committee estimated that British forces from Nigeria would require reinforcements to successfully invade the

Cameroons, so the committee decided to reconsider an operation there at a later time. In the Pacific, Germany had wireless stations and ports at the islands of Yap and German New Guinea. The committee advised the cabinet to request that Australia's commonwealth government send a force to strike these German holdings. In the same vein, the committee recommended that the cabinet invite forces from New Zealand to send expeditions against the German wireless stations and bases on the islands of Samoa and Nauru.[15]

The Offensive Sub-Committee met again on August 6 to try to improve on its initial recommendations. It decided that the India Office should send one force to attack Dar es Salaam and a second to reinforce the King's African Rifles in British East Africa. The committee also noted that the Admiralty should be informed of the proposed dates for the various operations to ensure that the naval situation remained favorable to attacks.[16] In his August 6 daily letter to the sovereign, Prime Minister Asquith reported that the cabinet had met that day and sanctioned immediate dispatch of an expeditionary force, of undetermined composition, to France. At the same meeting, the cabinet had also approved the principle of attacking German colonies to seize ports and wireless stations in Togoland, German East Africa, the China Seas, and Samoa. At a subsequent cabinet meeting, the War Council determined that the composition of the expeditionary force should be four regular divisions and a five-brigade cavalry division.[17] The timing of the meetings indicates that the cabinet decided on overseas expeditions before it committed to a size for the force it sent to the continent. Although not conclusive, this indicates that the cabinet had misgivings about sending the full expeditionary force to the continent until it resolved the important issue of the safety of the trade routes.

Colonial Secretary Lewis Harcourt wasted no time acting on the cabinet's decision to attack Germany's overseas territories. He simply directed the governors of Sierra Leone and the Gold Coast to mount an expedition against Togoland to eliminate the wireless stations there.[18] Because South Africa, New Zealand, and Australia were self-governing dominions, the cabinet requested rather than directed their cooperation. Harcourt drafted telegrams to the dominion governors informing each that if his "ministers desired and felt themselves able," His Majesty's Government in Great Britain would regard the seizure of nearby German ports and wireless stations "as a great and urgent Imperial service."[19] The cabinet invited the government of the Union of South

Africa to attack German Southwest Africa to seize the ports at Luderitzbucht and Swakopmund and also desired that the South African government disable or control the high-frequency wireless transmitters at those locations and in the interior. Any territory in German Southwest Africa that South African forces occupied had to be placed at the disposal of the imperial government for purposes of negotiating the end-of-war settlement. The Admiralty viewed seizing the wireless stations at Luderitzbucht and Swakopmund an urgent priority and recommended that a joint naval and military expedition up the coasts as the quickest option for capturing the facilities.[20]

Along with a wireless transmitter, Germany also had a built-up port at Samoa. Harcourt sent a telegram urging New Zealand's governor to send an expedition to Samoa to occupy the port and its wireless station. The telegram also reminded the governor that any German territory occupied would necessarily fall under the auspices of His Majesty's government for settlement at war's end. The Admiralty followed the telegram with a memorandum that pointed out the object of the New Zealand expedition should be the island of Upolu, Samoa, which would prevent Germany from using it as a base for commerce raiders and a center for wireless communication in the Pacific.[21]

With the same caveat that any German territory occupied would be subject to end-of-war negotiation, the cabinet suggested that Australia undertake operations to subdue German New Guinea and the islands of Angaur, Feys, Nauru, and Yap. The Admiralty set as specific objectives operations against the wireless and cable station on Yap and the wireless stations at Nauru. It also desired that Australia seize the port at Rabaul in German New Guinea and prevent the Germans from completing the nearby wireless station.[22] Feys and Angaur also had wireless transmitters, but these were of comparatively low power. Moreover, the ports at these islands were undeveloped, rendering their capture lower priority. Because both islands contained valuable phosphate deposits, however, Britain still considered their capture worthwhile. Feys and Angaur lay in the Pellew Island group, so their capture would possibly come as an extension of the operations against Yap and Nauru in the Caroline Islands.[23] The cabinet consulted the India Office to send an expedition from India against Dar es Salaam in German East Africa. The expedition's purpose remained to protect British trade by denying the port to German naval forces and commerce raiders. The cabinet also petitioned the India Office to put the wireless transmitter there out of commission.[24]

On August 8, the Offensive Sub-Committee met again and reconsidered the attack against the Cameroons. The committee advised the Foreign Office to inquire of the French government what steps it would be willing to take to coordinate an attack against the Cameroons with forces it had in West Africa. If France cooperated, it could provide the additional forces necessary to subdue the colony.[25] Great Britain's ambassador to France, Francis Bertie, replied to the Foreign Office's inquiries that France's Ministry of Colonies had already considered attacking Duala, Cameroons. A few days later, Bertie confirmed that France would provide naval cooperation to occupy Duala and would invade the Cameroons from the northeast simultaneously with a British offensive from the northwest based out of Nigeria. Until this operation began, the Admiralty intended to blockade Duala.[26]

Meanwhile, Foreign Secretary Edward Grey busied himself with Japan and China. Vice Admiral Maximilian Graf von Spee's East Asia squadron—consisting of the armored cruisers SMS *Scharnhorst* and *Gneisenau,* the light cruisers *Nürnberg, Leipzig,* and *Emden,* and assorted gunboats—constituted the greatest threat to commerce in the Pacific. Dominion naval forces sufficed to accomplish the missions requested of them, but they lacked the capacity to assume the additional task of hunting down and defeating Germany's East Asia squadron. Grey sought assistance from Britain's Japanese ally to meet the challenge.

In a telegram addressed to the British ambassador in Tokyo, Grey warned Japan about brewing hostilities with Germany. In the event that Germany attacked Hong Kong or Wei-Hei-Wei, Britain anticipated that Japan would lend its support.[27] Japan had already considered the possibility and sent a message indicating that it was willing to fulfill its alliance responsibilities toward its British ally if it came under German attack.[28] Japan, however, indicated that a war in Europe did not affect its interests and it preferred to wait for a specific invitation from Britain on contemplated action before determining its own course.[29] On August 6, Grey petitioned Japan to use its naval forces to intercept German armed merchant cruisers engaged in attacking British commerce. Grey acknowledged that Japan's participation constituted an act of war, but argued that help curtailing commerce raiding greatly assisted Great Britain. He regretted that the situation could not be avoided.[30] The terms of the Anglo-Japanese alliance did not invoke action for protecting maritime commerce. Japan remained willing to assist Great Britain, but did not wish to provoke Russia, so the government requested that Grey provide a statement as to the rationale for Japan's entry into the war and the assistance required.[31] Japanese diplomats worked steadily to draft a suitable declaration of war.[32] Grey requested repeatedly that Japan allow him to view and comment on the proposed declaration prior to formally issuing it.[33]

By August 8, correspondence between Tokyo and London indicated that Japan was contemplating an attack on the German port at Tsingtao. One report held that the French ambassador to London had inquired of Arthur Nicholson, the permanent undersecretary for foreign affairs, as to the feasibility of French and British participation in the planned Japanese attack on Tsingtao. He believed that French and British prestige would suffer if Japan reduced the port unilaterally.[34] Grey, however, denied to his ambassador in Tokyo that any conversations concerning a military operation against Tsingtao had taken place.[35] The latter nevertheless insisted that he intended to assign the naval attaché to observe Japanese naval forces in operations against Tsingtao.[36]

On August 9, Grey called on Japan to limit is wartime actions to protection of commerce to avoid spreading the war to China.[37] Later that day, Grey telegraphed the British embassy in Tokyo that he understood Japan's position that any warlike actions taken against Germany exposed Japanese trade to German predation worldwide, and that under those conditions, Japan considered eliminating the German military and naval presence in East Asia a necessity. He objected, however, to military operations on the Chinese mainland aimed at the German naval port at Tsingtao. If Japan's entry into the war included land operations in China, Grey preferred that Japan take no action at all.[38]

By August 11, however, Grey had accepted that Japan's entry into the war would be on its own terms and those terms included an attack on Tsingtao.[39] Grey sought to limit the damage by pleading for a commitment that limited Japan's operations to the geographic area immediately surrounding Tsingtao. As the dominion governments in Australia and New Zealand grew nervous over perceived Japanese expansionism, Grey even proposed the words he hoped Japan would use to announce its limited objectives. He asked the Japanese government to specify that its military operations would not extend to any islands or territories beyond the meager German holdings in continental East Asia.[40]

The next day, Grey reported that British military and naval forces had been instructed to cooperate with the Japanese government for any proposed operations inside those geographic constraints. He reaffirmed his intent to Britain's ambassador in Tokyo in a subsequent telegram. Grey attempted to make the point that Britain had no designs to add any Chinese territory to the empire, and that for the stability of China, Tokyo should follow London's example in this respect. Over several days, Grey pushed the point that Japan's declaration must include a statement to the effect that it had no designs on German-held islands in the Pacific; the self-governing dominions desired to deal with those themselves. Other European powers also desired a Japanese pledge that it would not attempt to use the situation to its advantage and seize their possessions, such as the Dutch East Indies.[41]

Japan ultimately issued its declaration to the German ambassador in Tokyo without allowing Grey to view it first. When Grey heard of it, his rebuke to his representative in Tokyo revealed his annoyance, "I assume [the] ultimatum has now been issued and it is therefore useless to criticize its terms." Grey continued to push for a statement that indicated the restricted scope of Japan's planned operations, stating that if the ultimatum contained specific parameters, he would simply quote from it. If it did not, however, he still considered it essential to assure the self-governing dominions, other European powers, and China of Japan's limited intentions.[42]

When the Japanese ambassador in London presented a copy of the declaration to Grey on August 17, Grey saw that it had no comforting statements circumscribing the scope and scale of Japanese ambitions in the Pacific. He admonished the ambassador that Britain would have to see how events developed to decide its course. Germany, he added, could simply cede Kiao-Chou back to China and send its ships to sea to prey on British commerce; he hoped Japan had a plan to deal with that exigency.[43] Japan explained that including a specific statement of geographic limitations would have implied that Japan acted under the direction of the British government. The British ambassador in Tokyo speculated that Japan's cabinet had refused to make a statement pertaining to geographic limits on the scope of the war because it had other plans.[44] A few days later, however, several Japanese papers reported the emperor's conciliatory statement to the effect that Japan's participation in the war remained in the spirit of the Anglo-Japanese alliance and that it had no desire for territorial aggrandizement.[45]

As events unfolded, Britain's enthusiasm for military operations in East Asia with Japan waned. On August 21 the War Office planned to commit a brigade consisting of two British infantry battalions and two Indian battalions to the Tsingtao operation, but a day later Grey told the Japanese that because of other priorities, the War Office would commit only one battalion of British troops.[46] Observing that Japan had naval forces available, the Admiralty requested that they operate alongside the Allies in the Mediterranean and in the waters around France and Great Britain.[47] This appeared to be a British attempt to garner Japanese support in a way that would materially aid the war effort while simultaneously minimizing Japan's potential to acquire additional territory.

Japan formally declared war on Germany on August 23. Four days later, Japan placed the Kiao-Chou bay and the German naval base at Tsingtao under blockade. Britain thus received the naval assistance it requested.[48] Japan agreed to protect trade north of Hong Kong, and French and British naval vessels patrolled the trade routes south of Hong Kong to Singapore. HMS *Yarmouth* and *Minotaur,* plus two promised Japanese cruisers and any Russian cruisers available, hunted German men-of-war and auxiliary cruisers in other areas.[49]

By October 23, weeks before Turkey entered the war, Great Britain had the India Expeditionary Force D (IEF D) in readiness at Bahrain. The Admiralty desired the force to protect its interests in Anglo-Persian Oil at Abadan in Persia. The India Office had additional reasons for concern. If Turkey induced Arab sheiks to incite a pan-Islamic jihad, Muslims in Afghanistan, Baluchistan, Egypt, and India might all rebel against British rule. The viceroy of India sought to prevent a jihad with a strong British show of force at the head of the Persian Gulf. The Arab rulers, particularly Sheik Ibn Saud, disliked Turkish rule. The presence of IEF D in the gulf sent a strong signal of support from Great Britain for the Arab cause. The India Office considered this insurance against Islamic rebellion in areas it governed.

Whenever the India Office wrote of operations in the gulf, it emphasized the need to prevent Muslim uprisings. In contrast, the cabinet and the Admiralty emphasized British interests at Abadan. Turkey declared war on November 5, and the ships carrying IEF D crossed the bar at Shatt al-Arab the same day. The force disembarked on November 6, and instead of joining with Arab tribes in the region to thwart Turkish plans, moved to the east where it reached Abadan on November 7 and set up a defensive position.[50] The operation's intent remained to meet the twofold purpose of countering a jihad and protecting the oil fields at Abadan, but the requirement to protect oil appeared to hold primacy.

Historians have put forth various reasons as the impetus for Britain's overseas expeditions. Two prominent arguments are that the cabinet desired to add territory to the empire, and to hold Germany's colonies as bargaining chips in postwar negotiation. Various memoirs and memoranda provide some evidence to support these claims. Prime Minister Asquith recalled the cabinet discussions held at the August 6 meeting where the idea for overseas operations generated enthusiastic support. He remarked that the cabinet members looked like "Elizabethan buccaneers" as they presided over dividing up Germany's colonies.[51] Colonial Secretary Lewis Harcourt's memorandum, "The Spoils," presented ideas on how to divide German colonies among the Allies.[52] The prime minister's memoir and Harcourt's memorandum both painted a picture of seizing Germany's colonies to add territory to the British Empire. Churchill remarked that respectable Liberal politicians would never have decided prior to the pressure of war to act with "malice aforethought" to seize German colonies. Germany posed a threat to sea communications that the "prompt denial of these bases of refuges to the German cruisers" could remove. He also considered German colonies hostages for the eventual liberation of Belgium.[53] Each line of reasoning deserves analysis.

First, Asquith's memoir misstates the reasons for invading Germany's colonies. Britain did not have a plan to seize all of Germany's colonies. In fact, Britain had no plan and no hope of seizing Germany's most important base in the Pacific, Tsingtao. Foreign Minister Grey had invited Japan's participation in the war to garner additional naval strength on the high seas. Ministers in Tokyo determined to seize Tsingtao in spite of Whitehall's attempts to deter that action. In addition, Britain had requested French assistance to seize the Cameroons because the operation posed too difficult a challenge for the British colonial forces available. Germany also claimed many islands dotting the Pacific, but the Offensive Sub-Committee initially considered only a few of these sufficiently important to warrant an expedition. The cabinet's enthusiasm stemmed from having, or at least it should have, a cogent plan to curtail German "buccaneers" from hampering Britain's trade.

Harcourt wrote "The Spoils" in March 1915, after the operations directed against German colonies had largely been successful. Pressure from allies concerning the ultimate disposition of Germany's territories compelled Harcourt to address the matter. Thus, Harcourt's ideas do not reflect initial war planning concerning threats to the British Empire. His memorandum concerns planning mid-war, specifically dealing with maintaining relationships within the Alliance when Britain's partners raised the idea of retaining Germany's colonies.

Churchill's remarks are half right. Extinguishing Germany's overseas ports and capturing its communications centers denied commerce raiders the logistics and information necessary to effectively disrupt British trade. The idea that Germany's colonies constituted effective bargaining chips for the eventual liberation of Belgium represents Churchill's wishful thinking. Unlike Great Britain, Germany did not derive its wealth and capacity to wage war from its colonies. Therefore, Germany suffered only limited harm from the loss of them. Consider that if Germany controlled Belgium completely, it would also likely gain possession of the Netherlands, Luxemburg, and Denmark. No German diplomat would trade control of developed, industrial nations that held the best ports on the continental side of the English Channel for undeveloped colonies in Africa or Pacific islands unless compelled to do so. Belgium alone remained more valuable than all of Germany's African and East Asian colonies.

Mahan discussed an analogous point in the American Revolution where a French officer proposed taking British West Indian territories as hostages to exchange for Gibraltar. Mahan felt it unlikely that Britain would trade an outpost as valuable as Gibraltar, the key to the Royal Navy's access to the Mediterranean, for a remote Caribbean island. More likely, Mahan postulated, one would have to threaten Britain's home islands with invasion before such a bargain could be struck.[54] Likewise, Germany's outright defeat, or the inevitability of that defeat, presented the only means of freeing Belgium.

The overseas expeditions were not designed to strip Germany of its colonies, but to seize ports, submerged telegraph cable junctions, and wireless transmission stations that provided logistical support and command and control for commerce raiders. Colonies and dominions became involved in overseas offensive operations at the discretion of the cabinet. Subsequent direction with specific objectives, however, came not from the War Office, but from the Admiralty. The department that directed the actions indicates whose interests were most affected. If the intent had been to seize the colonies—that is, to control the land and frontiers—the War Office would have necessarily taken the lead. The expedition's designs, however, focused on control of shipping lanes, so the Admiralty determined the tactical objectives. No more was required of the local colonial and dominion forces than to terminate commerce raiders' logistics, intelligence, and command and control capabilities. Hence the required targets became ports and communications systems. Moreover, dominion and colonial forces received instructions forbidding them to annex territory. This demonstrates that the scope of the operations was limited to the specific tasks assigned and not a plan that provided for the future disposition of Germany's overseas possessions. Admiral John Fisher, at the time retired but later to be recalled after war's outbreak, wrote to Asquith six months before the war, mainly about the dangers the submarine presented, and expressed the idea well, "The army should assist the navy in gaining command of the sea!"[55] The Offensive Sub-Committee designed the overseas offensive expeditions against Germany's colonies for exactly that purpose—to secure command of the sea.

7 WORLD WAR I IN THE COLONIES: EXECUTING THE STRATEGY

Soon after London declared war on August 4, 1914, Britain's colonial and dominion governments worked closely with the Admiralty to put together expeditions designed to seize Germany's overseas ports and high-frequency radio stations. At the same time, the India Office organized the expedition to Mesopotamia to protect the Anglo-Persian oil fields. The choices political, military, and naval leaders made with respect to the overseas expeditions demonstrated that London's decisions were foremost naval considerations. Whitehall's priorities for overseas operations were, in order of importance, maintaining the integrity of the trade routes, eliminating logistics and intelligence bases for German commerce raiders, protecting an independent source of fuel for the Royal Navy, capturing and destroying Germany's commerce raiders, and curtailing German trade.

PACIFIC ISLANDS

As July came to a close without an abatement of the European crisis, the Royal Navy attempted to shadow and track German warships and merchant vessels. At the war's outbreak, it knew little about the location of Germany's East Asia squadron, commanded by Vice Admiral Maximilian Graf von Spee. This lack of knowledge demonstrated that although a peacetime intelligence system had been implemented, diligent personnel at the ports still had to track and monitor warships' activities. On August 1, the German merchant vessel *Komet* was within clear communications range, about fifty nautical miles, of the British wireless station at Port Moresby in Papua. On the same day, the German armored cruiser SMS *Scharnhorst* communicated via high-frequency radio with the German wireless station on Yap, but the Royal Navy could not determine the warship's position. As of August 3, 1914, British naval intelligence knew that the armored cruiser SMS *Gneisenau* had departed Nagasaki, Japan, on June 23 but the warship's whereabouts were unknown. Intelligence believed *Gneisenau* had joined *Scharnhorst* and that these two marauders were near Tsingtao. The cruiser SMS *Nürnberg* had been at Mazatlan, Mexico, on November 13 the previous year. British intelligence believed the warship remained there or was transiting back to Tsingtao to rejoin its squadron. The cruiser SMS *Leipzig* was patrolling somewhere in the vicinity of Vancouver, British Colombia. The Admiralty knew, however, that the cruiser SMS *Emden* departed Tsingtao in company with four colliers on August 3. SMS *Grier,* an aging light cruiser, was transiting the Rhio Strait somewhere between Java and Singapore.

When war broke out on August 4, Australia's governor-general, Ronald Munro Ferguson, detained several German colliers in Australian ports, preventing them from potentially supplying von Spee's squadron. Nevertheless, some German colliers in port at Newcastle, New South Wales, slipped through Australia's bureaucratic net and hurriedly departed the morning of August 6.[1] Each of the East Asia squadron's warships remained in communications with the German wireless station at Yap, facilitating von Spee's ability to bring his ships together. By August 6, the Admiralty's intelligence branch indicated *Scharnhorst, Gneisenau,* and possibly *Nürnberg* were together in the vicinity of 8° south latitude and 162° east longitude, heading in a southeasterly direction.[2]

Rear Admiral George Patey, commander of Australian naval forces, rallied his squadron and planned to attack Simpsonhafen in German New Guinea unless he received specific reports of German warships' locations. His most recent intelligence postulated that the enemy's armored cruisers, *Scharnhorst* and *Gneisenau,* remained within 1,500 nautical miles of Australia, possibly at Simpsonhafen in company with *Komet,* and a survey ship, *Planet.* If true, Patey intended to surprise the German squadron in port with a superior force of his own. If the enemy warships were absent, the Admiral could still destroy the wireless station located there.[3]

Patey dispatched the cruiser HMAS *Sydney* and several destroyers to Simpsonhafen with orders to attack any ships there on August 11 at 9:00 p.m., which was about one hour prior to moonrise. *Sydney* would remain outside the harbor in support. Because Patey's priority was to sink the two larger armored cruisers, if the harbor were empty or only the smaller ships, *Komet* and *Planet,* were in the harbor, *Sydney* and accompanying destroyers would proceed to nearby Matupi harbor. Unfortunately, no German warships were found in either harbor. The *Sydney* flotilla also reconnoitered nearby Tilili Bay, which was also empty.

The following day, Patey landed a raiding party to find and destroy Rabaul's wireless station, but could not locate the transmitter. Fortunately, HMAS *Australia* stopped the German tanker *Talasea* outside of Rabaul. The ship's master divulged that the high-frequency transmitter sat several miles inland in the bush. Meanwhile, the Germans working the transmitter learned of the Australian squadron's presence and repeatedly broadcast Patey's ships' positions. In desperation, Patey informed Rabaul that he would shell the city unless the station ceased transmitting. The Rabaul district office administrator replied that he had no authority over the wireless company, and the governor was absent. Nevertheless, the radio station fell silent. *Sydney* crossed the bay to Herbertshohe in search of the transmitter. Patey's squadron scanned the coast but could not visually locate the wireless station. His squadron, low on fuel, departed to replenish. Shortly after leaving, Patey acquired additional intelligence that placed the transmitter on the Herbertshohe side of the bay, opposite Rabaul, about four miles inland.[4]

That same day, New Zealand's governor, Arthur Foljambe, 2nd Earl of Liverpool, asked Patey whether it was safe to proceed with a proposed expedition against the German territory in Samoa. The admiral knew nothing of the proposed expedition but supported it in principle because Samoa's capture denied Germany's commerce raiders an additional support base. Patey could not guarantee the safety of the expedition while the German East Asia Squadron's location remained unknown, so he told Governor Liverpool that the expedition could proceed if escorted by the fleet. Another factor that favored supporting the New Zealand expedition was that Australia's warships would then be in position to intercept von Spee's squadron if it headed for Samoa or attempted to escape toward the southeast.

Patey planned first to cover the movement of the Australian expedition to Rabaul; then he would escort the New Zealanders to Samoa. When the admiral received news on August 16 that the New Zealand expedition had already started, it surprised him. The Australian operation against Rabaul had been scheduled for August 19, so Patey believed that the Kiwis would wait until his forces were freed from escort duty before proceeding with their offensive. The Admiralty, however, had pressured Liverpool to begin as soon as he had his forces assembled, as it had also done with Australia's expedition. When Patey learned of this, he split his force to provide naval escort for both expeditions. In doing so, however, he suspended all other naval operations, which included searching for von Spee's warships.[5] The decision that Patey made, and the Admiralty's forcing the rapid dispatch of his expeditions, indicated that extinguishing potential naval bases and intelligence centers constituted a higher priority than destroying German warships.

Admiral Patey rendezvoused with the New Zealand force on August 17. He learned then that the Kiwis were escorted by the cruisers HMS *Psyche, Philomel,* and *Pyramus* and the French cruiser *Montcalm.* He added his ships, the battle cruiser HMAS *Australia* and the cruiser HMAS *Melbourne,* to the convoy. The force stopped to coal at the French port, Noumea, New Caledonia, and conducted rehearsals at Suva, Fiji. The expedition got under way again in order to arrive at Apia, Samoa, at dawn on August 30.[6] The New Zealand force also brought with them ten Fiji islanders knowledgeable of the local tribes on Samoa.[7]

The task force arrived at 7:45 a.m., slightly later than planned because of heavy weather. Immediately upon the New Zealand force's arrival, the German wireless station sent a coded message—the letters "S G"—four times. Seeing no enemy ships in the harbor, Patey directed *Psyche* to send a boat under a flag of truce to explain the situation to Samoa's German officials and request the colony's capitulation. The surrender documents *Psyche*'s delegation carried stipulated that the wireless transmitter must cease broadcasting immediately or the naval force would destroy it with gunfire. The German authorities protested Patey's threat of bombardment as a violation of the Second Hague Peace Conference, but nevertheless surrendered without resistance. The landing force disembarked at 1:00 p.m. and hoisted the Union Jack at the governor's house thirty minutes later.[8] The following morning, the invaders flew the British flag over the courthouse.[9] Although the *Montcalm* was present, the French did not unfurl their flag over the German colony.

The admiral left Apia in HMAS *Australia* at noon on August 31 for Rabaul. With Samoa secured, Patey prepared to seize Rabaul and Herbertshohe, in

German New Guinea, and capture the as-yet-unlocated wireless station. He intended to seize the towns and establish a base in the harbor for future operations aimed at Yap, Angaur, and Nauru. Meanwhile, because of repeated urging from the Admiralty, he dispatched HMAS *Melbourne* directly to Nauru to destroy the wireless station there. Once the wireless transmitter was inoperable, the island could be occupied at a convenient time later.[10]

The China squadron had already eliminated the German wireless at Yap, but a telegraph cable that connected to Shanghai, Guam, and Manado, in the Celebes archipelago, remained in service. The commander of the China squadron wished the wireless station at Angaur destroyed. He recommended that Allied forces forgo occupying the island because it was not connected to any other locations by telegraph cable, and he did not believe that it had adequate resources to serve as a base for German warships. He informed the Admiralty that he could not spare ships for the three-thousand-mile voyage to Angaur, but he was prepared to cut the telegraph cable at Yap if directed. Because the Yap cable landed at neutral territory, however, the Admiralty instructed the squadron not to cut it.[11]

Foreign Secretary Edward Grey disagreed with the China Squadron commander's recommendation against occupying Angaur. Grey had recently received information from the managing director of the Pacific Phosphate Company that Angaur was rich in phosphate deposits. The foreign secretary believed the phosphates ought to be secured as soon as possible.[12] Colonial Secretary Lewis Harcourt also desired that the Australians occupy the islands. His intelligence indicated that the Germans were ready for attacks on the wireless stations. They planned to hide parts to repair the stations, wait for the danger to pass, and then put the stations back in service. Harcourt believed that the only way to prevent the Germans from using the islands as centers for intelligence was to occupy them. The Allied garrisons could consist of small forces because German warships could not afford to detach landing parties from their crews to retake the islands.[13]

The Admiralty and the Colonial Office had not counted on occupying all the German territories in the Pacific. Intelligence received subsequent to the expeditions' departures from New Zealand and Australia pointed to the conclusion that Germany's Pacific islands might have to be seized and held to deny their usefulness to enemy communications. The Foreign Office concluded also that there might be minerals and other raw materials of value to the empire that warranted an island's occupation. When the cabinet approved the expeditions, however, neither of these facts was known. As a consequence, the Royal Navy and dominion governors planned to garrison some of the enemy islands and leave the other German territories alone after they could no longer contribute to Kaiser Wilhelm II's war effort. With receipt of this new information, however, the Admiralty and colonial military leaders revised their plans.

On August 31, the commander in chief, China, operating out of Singapore, asked Patey whether he intended to sweep the Caroline and Marshall Islands for SMS *Scharnhorst* and *Gneisenau*. The Admiralty had not only tasked Patey with invading Yap, Nauru, and Angaur, but two weeks earlier had also ordered the admiral to escort a future convoy of Australian troops to Aden. The cruisers HMAS *Melbourne, Sydney,* and *Encounter* would soon depart from Sydney to accompany the convoy. Patey's future movements hinged on whether he would lose ships from his squadron to perform that task. He informed the Admiralty and his colleague in Singapore that his current orders left him with insufficient warships to execute the expeditions to Yap, Nauru, and Angaur while simultaneously protecting a convoy bound for Aden.

With these requirements imposed on Patey's squadron, he could not engage in lower priority sweeps for German raiders. If the Admiralty permitted the Australian squadron to keep its ships by terminating the convoy escort, the admiral could search for *Scharnhorst* and company after subduing the three small islands. *Montcalm*, under the command of Rear Admiral Albert Huguet, returned to Noumea to pursue additional missions that the French government might desire. Huguet found his only orders were to fully cooperate with Australia's naval forces. *Montcalm,* therefore, left Noumea to rejoin Patey's squadron at Rabaul.

Meanwhile, Patey discovered that German trade in the Pacific had ceased at the beginning of the war. Because German ships were no longer running, provisions on Samoa were low.[14] The British cabinet was certainly aware of this development. Grey boasted to his ambassador in Tokyo that British cruisers operating throughout the world had brought German trade to a standstill. The German High Seas Fleet could not interfere at all with British trade because of the distant blockade. About 70 percent of all German merchant tonnage had been confiscated by the British; another 20 percent was sheltered in neutral harbors because of the danger presented by the Royal Navy if it moved. In contrast, British shipping carried on business as usual. Britain lost less than 1 percent of its ships as a result of their having been in German harbors at the start of war.[15] Grey may have provided this data to ease concerns from shippers in Tokyo who continued to inquire about the safety of the trade routes to Australia and the United States.[16]

Patey had to charter several shiploads of rice and other food to sustain the population of Chinese workers at Samoa. All of Germany's Pacific colonies suffered similar shortages. *Melbourne,* en route to Nauru, was due to arrive there on September 9, render the wireless transmitter inoperative, and rejoin Patey at Rabaul on September 12. In radio exchanges with the Admiralty, Patey relayed his misgivings about having to care for the inhabitants of the German colonies. He expected *Melbourne* would report that Nauru's inhabitants required provisions. He also recommended that Australian naval forces only disable the radio transmitters at Nauru and Angaur, leaving the islands unoccupied. By this course, Patey hoped to avoid responsibility for the islands' inhabitants. *Melbourne* completed the mission on September 9 and captured two German engineers maintaining the high-frequency station on Nauru.[17]

The German facility at Yap possessed both a wireless transmitter and a submerged telegraph cable connection. Despite the fact that Patey's forces were spread thin, he saw no alternative but to occupy the island. Moreover, the Naval Board notified Patey that it still expected him to release *Melbourne* and *Sydney* to escort the Australian convoy scheduled to depart for Aden on September 22. Patey anticipated completing occupation of Simpsonhafen by September 12. He believed he could safely release *Sydney* and *Melbourne* for convoy duty following that operation, but knew that *Melbourne* might not actually be ready until September 23.

Naval intelligence received on September 9 told Patey that there might be two wireless stations in the Rabaul area. One was possibly located about four miles up a road leading out of Herbertshohe and a second just inland from a plantation near Kabakund. The personnel staffing the intelligence branch reported that one of the two stations was in operation and the other under construction. Intelligence, however, did not know which of the stations was operational.

Admiral Patey's force arrived at German New Guinea on September 11. The main body would proceed to Simpsonhafen while *Sydney* and Patey's destroyers reconnoitered the nearby harbors at Simpsonhafen and Watupi. The harbors were empty when *Sydney* arrived at 3:30 a.m. The cruiser landed two parties of twenty-five men: at Herbertshohe, consisting of a mixture of naval reserve volunteers and infantry from the Australia Naval and Military Expeditionary Force to seize the wireless transmitter in that vicinity, and at Kabakund, about four miles away from Herbertshohe, to find and capture the high-frequency radio station reported to be there. A short time later, *Sydney* stopped the Norddeutscher Lloyd collier *Sumatra* en route to Rabaul, a clear sign that German merchant vessels had little intelligence on Australian navy activity. The party that had landed near Herbertshohe returned to the town without locating a wireless station. The force occupied Herbertshohe and hoisted a British flag there at 7:30 a.m. on September 11. The party put ashore at Kabakund encountered resistance as it worked its way inland. *Sydney* landed reinforcements to assist the original party, which located and captured the radio transmitter at about 7:00 p.m. that day. Patey's main force occupied Simpsonhafen and Rabaul as well. The German government had not yet surrendered, but occupation of the towns occurred without incident.[18] The locations the Australia and New Zealand expeditions had occupied had little to fear from Admiral von Spee's squadron except a possible shelling because the Germans had no personnel to spare for landing forces.

The Australians received information that SMS *Geier* was at Kawing arming a large German merchant steamer. Patey dispatched *Melbourne* and the destroyer *Warrego* to investigate the report while on their way to Sydney for convoy duty. *Melbourne* found the German yacht *Nusa* and learned that the *Geier* had been in the area, but departed September 7. *Melbourne* proceeded to Sydney, and *Warrego* returned to Simpsonhafen. A rumor cropped up that German reinforcements had landed and were marching to retake Rabaul. Patey conducted searches for landing parties, but the only evidence found was the wrecked German ship *Koloniel Gesellschaft*, which had run aground and burned. The wrecked ship's hold contained a dismounted gun, evidence that supported Admiralty suspicions that German merchant ships had the potential to arm themselves on the high seas. German warships prowled the area, most likely somewhere northwest of New Guinea.

On September 14, SMS *Scharnhorst* and *Gneisenau* had appeared off Apia, Samoa.[19] SMS *Emden*'s activity in the Bay of Bengal also began to concern British shippers. Additionally, the governor of German New Guinea surrendered on September 15. Patey's next priority was to organize the convoy of Australian troops for Aden. The convoy, originally consisting of twenty-seven transports, would be joined by fifteen troop carriers full of New Zealanders bringing the total ships needing escort to forty-two. When Patey learned of these developments, he postponed the convoy's departure until September 27 so he could attempt to deal with the German threat. Patey directed *Melbourne* to continue to Sydney while he proceeded with *Australia* and *Sydney* to Rabaul. The admiral reasoned that since Admiral von Spee had determined that Samoa was occupied, the German might steam to Rabaul for intelligence and fuel. Because Apia lay at the far southeast reaches of German territories, any help that von Spee's squadron might have received would have come from the north and west. Rabaul was the closest friendly base from which Germany's East Asia squadron could draw fuel and information.

The Australian warships arrived at Rabaul on September 19 and refueled. Patey calculated that von Spee's raiders could reach Rabaul by September 22. Patey, however, had guessed von Spee's intentions incorrectly. Von Spee had continued eastward, abandoning his own bases of supply, electing to survive off of what he could possibly seize from the Allies.

Patey sent *Sydney* to Angaur to destroy the wireless station and then to check a known rendezvous point for German colliers in the open ocean on the equator. *Australia* and the remainder of Patey's ships patrolled the vicinity north of New Guinea, looking for *Scharnhorst* and *Gneisenau*.[20] HMAS *Sydney* arrived at Angaur on September 26 and promptly put the high-frequency wireless station out of commission. The situation regarding provisions at Angaur was similar to that found at Samoa. Patey informed the Admiralty of the food shortages in the German territories and recommended that the Australians forgo occupying Angaur, Yap, and Nauru until they had made arrangements to properly care for the inhabitants. Supply shortages were the natural consequence of nearly completely curtailing German trade. Placing additional personnel on the islands without regular replenishment would only heighten the food deficit. The Admiralty, aware of Patey's concerns, requested help from the Colonial Office to supply Germany's Pacific islands.[21]

TSINGTAO

Alfred William Meyer-Waldeck, the governor of Tsingtao, held the rank of captain in the German navy. He had 4,390 men available to defend the base there once he consolidated his available reserve forces. The defenders at Tsingtao consisted of about sixteen hundred marines from the III Seebatallion, plus a hodgepodge of other forces, including a contingent of Chinese colonial troops, naval personnel from four small German gunboats, and sailors from the Austro-Hungarian cruiser *Kaiserin Elisabeth.* Several fortifications guarded Tsingtao, but the main defenses were oriented landward for an anticipated attack from technologically inferior Chinese forces. The gun emplacements held artillery that the Germans had acquired during the Boxer Rebellion in the early 1900s and from the Franco-Prussian War in 1871. The German East Asia squadron and mines nominally protected the base from attack by sea. Von Spee's orders, however, indicated that the squadron's first duty in a war with Great Britain was to inflict as much damage on British trade as possible. With the looming, combined Anglo-Japanese naval threat, Von Spee's force risked becoming blockaded if it were in port when war broke out. As events unfolded, however, Germany's East Asia squadron found itself widely dispersed on August 4, which made Tsingtao vulnerable to an amphibious landing.

Japan's naval blockade rendered the port useless for German naval activity after August 27. On September 2, the Japanese landed a small detachment from the 18th Division at Lungkow, on the north side of the Shantung peninsula, to isolate Tsingtao from the mainland. On September 18, the Japanese began landing the bulk of their 18th Division at Laichow, in Lao-Shan Bay, about four miles northeast of Tsingtao. Delayed by weather, General Mitsuomi Kamio eventually built a force of 23,000 men that included a promised 1,500-strong British and Indian force—a combination of 925 to 1,000 soldiers of the 2nd Battalion South Wales Borderers and about 300 to 500 men of the 36th Sikhs—under the command of Brigadier General Nathaniel Walter Barnardiston. This mixed British-Indian force, although largely symbolic, likely constituted the first British force to fight under a non-European commander. Kamio's plan called for a siege of Tsingtao supported with massed artillery consisting of 142 modern siege guns. Meyer-Waldeck held out for two months. Low on ammunition and artillery shells and greatly outnumbered, the governor surrendered on November 7. With the fall of Tsingtao, Germany's powerful radio transmitter, the key link to the outpost at Yap, was also put out of service.[22]

TOGOLAND

On August 6, Captain Frederick Carkeet Bryant, British army, found himself in acting command of the Gold Coast Regiment because the unit's commanding officer and his deputy were both on extended leave in the United Kingdom.[23] Bryant sent his subordinate Captain Edward Barker under a flag of truce to the Germans at Lomé, Togoland. Barker communicated the situation to the German authorities and demanded the town's surrender. The government at Lomé did not immediately reply, but when Barker returned the following day, the Germans had abandoned the town. The district commissioner presented Barker a letter surrendering Lomé and all of Togoland inland for 120 miles.[24]

The London Cable Telegraph Company had intercepted an unencrypted message from Togoland's governor, Adolf Friedrich of Mecklenburg, to Berlin. The message indicated that the governor did not intend to surrender, but instead planned to withdraw from Lomé and prepare defenses inland, about 120 miles, at Kamina to protect the wireless station located there.[25] The governor therefore surrendered Lomé immediately to avoid destruction of the city. Defending the wireless station at Kamina constituted the governor's primary responsibility.[26] London rejected the terms of the surrender because it would leave an important wireless station in operation to pass instructions and intelligence. Under the direction of the Colonial Office, Bryant proceeded to Kamina to seize the radio station.

On August 8, Major J. J. F. O'Shaughnessy, a telegraph engineer, arrived in Lomé with a team of technicians. The British team brought with them sufficient materials to establish and operate a temporary telegraph system.[27] The Germans had dismantled a smaller wireless transmitter located at Lomé and transported it inland with them.[28] O'Shaughnessy's team located Germany's submerged telegraph cable that connected Lomé with Monrovia and Duala, picked it up from the sea bed, cut it and sealed the ends.[29] The operation severed German communications, but permitted the British to easily repair the cable or connect it to another line at a later time, demonstrating a technical capability that most other nations lacked.

Charles Noufflard, lieutenant governor at the French colony of Dahomey, corresponded by letter with the Gold Coast on August 8 to coordinate the two colonies' offensives against Togoland. He reported that French troops had occupied Togoland in the vicinity of the Little Popo and Maro Rivers. One day later, British forces under Captain Barker were working directly with the French troops there. The governor general of French West Africa, Amédée Merlaud-Ponty, also volunteered his forces, offering to coordinate by invading Togoland from the north.[30]

Captain Bryant received the temporary rank of lieutenant colonel so that he could outrank his French peers and command the military drive inland toward Kamina. The Allied forces overcame German opposition after a few battles. The Germans garrisoning the Kamina outpost destroyed the wireless station before surrendering to prevent the British from acquiring a working wireless transmitter. When German colonial troops, retreating from the final battle, arrived at Kamina, they found that the garrison had already completed demolition; all nine radio towers were down, and the building housing the diesel generator was burning.[31]

Bryant reported on August 26, that all German forces in Togoland had unconditionally surrendered. British and French colonial forces occupied the site of the Kamina high-frequency radio station at 8:00 a.m. the following morning.[32] Later that day at a meeting of the cabinet, Colonial Secretary Harcourt reported that the Togoland expedition had succeeded.[33]

The Cameroons

Early in the war, Britain, Belgium, and France decided on a combined operation against the Germany colony of the Cameroons. The plan called for two British forces to attack, one from the sea and one overland from Nigeria. The Belgians were to advance west from the Belgian Congo. Meanwhile, French forces from Chad and Congo would strike from their territories in the north and south, respectively.[34] London proposed that British general Charles Dobell command the joint expedition. Francis Bertie, the British ambassador in Paris, assured the French that Dobell's appointment would not prejudice the final disposition of the colony.[35] The Foreign Office recommended leaving the choice of hoisting flags over captured German territory to the discretion of the field commanders. Secretary Grey attempted to push the Allies to agree that none of them would claim any German territory until the conclusion of a negotiated peace. In the opinion of the office's ministers, having no policy in place was preferable to a policy to which the Allies might object.[36]

German military personnel in the Cameroons numbered almost three thousand, but they were scattered widely among roughly forty separate outposts. The Cameroons defense plan called for the troops to delay Allied forces as long as possible while attempting to concentrate and escape into Spanish Guinea.[37] This put a premium on preserving troops rather than retaining the colony. The

Allied expedition against the Cameroons began following the German surrender in Togoland. British naval operations against Duala commenced on September 4, 1914. After about three weeks of fighting, the Germans destroyed Duala's wireless transmitter and capitulated on September 27.[38] Duala's surrender did not, however, signal the end of the Cameroons campaign. As British forces advanced, the cabinet decided that the War Office would assume responsibility from the Colonial Office for the military operation. The Colonial Office presided over all other matters, including administrative appointments and trade. The War Office could not move colonial forces from Nigeria to support the campaign without prior Colonial Office approval.[39] Fighting would continue until the last Germans surrendered at Mora on February 18, 1916.[40]

Early in the campaign, British forces had captured two German ships in the harbor at Duala. One of them, *Max Brock,* had a cargo that Admiralty officials determined was neutral. The cargo was transferred to a British ship for delivery, thus emptying *Max Brock.* If the ship were condemned as a prize of war, the Colonial Office believed it could make use of the vessel. The Admiralty recommended that both captured ships, SS *Max Brock* and SS *Kamerun*, become transports that the Colonial Office could use for subsequent operations. Both ships were condemned and sold to British shipping firms.[41]

GERMAN SOUTHWEST AFRICA

When South Africa learned of war with Germany on August 4, it volunteered to employ its dominion troops for self-defense so that regular British troops would be available for use elsewhere. On August 7, Whitehall suggested that South Africa seize parts of German Southwest Africa. London was particularly interested in the ports Luderitzbucht and Swakopmund as well as the wireless station in the interior.[42] On August 10, the government of South Africa agreed to proceed with the expedition. The South Africans already had a plan for an offensive against the neighboring German colony, so preparation for the expedition moved rapidly.[43] The plan's author, General Paul Sanford Methuen, argued for an immediate offensive, reasoning that this would help the country put its internal disputes aside as well as deprive the Germany navy of its colonial ports. He also thought that a defensive posture would facilitate German attempts to agitate nationals and foment rebellion.

At the beginning of the war, the Royal Navy maintained three cruisers in South African waters. HMS *Pegasus* stayed in the vicinity of Zanzibar, while the Admiralty tasked HMS *Hyacinth* and *Astraea* to escort regular army troops bound for Europe. The convoy was scheduled to depart August 26. *Hyacinth* would not return for three to five weeks and *Astraea* not until September 10. With the cruisers gone, South Africa had only one armed merchant cruiser to escort local forces on the operation against German Southwest Africa. The officer administering the government of South Africa, John H. DeVilliers, and his ministers believed the operation too risky without better naval support, all the more so with the location of Germany's East Asia squadron unknown. DeVilliers proposed delaying the operation that had been agreed to on August 10 until sufficient naval support became available.[44]

While waiting for adequate naval support, however, South Africa continued to make preparations for the operation, including posturing troops near the land border with German Southwest Africa. Methuen's prewar assumptions regarding uprisings proved wrong. It was South Africa's offensive against German Southwest Africa that provoked unrest. During the Second Boer War twelve years earlier, Germany had provided much needed moral support for the Boers against their British foes. Many Boers remained sympathetic toward Germany, and several thousand Boers, including some of the troops in the vicinity of the Transvaal and the Orange Free State, objected to expeditions against Germans in the neighboring colony. To avoid participating in South Africa's campaign against German Southwest Africa, they rebelled against the South African government by declaring themselves free and independent. Because of the revolt, South Africa was forced to recall the expedition against Swakopmund.[45] The situation in German Southwest Africa was so adverse that the cabinet considered diverting the Australia and New Zealand (ANZACS) contingent that was about to start for Aden and send it to the cape instead. To make the trip, the troop transports would require coaling at Colombo, prompting Whitehall to initially order the convoy to proceed there to await developments. Depending on how the campaign unfolded, the cabinet could then decide whether to divert the ANZACS.[46]

South African general Louis Botha, himself a Boer, put down the internal rebellion. With rebels surrendering in large numbers, the situation in South Africa improved to the point that the campaign against German Southwest Africa could resume.[47] While General Jan Smuts advanced from the south at Luderitzbucht, General Botha pressed forward from Swakopmund, beginning on February 7, 1915. Both forces moved inland along the major railroad beds. On May 12, the town of Windhoek, the capital of German Southwest Africa, surrendered to Botha with its wireless station undamaged. The German colonial government had withdrawn to Grootfrontein, in the north. On July 9, 1915, all German forces in German Southwest Africa surrendered.[48]

German East Africa

In German East Africa, a small force commanded by Lieutenant Colonel Paul von Lettow-Vorbeck had made repeated raids into British East Africa to cut the Uganda rail line. On each of these occasions, however, the local defense force, the King's African Rifles, had repulsed the German forces. The crown forces in the British colony of Rhodesia, assisted by Belgians from Katanga, had also repulsed several German incursions into their territories. In Nyasaland, British forces remained in a defensive posture but had managed to disable the German steamer *Von Wissmann* on Lake Nyasa and gain control of the lake.[49] The British cabinet had already decided to attack German East Africa to help the Royal Navy take control of the seas, but decided subsequently that only the conquest of German East Africa would prevent an invasion of British East Africa. Colonial Secretary Harcourt reported to the cabinet on September 14 that the situation in East Africa had slightly improved. He cautioned, however, that the cabinet should not contemplate aggressive action until reinforcements could be brought forward from India.[50]

The King's African Rifles were the only full regiment in eastern Africa, so the troops from India provided the needed reinforcements to go on an offensive.[51] Consequently, the planning and conduct of the expedition fell to India. The India Office in London directed that the dominion government provide all troops and logistics for the operation and that India also coordinate with the Admiralty, Colonial Office, and the cabinet. The War Office, preoccupied on the European continent, had no interest in German East Africa.[52]

The India Office formed two expeditionary forces to reinforce British interests in East Africa. The India Expeditionary Force (IEF) B, under the command of Major General Arthur E. Aiken, consisted of the 27th (Bangalore) Brigade from the 9th Secunderabad Division, an imperial service infantry brigade, a pioneer battalion, a battery of mountain artillery, and some engineers. Five other battalions (the 29th Punjabi, and a battalion each from Jind, Bharatour,

Kaparthala, and Rampur), the 22nd (Derajat) Mountain Battery (a 15-pound artillery battery of volunteers), and a maxim gun battery comprised IEF C, under the command of Brigadier General J. M. Stewart. IEF B formed the main offensive unit for invading German East Africa. The British island territory of Zanzibar, off the coast of German East Africa near Dar es Salaam, became the staging area for the planned operation. IEF C reinforced the King's African Rifles in defense of British East Africa.

India's scheme for command and control placed General Stewart and IEF C under the authority of Governor Henry Conway Belfield of British East Africa, who controlled the King's African Rifles and fell under the authority of the Colonial Office. IEF B also fell under Belfield's authority when it reached Zanzibar. When IEF B actually entered German territory, however, General Aiken, working for the India Office, controlled the expedition. Similarly, when IEF C entered German East Africa, it also fell under the control of the India Office. This was apparently not so with the King's African Rifles, which remained under the Colonial Office's authority. The general plan relied on an overland thrust by the King's African Rifles and IEF C into German territory along a line from Kilimanjaro to Tanga to threaten Moshi, about halfway along that route. As a sequel, these forces would occupy a line from Tabora to Dar es Salaam. Their purpose was to fix German East African forces in the west so that IEF B could attack Tanga from the sea.[53]

From November 2 through November 5, IEF B assaulted Tanga, and German troops repulsed the attack. Aiken reported that locals in Mombasa knew of his force's arrival, therefore the Germans probably also knew of the impending attack. IEF B had not achieved any level of surprise at Tanga. Instead of having been drawn westward and fixed by Britain's overland forces, the Germans had the coastal city defended. Despite this, Aiken believed he could have succeeded at Tanga with the addition of two reliable battalions. He also had difficulty obtaining the support he needed from local naval authorities.[54] No doubt, Aiken's inability to obtain the cooperation he required was exacerbated by the expedition's convoluted command relationship. In spite of the aforementioned problems, IEF B nearly succeeded: Aiken lost confidence in his attack and ordered an evacuation at nearly the same time that Lettow-Vorbeck decided that defending the city was untenable.[55]

Contributing to the expedition's coordination problem, the Admiralty had given guidance to the local naval forces that set their priorities farther to the south. In early August 1914, two Royal Navy cruisers steamed into Dar es Salaam searching for SMS *Königsberg*. In order to prevent the unnecessary destruction of the city, German East Africa's governor, Heinrich Schnee, brokered a deal in which he agreed to cease operating the high-frequency wireless station and close the port. So that Tanga, German East Africa's second largest city and farther to the north, could not support German commerce raiders, the agreement also conferred neutral status on the city. In late October, British naval forces located *Königsberg* hiding in the Rafiji River delta, south of Dar es Salaam. The Admiralty directed the local squadron to prevent the German raider's escape and destroy it as soon as possible.[56] With German ports prevented from providing logistics to commerce destroyers, the wireless station shut down, and the primary menace to trade bottled in the Rafiji River, the Admiralty achieved its objectives in the region.

Local naval commanders had also hesitated to support the Tanga operation because of the prior agreement with governor Schnee declaring that port neutral. Moreover, resourcing the Tanga operation would have diverted some of the ships from the Rafiji delta and risked *Königsberg*'s escape. As long as Schnee held to the agreement, the Admiralty could accept the status quo. The Royal Navy's interest in subduing the entire German colony waned.

Following the failed Gallipoli campaign confidence in Asquith's Liberal government faltered. This forced him to form a coalition government in late May 1915 that included several cabinet members from the Conservative party. As a result of reforming the cabinet, Andrew Bonar Law replaced Harcourt as Colonial Secretary. Additionally, Churchill was sacked as First Lord of the Admiralty, Arthur Balfour replacing him. Bonar Law believed that British prestige and the ability to rule in Africa required the outright defeat of the remaining German forces. General Jan Smuts, previously victorious in German Southwest Africa, took command of the operations in East Africa. Fighting continued throughout the war, and the Allies kept committing troops to the theater without defeating the elusive German commander. Lettow-Vorbeck was the last German to surrender in the Great War. Despite his prolonged resistance, however, the German navy was never again able to threaten British trade in the Indian Ocean.[57]

MESOPOTAMIA

The India Office promised the empire two army divisions and a cavalry brigade for the war. London could exceed that limit and use three Indian divisions, however, for a serious emergency. After the War Office took more troops than those India had offered and replaced them with ill-trained, poorly equipped territorial forces, the viceroy complained to the secretary of state for India. The cabinet had tasked India with protecting the oil fields and pipeline at Abadan, as well as sending forces to invade German East Africa and to defend the Suez Canal. Each of these requirements used one Indian division. The viceroy argued that any reduction in troop levels beyond India's current level attended too much risk for the army of India to retain imperial territory.[58]

The Indian Expeditionary Force (IEF) D, under the command of Lieutenant General Arthur Barrett, had been sent to Basra, just to the north of Abadan, to establish the defense of the region. The Turks had amassed forces in Baghdad for an offensive to the south that made the Arab sheikhs uneasy and threatened Basra directly. The security of Britain's position in Mesopotamia hinged on continued Arab support. The 12th Brigade (India) was en route to Basra to reinforce IEF D, but would not arrive until February 7, 1915. IEF D required more forces upriver in the vicinity of Ahwaz to demonstrate commitment to the sheikhs. Barrett believed a battalion at Ahwaz would be sufficient to quiet the Arabs and guard against Turkish raids.

Without Arab support, the division that constituted IEF D would be insufficient to hold Basra. The additional brigade could remedy that problem, but it might arrive too late. Troops at Karna would shift to backfill Basra while another battalion proceeded from the latter to reinforce the Arabs at Ahwaz.[59] The viceroy and the undersecretary of state for India agreed that they should press the War Office to release the Indian divisions from Egypt to reinforce IEF D in Mesopotamia. With two full divisions at Basra, IEF D could advance on Nasiriyah and Amara. Basra, they argued, would remain secure once that offensive drove away the Turks.[60]

The viceroy understood the War Office's desire to retain an Indian division in Egypt. Nevertheless, in a letter to the War Office dated February 10, he argued that India had a more pressing need in Mesopotamia. If the Turks obtained a victory at Basra, Muslim communities in Persia and Afghanistan would perceive the Turks as strong rulers. As a result, these Muslims would likely side with the Turks, eroding loyalty to the British among the Muslim population and Muslim troops. Not only did the empire risk losing access to Mesopotamia and its oil, but also, without the loyalty of Muslim troops in Persia and Afghanistan, the whole of India faced the risk of a pan-Islamic jihad.[61]

A reply, apparently from the War Office, written in the margins of this correspondence suggested that the India Office instruct the viceroy that troops engaged in other regions were not in a position to rapidly withdraw. Moreover, the note suggested that India had made a mistake when it decided on an offensive campaign in Mesopotamia when it should limit its endeavor to the security of Abadan, an objective that its force was sufficient to guarantee.[62]

Buoyed by previous success and despite the War Office's admonition, India determined to mount an offensive. Lieutenant General Sir John Nixon assumed overall command in April 1915. He sent Major General Charles Townshend with the 6th Indian Poona Division north along the Tigris and Euphrates Rivers to seize Kut al-Amara and Baghdad. Initially Townshend met with success; by October 1915, the army was encamped thirty miles south of Baghdad. Then the Turks counterattacked and repulsed Townshend and his force on November 22 in a five-day battle at Ctesiphon, about twenty-five miles south of Baghdad. Townshend fell back to Kut al-Amara and subsequently became surrounded when the Turkish 6th Army pressed its advantage.[63]

Nixon sent Lieutenant General Fenton J. Aylmer with a force to Townshend's aid. Aylmer's attempt to rescue IEF D failed. The setback prompted the War Office to intervene, and it immediately replaced Nixon, who had reportedly also become ill, with General Percy H. Lake. Lake sent Alymer again to attempt to raise the siege of Kut al-Amara, but without success. Lake replaced Alymer with Lieutenant General George Gorringe, who also failed to break the Turks' stranglehold on Kut. Townshend eventually surrendered on April 29, 1916.[64]

The Mesopotamia campaign embarrassed the British army. Whitehall recalled Lake to stand before the Mesopotamia Commission, established to inquire into the failures of the campaign. Lieutenant General Frederick S. Maude, originally sent to relieve Gorringe, assumed command of Allied forces in Mesopotamia. The War Office wrested control of the campaign from the India Office and then gave Maude newer equipment and reinforcements. For the remainder of the war, British forces advanced steadily northward, which allowed the War Office to erase the stain of Townshend's surrender.[65]

Nixon's initial decision to advance toward Kut al-Amara from Basra constituted a serious strategic blunder. The singular reason Whitehall had for sending IEF D to the Shatt al-Arab was to secure the Abadan oil fields. The terrain around Kut al-Amara was no more defensible than that surrounding Basra.

Moreover, Kut al-Amara was isolated along difficult and long lines of supply, whereas Basra was easily supplied via the Shatt al-Arab by sea. Had the Turks attempted to dislodge IEF D, the Ottoman forces would have had to overcome the same logistical difficulties to move south as the British did moving north. Moreover, the 6th Indian Poona Division's defeat at Kut al-Amara did not lead to the Turkish 6th Army advancing on Basra, probably because the Ottomans could not solve the logistical problems involved in conducting a successful campaign southward, from Kut al-Amara to Basra. The British, therefore, controlled the Abadan oil fields throughout the war.

OBSERVATIONS ON THE CAMPAIGN

Each of the overseas expeditions had objectives related to protecting trade. Threats to Britain's lifeblood came not only from marauders prowling shipping lanes in search of British-owned cargo vessels, but also from the Turkish army possibly seizing the Suez Canal and the Abadan oil fields. Had the Turks closed the Suez Canal, trade between India and Great Britain would have had to travel around Africa. The longer journey would effectively diminish the number of cargoes delivered to the home islands because each ship would require additional weeks to make the journey, meaning fewer round-trips each year. This in turn would contribute to a scarcity of freight capacity, driving up consumer prices. Oil from Abadan was an important British-controlled source of fuel for the Royal Navy. Loss of these oil fields would increase Britain's vulnerability to fuel price fluctuations and pressure from foreign governments. The expeditions targeted German colonial ports and high-frequency radio transmitters to eliminate logistics and intelligence support for commerce raiders. The objectives for each of these operations show that they were subsidiary efforts supporting an overarching campaign designed to protect British trade.

Securing the integrity of the trade routes where they were vulnerable to direct overland attack, as at the Suez Canal, constituted a higher priority for British and imperial troops than protecting the oil fields at Abadan or conquering German East Africa. The War Office denied requests from the viceroy and the India Office to divert forces from the defense of Suez to Abadan and to increase the commitment to German East Africa. In the Indian Ocean, IEF D proceeded to Abadan with escort while *Königsberg* remained at large, but this operation's priority was not sufficient to divert troops from other operations in

East Africa or Suez. The oil fields were important, but the fuel it supplied was useless if it could not safely transit the trade routes. Security of the shipping lanes was a prerequisite for the continued utility of the oil fields.

London had originally conceived of the expedition to German East Africa as a means to assist the Royal Navy in its task to secure Indian Ocean trade. Later, the Colonial Office determined that subduing the entire German colony would be expedient for protecting neighboring British territory. The War Office showed no interest in resourcing the expanded goal. Similarly, the Admiralty hesitated to support the Tanga operation when the navy had already achieved its assigned objectives. The Admiralty's priority was to protect the shipping lanes. The threat to the ocean's highways came from German raiders (whether warships or merchant vessels converted to auxiliary cruisers), the ports that could serve as logistics bases, and the network of high-frequency wireless stations that helped provide direction and intelligence. Hence, the Admiralty fixed its attention on Dar es Salaam, to the south of Tanga, where robust port facilities and the wireless station were located, and *Königsberg* trapped in the Rafiji River. The War Office also showed no interest in planning the expedition to German East Africa. Additional forces for the conquest of this important German colony arrived only after Germany's other African territories had surrendered. Logically, the justification for denying troops to the East Africa expedition was that conquering German territory held a lower priority than extinguishing support to commerce raiders.

The higher priority of sapping the support available to German commerce raiders was evident in the Pacific as well. The Royal Navy and the Australian government avoided occupying German territory that could be effectively neutralized with a straightforward raid. Patey's decision to halt searching for von Spee's squadron in order to simultaneously support his convoys, the Samoa expedition, and the Rabaul expedition illustrates the relative priority of these tasks. Searching for the German East Asia squadron ceased so Patey could support the other operations, even though von Spee's ships constituted Berlin's greatest naval threat outside of the North Sea and their whereabouts were unknown for a significant period of time. The Admiralty focused on the potentially high payoff of eliminating Germany's logistics bases rather than futile pursuit of dispersed commerce destroyers. Without logistics, the kaiser's war on British trade would eventually cease.

Far from racing to seize Germany's colonies, the forces involved in the overseas expeditions were reluctant to occupy any more of them than necessary to prevent the kaiser's navy from using overseas ports and wireless transmitters. The manner in which Great Britain executed the sub-campaigns does not support the conclusion that their purpose was to add territory to the British Empire or to hold the kaiser's colonies as bargaining chips for end-of-war negotiations. The mere act of German colonies surrendering made them available for bargaining chips or expanding the Allies' imperial holdings, but those outcomes were incidental to the campaign.

The Admiralty strategy relied on severing German commerce raiders' logistics and intelligence to limit the range and duration of their threat to shipping. Only Royal Navy warships beyond those necessary to support the higher priority overseas expeditions and convoys hunted for German raiders. Individual commerce destroyers that could replenish from their victims, such as *Kaiser Wilhelm der Grosse* and *Emden,* remained at large the longest. As Germany's overseas ports were overrun, the kaiser's raiders relied on the extensive Etappen system extant in neutral countries for logistic support. The use of neutral ports placed the German navy's logistics out of reach of the Royal Navy, and military expeditions were not a suitable solution either. Halting Germany's remaining naval activity required a significant diplomatic effort.

8 DIPLOMACY AND THE STRATEGY'S EFFECTS

Curtailing Germany's trade and logistical support for its overseas warships and auxiliary cruisers exceeded the capabilities of the Allied navies. Put simply, German marauders possessed too many ways to evade their pursuers. While Allied colonial and dominion forces overran Germany's overseas bases to eliminate their potential to serve as bases for supplies and intelligence by capturing ports, cutting submerged telegraph cables, and destroying high-frequency radio transmitters, Whitehall implemented another set of plans to disrupt German intelligence and other attempts by commerce raiders to use neutral countries for support via Berlin's elaborate Etappen system. Therefore, in conjunction with Allied overseas expeditions and the naval war, British ministers exerted considerable diplomatic and economic pressure on neutral countries in order to bring Germany's commerce destroyers to heal.

According to German historian Ernst Bischoff, the general understanding of the situation between the German navy and its British counterpart in hindsight was that the Royal Navy dominated the Imperial Kriegsmarine. Most historical accounts conclude that the Royal Navy swept German cruisers, commerce raiders, and auxiliaries from the oceans while simultaneously transporting the British Expeditionary Force to the European mainland for the land war. The official British version, Bischoff contends, is London's one-sided propaganda and is therefore only half true.[1]

Bischoff explained that one of the Royal Navy's missions was halting German merchant shipping. Moreover, the relative strength of the British and

German fleets was beyond dispute. Given the straightforward task of curtailing German commerce and the Royal Navy's clear superiority, one would have expected Britain's success. Bischoff reminded his readers that the German navy's function was not to dominate the Royal Navy's Home Fleet or even to protect Germany's merchant marine, but to hinder or damage Great Britain's merchant shipping. Bischoff argued that the situation in the North Sea was always desperate and that Germany's High Seas Fleet was fated to be blockaded, scuttled, or interned. What it accomplished accorded with Tirpitz's risk theory. The fleet tied down significant British naval forces to such an extent that German cruisers and auxiliaries outside of the North Sea blockade could inflict losses on a larger number of British ships overseas. With relatively few overseas cruisers and auxiliaries, Bischoff maintains that Germany enjoyed high operating success against British shipping.[2] The overseas cruisers and auxiliary cruisers captured or sank fifty-six British merchantmen from August 4, 1914, through the end of March 1915.[3]

At the outbreak of war, several German steamships were immediately placed into service as auxiliary cruisers. With the exception of SS *Kaiser Wilhelm der Grosse*, each of the ships converted to war service was overseas. During the course of the war, Germany would place additional steamers into naval service.[4] The German Naval Staff intended that the cruisers' patrols would destroy a large number of Allied merchant vessels, disrupt normal trade, and produce grave damage to the enemy's economy. Ultimately, although Germany's cruisers endured hardship and executed their missions with skill and daring, Allied warships relentlessly pursued them until they were finally forced to fight and were sunk.

Bischoff strove to dispel the myth promulgated by London's propaganda mills that British warships were better equipped and better crewed than their German counterparts. His history, therefore, concentrates on the exploits of the German raiders, noting that German naval tactics matched and at times exceeded those of the British. Bischoff also notes, however, that British, French, Japanese, and Russian armed forces steadily denied Germany's commerce destroyers intelligence and cut off raiders from their bases of support.[5] Even if one concedes Bischoff's point about the skill of German sailors, Whitehall still accomplished its naval objectives through a superior and better executed naval strategy. Britain's overseas expeditions, coupled with its diplomacy, provide evidence for a comprehensive and effective strategy and its execution, providing important lessons for those who study naval warfare.

GERMAN EAST ASIA SQUADRON

When war broke out, Admiral Maximilian Graf von Spee's warships were dispersed throughout the Pacific. The British Post Office immediately terminated all German traffic over British-owned telegraph cables and disconnected German cables that passed through British territory. Germany's East Asia squadron quickly suffered from a lack of information. Admiral von Spee collected his squadron at Pagan Island in the Marianas chain and from there sent SMS *Nürnberg* to Honolulu to fetch newspapers for the latest war news.[6]

The British consulate in Hawaii promptly reported *Nürnberg*'s visit. The British agent in Honolulu calculated that five hundred tons of coal would permit *Nürnberg* to reach Yap, in the Caroline Islands, governed by German New Guinea, the nearest German port. The consul's report indicated that the German raider only stayed the permitted one day, but loaded more than the required coal and still had plenty of that commodity in its bunkers. He judged that local American authorities had not abided by the rules required of a neutral nation. The Admiralty petitioned Foreign Secretary Edward Grey to make the appropriate protests to the U.S. government.[7] No Royal Navy cruisers were on station to chase *Nürnberg*, which allowed it to execute an unhurried departure.

Nürnberg rejoined the East Asia squadron near Christmas Island. Armed with U.S. newspapers, von Spee learned that New Zealand had occupied Samoa. Calculating that British shipping would remain in Apia harbor to support the New Zealand contingent, the German raiders proceeded there to destroy any Allied vessels present. When von Spee arrived, however, the harbor was empty. All British ships had departed three days earlier. This was fortunate for the Germans because HMAS *Australia*, a battle cruiser escorting the recently departed convoy, possessed enough firepower to sink the East Asia squadron unassisted. The island's garrison sighted SMS *Scharnhorst* and *Gneisenau* and immediately reported their presence. Von Spee did not attack because his primary responsibility was to destroy and disrupt Allied shipping. His ammunition and fuel would be necessary to defend his squadron and attack enemy vessels, so he led the German East Asia squadron to Papeete, Tahiti, to attack French shipping.[8]

Von Spee's luck was little better at Tahiti. The French fort at Papeete opened fire on the Germans, but was soon silenced by the cruisers' shells. *Scharnhorst* and *Gneisenau* sank the small French gunboat *Zélée* and the German freighter *Walküre,* which had been captured by *Zélée.* The French burned the island's coal supply to prevent the Germans from seizing it.[9] With Japan's entry into the war as a British ally, von Spee knew that his squadron was outmatched in the Pacific. Because the admiral had little chance of sustaining his squadron cruising the South Pacific, he considered a foray into the India Ocean. His prospects of sustaining the squadron in the Indian Ocean appeared little better, so he drafted a general plan to evade Allied warships and make his way to South America, where there were a number of reliable agents, and eventually rejoin the German navy in the North Sea.

Von Spee's only hope was to keep moving. Any time he entered a port for refueling, British agents there would report his squadron's presence. Neutrality laws only permitted port authorities to provide enough coal for his ships to reach the nearest German port. To avoid becoming interned or forced to fight, von Spee would have to remain ahead of the British intelligence system, which would inexorably direct British cruisers toward his ships.[10] The German East Asia squadron drew supplies at the Marquesas Islands and then headed for the Galapagos Islands, where on October 12, 1914, SMS *Dresden* joined von Spee's squadron. The outbreak of war had caught *Dresden* headed for Germany. Upon receiving orders to commence commerce raiding, the cruiser headed for the South Atlantic. *Dresden* sank two British ships, *Hyades* and *Holmwood* and subsequently passed through the Strait of Magellan into the Pacific to rendezvous with the East Asia squadron.[11]

Intercepted radio transmissions, reported sightings from British steamers, and agents in various ports kept the Admiralty in pursuit of Germany's East Asia squadron. At Rear Admiral Christopher Cradock's suggestion, Whitehall also directed the aging battleship HMS *Canopus* from the station at the Canary Islands to the Falklands in anticipation of the German East Asia squadron passing through the Strait of Magellan. If von Spee managed to evade or escape the British squadron on the west side of South America, Cradock believed that the Falklands, English Bank, and Abrolhos coaling stations would become vulnerable to attack. Royal Navy warships in the vicinity of the Falkland Islands would prevent an attack on British coaling stations and likely bring the German squadron to action if it had not already been destroyed in the Pacific.[12]

Despite von Spee's attempts to evade the Royal Navy, his squadron encountered and fought Admiral Cradock's force off the coast of Chile, near Coronel, on November 1, 1914. The Germans emerged victorious, but in doing so spent precious fuel and ammunition.[13] When news of the defeat reached London, the Admiralty took additional steps to meet the German squadron. Naval intelligence was certain that von Spee was proceeding from the Pacific to the Atlantic and possibly toward the Cape of Good Hope. The cruisers HMS *Minotaur* and *Dartmouth* reinforced the Royal Navy's Cape squadron as a precaution.[14]

Meanwhile, HMAS *Sydney,* while escorting a convoy of Australian troops to Aden, caught and sank the cruiser SMS *Emden* on November 9, 1914. The German cruiser had been in the process of raiding a British outpost and telegraph station at Direction Island, in the Cocos archipelago, when *Sydney* arrived. Responding to calls for assistance from Cocos, *Sydney* transmitted on its wireless at half power. This tactic deceived *Emden*'s commanding officer, Karl von Müller, into believing *Sydney* was too distant to respond in time.[15] *Emden,* originally part of Germany's East Asia squadron, had been one of Germany's most successful commerce raiders. From the beginning of the war until its destruction, *Emden* captured or sank a total of twenty-five Allied merchant and warships in the Indian Ocean and South Pacific.

With the *Emden*'s menace to trade removed, the Admiralty took stock of the remaining German raiders to evaluate the extent of the threat they still posed to commerce in the Pacific. The SMS *Geier* had gone to Honolulu and remained there. The Admiralty also knew that the cruiser SMS *Königsberg* was blocked in the Rafiji River, in East Africa, so it assessed that the Pacific Ocean trade routes were safe enough to spare the HMAS *Australia;* the other warships in the Pacific were sufficient to fulfill required convoy duties. London, therefore, directed *Australia* to join the Japanese battleship *Hizen* and the armored cruisers *Idzumo* and *Asama* and the Royal Navy cruiser *Newcastle* near San Diego. The combined squadron would search southward along the Pacific shore of South America for the German East Asia squadron.[16]

With the Royal Navy closing in, von Spee's ships replenished at Valparaíso, Chile, but would require more coal to cross the Atlantic. To attain the necessary fuel, von Spee planned a bold raid on the Falkland Islands. When the German squadron arrived at the archipelago on December 8, 1914, it found that the Royal Navy had dispatched two battle cruisers, HMS *Inflexible* and *Invincible,* to protect the South Atlantic shipping lanes. The aging battleship *Canopus* and five cruisers—*Bristol, Carnarvon, Cornwall, Glasgow,* and *Kent*—were also waiting there to ambush the German squadron. Vice Admiral Frederick Doveton Sturdee, commanding the British squadron, pursued the fleeing Germans. Only one ship, *Dresden,* escaped. Sturdee sank the rest.[17]

Given Cradock's humiliating defeat at Coronel, First Sea Lord Winston Churchill cheerfully reported the Royal Navy's success at the Falklands. In his report, he stated that he thought that *Dresden* and *Nürnberg* would soon be caught. Only *Karlsruhe* would remain loose on the seas.[18] Churchill had apparently been unaware that *Nürnberg* had been sunk at the battle of the Falklands. He was, nonetheless, convinced that the Royal Navy's efforts had nearly secured command of the seas. Believing that the naval war now raged only in the North Atlantic, Churchill directed the ships of the Australia squadron—HMAS *Australia, Sydney,* and *Melbourne*—to fall in on the West Indies station at Jamaica.[19]

THE JAPANESE OCCUPY YAP

Once the Australians had decided to occupy Yap, they found that Japan had already placed a garrison there. The Australians reported Japan's presence to the Colonial Office and emphasized that the German surrender in New Guinea explicitly included all other German possessions in the Pacific, because each was controlled by the government in German New Guinea. Colonial Secretary Lewis Harcourt's correspondence with Foreign Secretary Grey illustrates that the Australians and Whitehall were surprised by the Japanese action. Harcourt asked Grey why the Japanese were occupying the islands when Australia intended to do so. Grey cautioned Harcourt to have the Australian contingent wait for a resolution while Grey pressed his own office to report any exchange with Japan on the subject.[20]

Grey had previously informed the Japanese government of the Australian and New Zealand expeditions. The foreign minister had told Tokyo that they were under way and would seize Samoa, German New Guinea, and the Caroline Islands. In fact, when Grey told Tokyo, only the New Zealand expedition had started. Grey stretched the truth because he hoped that knowledge of British movements in the Pacific would dissuade Tokyo from taking any action of its own to acquire Pacific islands. Grey's desire remained that Japan limit the scope of military operations to those necessary to seize Tsingtao.[21] Ultimately, with the Japanese occupation a fait accompli, the Admiralty and Colonial Office no longer desired to send Australian troops to Yap. Instead, they asked the Foreign Office to arrange with Tokyo for continued Japanese occupation. Japan now controlled the telegraph communications there, and the Admiralty recommended that the Japanese navy decide whether it was necessary to interfere with the submerged telegraph cable that connected the island to Shanghai.[22]

HUNTING THE SMS *KÖNIGSBERG*

At the end of October, Royal Navy cruisers found SMS *Königsberg* hiding up the Rafiji River to the south of Dar es Salaam. The British warships blockaded the river's mouth to prevent the German cruiser from leaving.[23] The Admiralty felt particular relief having bottled up this German menace to commerce. Months earlier, as the threat of war loomed, *Königsberg*'s commanding officer, Lieutenant Commander Max Looff, prepared to raid enemy commerce. Looff planned to remove the armament from *Möwe,* an obsolete German gunboat and survey ship stationed at Dar es Salaam, and provide the guns to the first suitable German-owned merchant vessel that arrived in the harbor. Three ships—*Somali, König,* and *Tabora*—were already at Dar es Salaam. Of these, only *Tabora* could function as an auxiliary cruiser. As tensions escalated between Great Britain and Germany, Looff received a report of three nearby British cruisers. Fearing a Royal Navy blockade would trap *Königsberg* the instant war was declared, Looff proceeded to sea while Captain Gustav Zimmer of *Möwe* remained in charge of the harbor.[24]

The British cruisers HMS *Astraea, Hyacinth,* and *Pegasus* quickly caught up with and began trailing *Königsberg.* If war had been declared, the three Royal Navy cruisers would have destroyed Looff's ship immediately. Knowing of the impending war declaration, Looff evaded his British stalkers in a desperate maneuver by steaming into a rainsquall. After war was declared, the British merchant vessel *City of Winchester* ran afoul of the German cruiser on August 6 and became the Great War's first casualty to commerce raiding. Next, Looff proceeded to Aden to destroy Allied shipping, but found only an empty harbor. A Japanese steamer had sighted and recognized *Königsberg* and reported the warship's presence. The Admiralty immediately ordered all Allied ships to clear the shipping lanes leading to the Gulf of Aden and the Suez Canal.[25] The

Admiralty also instructed the naval commander in the East Indies to provide at least two escorts, one of which had to be superior in guns and armor to *Königsberg,* for Allied transports and merchants prior to their transiting the area.[26]

Königsberg intercepted radio transmissions from several British warships that helped it evade pursuers. The East Indies squadron, the pre-dreadnought battleship HMS *Swiftsure,* the cruisers *Dartmouth* and *Chatham,* as well as the armored cruisers *Black Prince* and *Duke of Edinburgh* were searching for the German cruiser near the Arabian coast. The German raider, however, had not heard from Dar es Salaam for several weeks.[27] Unknown to Looff, *Pegasus* and *Astraea,* two of the cruisers he had evaded just prior to the war, had gone to Dar es Salaam on August 8 in search of his ship. While there, the British cruisers had shelled the radio tower. Governor Heinrich Schnee agreed to keep the city neutral in order to prevent harm to the populace. He also destroyed the radio station. The Royal Navy forces accepted his pledge as well as its extension to the city of Tanga.[28] The navy's understanding that Tanga was, from this time, a neutral city constituted part of the problem Major General Arthur E. Aiken would have gaining appropriate naval support for his assault on Tanga later in November.

Nearly out of coal, *Königsberg* anchored in the lee of Sacotora Island, a designated rendezvous, and waited for *Somali.* The warship lacked the fuel to reach Dar es Salaam and had not been able to supply itself from prizes. The Reichsmarine in Berlin had calculated that German warships with a five-thousand-mile cruising radius prowling the oceans could cripple British shipping. In practice, however, Looff expended 120 tons of coal, a fifth of his bunker capacity, in one night evading Royal Navy cruisers prior to the outbreak of war. He knew now that the figure used for cruising radius was a dangerously unrealistic assumption not suited to actual wartime demands. If he could not refuel *Königsberg,* the warship's threat to shipping was over. Two days later, *Somali* arrived. Looff coaled from his support ship and proceeded south to Madagascar to harass French shipping. Five days later, *Königsberg* arrived at Majunga, Madagascar, only to find the bay empty.[29] Without radio communications, Looff lacked intelligence on Allied shipping, so his ability to interdict trade relied on sheer luck.

Königsberg met *Somali* again to refuel. The rough weather prevented transferring coal on the open ocean so the two ships steamed up the Rafiji River to calmer waters. Looff sortied one last time when he heard the HMS *Pegasus* was at anchor in Zanzibar. *Königsberg* surprised the British cruiser, sank it, and returned to hide in the Rafiji River. The Royal Navy gained the critical intelligence necessary to locate *Königsberg* when it stopped the German merchant *Präsident* on its way to replenish the elusive cruiser.[30] The Royal Navy cruisers HMS *Chatham* and *Fox* and the battleship HMS *Goliath* set a blockade at the mouth of the Rafiji. The warships experienced difficulty engaging *Königsberg* because it and the escort *Somali* were well-sheltered up the river in Portuguese waters. Churchill directed the local forces to press the attack to destroy *Königsberg* irrespective of Portuguese neutrality.[31]

The second-rate battleship *Goliath* came on the scene because it had been transferred from the 8th Battle Squadron in the Channel Fleet to the East Indies station to support convoys moving India Expedition Force (IEF) D to the Persian Gulf and IEF B and C to German East Africa. Despite the truce, *Goliath* and a small force of cruisers shelled Dar es Salaam on November 28 and again on November 30, 1914. The Germans viewed the bombardment as an unnecessary and lawless act. The cruiser HMS *Fox* reported, however, that it had been fired upon from a position inside Dar es Salaam while under a flag of truce and had taken casualties. *Fox* retaliated by shelling prominent buildings in the city.[32]

By November 24, *Somali* had been shelled repeatedly and completely burned and *Königsberg*'s crew had stripped the cruiser of its mounted armaments to help defend German East Africa.[33] Even though the German cruiser remained bottled up in the Rafiji River, it took the Royal Navy until summer 1915 to devise a way to effectively attack it. Using aerial observation to direct mortar fire from barges, the British finally found their mark. *Königsberg* took such heavy fire that Looff abandoned ship and ordered it scuttled. At 2:00 p.m. on July 11, charges set in the keel of the German cruiser detonated and the ship settled on the river bottom.[34]

Despite Governor Schnee's pledge, Dar es Salaam's neutrality remained problematic because IEF troops could not enforce the edict. *Königsberg*'s destruction, however, ended the threat to Allied shipping in the Indian Ocean. German general Paul von Lettow-Vorbeck and his soldiers, the Schütztruppen, continued to threaten neighboring Allied territories for the remainder of the war. To deal with Lettow-Vorbeck, the cabinet requested that France dispatch reinforcements from Madagascar to assist British troops in German East Africa.[35]

Eventually, London sent General Jan Smuts from South Africa with troops to East Africa to help combat the tenacious German force.

DIPLOMATIC CHALLENGES TO BRITAIN'S ECONOMIC PRESSURE AGAINST GERMANY

The Allies interned German and Austrian merchant marine ships that happened to lie in an allied port at the beginning of the war. They also soon captured other enemy steamers on the high seas and brought those as prizes into allied ports. Many other tramps and liners belonging to the Central Powers evaded Allied navies and sought safety in neutral ports, where they remained, useless for trade or transformation into marauders, as if they had been interned.[36] The fact that so many German merchant vessels sought safety in neutral ports signals that Wilhelmstrasse planners did not understand the way the war would impact a shipmaster's plan to continue a voyage as well as Whitehall's ministers assessed it. Hence, Berlin did not anticipate the need for an effective plan, such as a national insurance scheme, to induce its nation's merchant vessels to return home, where many of them could later be fitted as auxiliary cruisers.

Germany lost most of its nationally owned cargo-carrying capacity early in the war. Nevertheless, it initially continued a thriving trade through neutral ports and neutral ships. The volume of food imported from the United States into neutral Danish, Dutch, and Swedish ports increased approximately tenfold during the first month of war. British authorities concluded that these neutral European nations profitably reexported nearly all of the excess food to Germany.[37] The same neutral ships that brought food in also carried German exports out.

At first, the Royal Navy let such cargoes, carried in neutral vessels, pass. The Allies had not officially declared a blockade because a traditional blockade could not extend beyond the ports or coasts belonging to or occupied by the enemy. The Royal Navy could not blockade the coasts of neutral Denmark, the Netherlands, and Sweden, so London directed its cruisers to exercise a belligerent's right to stop any vessel on the high seas and search for contraband. Food and items such as iron ore, copper, rubber, and phosphates only counted as conditional contraband. To seize them, Great Britain had to show that they were destined to the enemy government or the fighting forces. Obtaining such evidence proved difficult because German agents purchased the goods via legitimate businesses in neutral countries. The key to halting Germany's trade then became a matter of expanding the list of goods that constituted contraband.[38]

Great Britain informed the governments of Denmark and the Netherlands that they would continue to receive exports of British coal only if they agreed that the fuel would not be resold to Germany. As an added measure, Britain threatened the Netherlands with cutting off its coal supply if it sold wheat to Germany. With the threat of embargo, Britain effectively prevented Germany from importing goods even though a blockade against the German coast could not extend to ports in these neutral countries.[39] London also forbade Canada to sell coal to Denmark, Norway, and Sweden until the Admiralty granted its approval to fill the orders and the Scandinavian nations agreed that the fuel would not be resold.[40]

In addition, the Admiralty asked the Colonial Office's assistance in regulating coal export from the colonies. For commerce to proceed normally, the colonies required regular coal shipments to sell to merchant ships. The Admiralty desired that specific colonies retain a designated minimum stockpile available strictly for Royal Navy use. With Colonial Secretary Harcourt's approval, the Admiralty issued the necessary instructions.[41] Colonial authorities also regulated coal sold to neutrals. U.S. ships, for example, could not purchase coal if it would be resold to Britain's enemies.[42]

Because Britain had not formally declared a blockade, the United States insisted that the Royal Navy had no authority to capture conditional or non-contraband goods in neutral ships. All neutral powers were free to trade, especially if the cargo's destination was a neutral port. To tighten the economic pressure on Germany, Whitehall declared in September 1914 that food that could be used for feeding the army, items routinely used to manufacture munitions, as well as cloth and leather that could be used for uniforms would be considered outright contraband. London's interpretation of contraband drew a sharp protest from Washington.[43] Britain and the United States eventually worked out a compromise, which was published in a new British order of council on October 29, 1914.[44] To help make a case, the Foreign Office used Otto von Bismarck's logic to argue that the Royal Navy's action was legal. Bismarck had written that a naval blockade, similar to a siege in land warfare, had as its object "shortening the war by increasing the difficulties of the enemy" and that intercepting food supplies was "a justifiable step if uniformly enforced against all neutral ships."[45]

Meanwhile, Germany had begun laying mines in the North Sea. SS *Königin Luise,* a passenger ferry converted to a minelayer, scattered mines outside of Britain's territorial waters, where HMS *Amphion* ran afoul of the new weapon's destructive potential and sank. The international community found the act by the Germans shocking because the mines were in the international shipping lane and imperiled neutral shipping. Neutrals chided the Royal Navy for halting their ships and attempting to seize cargoes as contraband because it created delays and potential financial loss. On the other hand, Germany's mine laying constituted a threat with consequences far more grave, including the loss of the ship, the cargo, and perhaps the lives of the crew.[46]

The German minelayer *Albatross,* in company with two cruisers, *Mainz* and *Stuttgart,* laid mines about thirty miles off the English coast near the entrances to the harbors at Humber and the Tyne. A Danish trawler became the first victim of this minefield. A British fishing boat caught a mine in its net and alerted the Admiralty. Two more neutral trawlers and two minesweepers sank before the Royal Navy determined the full extent of the field. The Admiralty chose to mark the location rather than sweep the field because its location tended to protect the approaches to the English coast.[47] No doubt Whitehall hoped that the minefield also served as a reminder to neutrals that Germany continued to lay mines in international waters.

London used the danger of mines in open waters as a pretext to declare portions of the North Sea a war zone. Initially, the Admiralty believed that Germany was using fishing vessels and merchants disguised as neutrals to deploy mines. Therefore, the war zone banned all types of neutral fishing vessels, closing an area from thirty to one hundred miles from Britain's shores. The Admiralty also desired to divert neutral merchant ships to port for more detailed inspections. Sending a neutral's cargo vessel into port also bought British agents more time to discern the ultimate destination of a cargo, making it more likely that the navy could find and seize conditional contraband.[48]

The United States also opposed this new Allied measure, arguing that a belligerent had the right to search a vessel at sea, but that accepted law precluded diverting a vessel significantly from its intended track. France and Britain responded that the new weapons of war, namely, mines and torpedoes, rendered extended stopping of a ship on the high seas to conduct a thorough search extremely hazardous. The two powers also pointed out that during the

U.S. Civil War, the U.S. Navy had required British ships to deviate from their tracks to enforce the blockade of the entire southern coastline. Belligerents in the Russo-Japanese and the Crimean Wars had also routinely diverted British merchant ships. In this case, the Admiralty held its ground.[49]

Naturally the neutrals also objected to the closure of a portion of the North Sea. In 1914, a nation's territorial waters extended only three miles from the shoreline. Britain defended its action as being in the interest of international commerce. London's goal remained to thwart additional mine laying that constituted an indiscriminant menace to international shipping. In essence, the area was de facto a war zone because of actions Germany had taken. Britain, by formally declaring the war zone, enhanced safety by warning all nations of the danger.[50]

When the dreadnought HMS *Audacious* struck a mine and eventually sank, the Admiralty realized that it had done little to abate the danger. Admiral John A. Fisher, the First Sea Lord, reacted by declaring the whole of the North Sea a war zone, except the three-mile territorial waters of Denmark, the Netherlands, Norway, and Sweden. Fisher's decree also mandated that neutral shipping approaching the area from the south and west enter the North Sea via the English Channel. By this expedient, the Admiralty hoped to facilitate inspections by requiring ships to check in and present papers. In return, the Royal Navy would sweep a route daily and escort all cleared ships so that the vessels could reach their destinations safely. The navy refused to guarantee the safety of any ship that deviated from the swept route.[51]

Britain's action held no precedent in international law and therefore, according to neutrals, constituted an illegal act. London justified the war zone as a reprisal for Germany's illegal acts.[52] The scheme, if neutrals complied, allowed Britain unfettered access to neutral ships' manifests. Moreover, because the Royal Navy ensured that the merchant vessels transited along a swept route, Britain could lay mines of its own to retaliate against Germany. British mines had the further effect of constraining the routes any German ship could use to evade the blockading Royal Navy cruisers.

The war zone had little effect on Germany's trade through the end of 1914, but Britain's efforts began to tell from early 1915 on. Walter Hines Page, the American ambassador to London usually raised the objections to Britain's attempts to extend the informal blockade. London understood U.S. business interests, so Foreign Secretary Grey and the British ambassador to the United States, Cecil Spring Rice, always attempted to negotiate. Page, along with acting secretary of state Robert Lansing, and President Woodrow Wilson also desired maintaining a lively dialogue. In general, the three favored the Allied position but found it necessary to placate U.S. business interests.

Lansing suggested to Spring Rice on September 28, that Britain attempt to reach an agreement with the Netherlands to prohibit the reexport of specific articles that Britain considered conditional contraband rather than making specious arguments to extend the contraband list. On November 3, the Foreign Office sent a memorandum to all of the neutral countries bordering the North Sea. The document stated that Britain desired to exercise its rights as a belligerent with respect to neutrals conveying contraband while simultaneously creating the least inconvenience to neutrals' bona fide trade. To those ends, London proposed that the nations agree to prohibit the export of all classes of goods and material in the contraband and conditional contraband lists that they desired for their own consumption. Moreover, if the neutrals would guarantee that the cargoes bound for their commercial centers were consigned to specified importers in their nations, then Great Britain would only detain those ships carrying cargoes to unspecified consignees or to order. Without U.S. backing for their protests, the neutrals settled into a routine with Great Britain, and the economic pressure on Germany took hold.[53]

Keeping Trade Moving

In the early days of the Great War, colonial governors hesitated to send merchant ships to sea without Admiralty assurance that the trade routes were safe. To reiterate the government's position, Foreign Secretary Grey telegrammed British officials worldwide to tell them that the government insurance scheme applied to any cargo on an approved voyage in British vessels. The ship in question simply had to belong to one of the contracted war risk clubs and all requests for insurance would process through the clubs. He stressed that the scheme applied globally.[54]

Many ships in the colonies, however, did not belong to a war risk insurance club. New Zealand governor Arthur Foljambe had ships to carry frozen meat to Great Britain, but they would go as transports chartered by the New Zealand government. He desired to know whether the government insurance scheme for cargoes covered this shipment, and if so, who issued the policy. If the shippers failed to acquire the necessary insurance in New Zealand, local bankers would refuse to finance their cargoes. Hence all trade from the dominion to Great Britain would be suspended.[55] Shipowners in Newfoundland had the same problem. Newfoundland's governor requested that London extend the war insurance scheme to colonial ships not enrolled in one of the approved war risks associations.[56]

The Admiralty recommended that the government extend the insurance scheme to the vessels not belonging to war risk clubs provided that the vessels followed instructions. The Admiralty directed that all vessels leave port after dark, make a good distance from port prior to dawn, keep off the usual trade routes, dim lights, and avoid passing constricted waters by day. These precautions constituted the usual rules that the Admiralty prescribed for ships, and if followed, there were no undue risks posed by the enemy to the trade routes.[57] The British government intended to charter fifteen vessels from companies in Australia and ten additional vessels from New Zealand businesses. London desired that the twenty-five vessels transit to the homeland fully loaded with cargo. All of the ships would fall under the government insurance scheme and be fully covered for the voyage.[58]

Moreover, the Admiralty requested that Colonial Secretary Harcourt send a message to all self-governing dominions and colonies explaining Admiralty policies. The Admiralty's purpose was to prevent colonial officials from closing trade routes or holding ships in port, as these practices were counterproductive to London's war effort. Two months of war experience demonstrated that this practice did nothing to reduce captures. When an enemy cruiser disgorged prisoners from captured vessels, it invariably disclosed its location. To avoid Allied warships, the commerce raider immediately moved to another location to continue attacking Allied trade. What location the marauder chose next would be a matter of conjecture. Closing trade routes in response to the past presence of an enemy raider, or holding up voyages in an ill-conceived attempt to avoid capture of merchants, simply fulfilled the kaiser's goals for attacking British trade.[59]

The Admiralty War Staff's Trade Division circulated a report among the shipping companies about SMS *Emden*'s captures. The trade division distributed the information to ensure that Britain's merchant marine complied with Admiralty orders. The report emphasized that the most effective means of avoiding capture remained to abandon the regular trade tracks, deviating from them by about one hundred miles. Ship's captains had to familiarize themselves with the trade routes that they did not regularly use. In at least three instances, while obeying the rule to avoid their regular track, captains unwittingly placed their ships on another regular trade route with which they were personally unfamiliar.[60]

The Admiralty's intelligence system provided reports on British merchant vessels stopped by the enemy in as quickly as two days. The insurance scheme and embassies tracked each ship, its gross tonnage, the port last left, its destination, and expected arrival. British agents in oversees and foreign ports reported overdue ships promptly. Ships stopped by the enemy and allowed to proceed provided timely data on enemy raiders. *Dresden* detained two merchant vessels on the southeast coast of South America on August 6. The German raider destroyed the wireless radios on them and then allowed the ships to proceed. Similarly, *Kaiser Wilhelm der Grosse* stopped one ship on August 15 and another on August 16 off the coast of West Africa, disabled the wireless radios, took some officers prisoner, and allowed the ships to continue. German raiders intercepted the merchant *Arlemza* on August 16, and the details were included in a report only two days later.[61]

The Admiralty also compiled similar data on merchants lost or sunk. By late September 1914, German raiders had destroyed or captured twelve ships. *Königsberg* had captured one, as had *Karlsruhe,* while *Dresden* and *Kaiser Wilhelm der Grosse* had each sunk two and the *Emden* six. Such data helped the Admiralty determine the raider's favorite cruising ground and allowed Whitehall to vector the merchant traffic around the enemy's suspected location. While the intelligence did not prevent all shipping losses, sixteen other British and neutral vessels were sunk by mines in the North Sea, it provided a measure of safety superior to what Berlin could give its shipping industry. As of September 23, 1914, Great Britain had lost eighty-six ships detained in port or captured at sea. In contrast, by the same time, the Allies had seized 327 ships from Germany.[62]

The public knew by late January 1915 that German commerce raiders had for all practical purposes been halted by the Royal Navy. Nevertheless, the public still paid more for food than it had before the war. Having diminished the direct threat to trade did not mean that trade resumed as before the war. Rather, it continued to evolve because of the war. New markets became available, old markets remained closed, and the number of ships available for transport fluctuated. Freight costs drove most of the increase in elevated food prices. The Royal Navy had not only cleared the trade routes of German commerce raiders, but had effectively swept the seas of all German merchant vessels as well. The German merchant marine represented on the order of 20 to 25 percent of available worldwide carrying capacity before the war. Its loss thus had a significant impact on freight rates. The citizens of Great Britain also suspected that German agents in the United States had bought wheat to stockpile solely for the purpose of denying its export to Great Britain.[63]

On the other hand, with German and Austrian ships no longer delivering goods manufactured in their countries, Great Britain gained an opportunity to capture markets previously supplied by its enemies. Walter Runciman, president of the Board of Trade, met with several foreign representatives to showcase British goods that could replace those no longer available from the Central Powers. Several British firms accepted orders as a result of the informal meetings. Runciman proposed government-sponsored trade fairs to increase British exports while the Royal Navy stifled Germany's trade.[64]

The War Office became aware of an impending meat shortage in Great Britain because Australia could garner higher prices for its frozen meat in the U.S. market. As a result, Australian meat producers prepared to ship to the more lucrative market rather than to the British Isles.[65] Because of the meat issue, Australia's governor general, Ronald Munro Ferguson, queried the home government about prohibiting the sale of goods useful to the war effort to neutral countries. He needed guidance because stopping the sales ran counter to the overall policy of minimizing interference with the normal course of trade.[66]

Trade behaved normally, though not in the respect that it returned to what it had been prior to hostilities, but in that it responded to market forces emerging from the war. A shortage of cargo vessels drove increased freight prices. Moreover, sellers desired to ship their goods to locations that garnered higher prices. In a free market, buyers in London had to pay going rates to get the goods they desired. If Whitehall wished stable prices, government policy had to adapt to keep up with changing circumstances as well.

Attacking German Raiders in Neutral Waters

British naval intelligence finally located SMS *Dresden*, anchored in Cumberland Bay, at Más a Tierra, in the Juan Fernandez archipelago. The Juan Fernandez Islands, about a thousand miles due west of Santiago, belonged to Chile. On

March 11, 1915, Grey provided this information to his ambassador in Santiago, Francis Stronge, and prompted him to ask the Chilean government to intern the German cruiser. Chile consented and agreed to send a warship to Cumberland Bay. As Stronge understood his exchange with Chilean officials, if *Dresden* refused to comply with Chilean authority, Whitehall was free to act as it thought best.[67] Three days later, however, a short engagement took place between *Dresden* and two Royal Navy cruisers, HMS *Glasgow* and *Kent*. *Dresden* sank either as a result of scuttling charges or succumbing to *Glasgow*'s shelling.[68]

The Chilean government strongly protested the action, claiming that Great Britain had violated the nation's neutrality by attacking the German ship after it had already been interned. As further evidence of its good intentions, Chile's minister in London presented Grey a copy of the protest his government had made to Berlin concerning the presence of *Dresden* in Chilean waters. *Dresden* entered the harbor at Más a Tierra at high speed on March 8 and requested to remain eight days to make repairs to its engines. Chile's minister pointed out that his government had refused. The cruiser was obviously seaworthy and could transit with sufficient speed that repairs to its engines were not urgent. *Dresden*'s captain then asked to remain twenty-four hours, but after a day's time had expired, the raider remained at anchor.[69] Chile awaited Britain's reply.

Stronge provided Grey with additional information on *Dresden*'s activities in Chilean waters. The ship had visited Easter Island in October 1914 with the rest of Germany's East Asia squadron and had remained there more than twenty-four hours. The cruiser had used the Juan Fernandez Islands between November 7 and 18 to coal and resupply. Stronge acknowledged that Chile had lodged a protest with the German government on both of these occasions. On December 12, less than the required three months permitted between visits by warships of nations engaged in war, *Dresden* received coal and provisions at Punta Arenos and had stayed thirty-one hours. The warship remained inside Chilean waters in the southern channels between December 14, 1914, and February 26, 1915. During that time, the Chilean steamer *Explotador* supplied the German raider with stores. Finally, *Dresden* arrived at Más a Tierra, where British cruisers engaged the elusive foe. Moreover, the German cruiser was in radio communication with a supply ship, *Alda,* to coordinate resupply.[70]

Britain used the information that Stronge provided to argue its own case. This incident bore similarities to HMS *Highflyer*'s sinking of *Kaiser Wilhelm der Grosse* earlier in the war, on August 17, 1914. *Highflyer* surprised and sank the German raider at Rio de Oro, Western Sahara. Because Spain claimed the North African territory as a protectorate, the sea battle apparently violated that nation's neutral rights. The Admiralty stressed that a key element of neutrality was to either provide or deny trade and facilities equally to each belligerent. Moreover, the country proclaiming its neutrality must enforce its rights. Because Spain had not prevented German raiders from using its remote waters, the aggrieved belligerent, the United Kingdom, looked after its own interests.[71] The case with *Dresden* in Chilean waters was much the same.

Chile was actually glad to be rid of *Dresden* but needed to remain in good standing with Germany as well as Great Britain. Santiago needed a response from London to satisfy its pride. The Foreign Office explained Britain's position and drafted an apology to the Chilean government.[72]

CURTAILING GERMANY'S USE OF NEUTRAL HARBORS FOR REPLENISHMENT

The intelligence network that the Royal Navy had put together before the war provided London with a considerable advantage in locating German ships. Lloyd's of London knew the locations of most large merchant vessels every day and provided consolidated data to the Admiralty War Staff's Intelligence Division. The Admiralty circulated the intelligence among the cabinet and provided the Lloyd's data to the Colonial Office to keep the colonies and dominions informed.[73]

Civilians in the employ of the British government overseas also used the information to monitor German shipping. In Buenos Aires, Mr. Mackie observed *Cap Trafalgar* and reported that he believed the German merchant vessel had guns already on board with which to arm itself and additional guns to provide to other steamers. Mackie filed his reports at the embassy in Buenos Aires with Mr. H. Norman, who also passed the information to his French counterpart, Mr. Jullemier. Norman and Jullemier each brought *Cap Trafalgar*'s activities to the attention of Dr. Murature in the Argentine government, pressing him to ensure that Argentina fulfilled its duty with respect to remaining neutral in the war.[74]

The Royal Navy's auxiliary cruiser HMS *Carmania* engaged and sank *Cap Trafalgar* on September 14, 1914, confirming that the German liner had undergone conversion to a commerce raider. Mackie assembled the details of the engagement into a reliable narrative. He confirmed the identity of the ship that *Carmania* had sunk, but he could not definitively prove that *Cap Trafalgar* had obtained its armament while in Buenos Aires. The official account from the German chargé d'affaires in Buenos Aires was that the armaments had come from the gunboat SMS *Eber,* which transferred the guns at sea and provided *Cap Trafalger* with its naval commander and crew. *Eber* had also removed the ship's civilian crew and brought them into Bahia, Brazil. Mackie insisted that the German chargé d'affaires had concocted the story as a plausible cover instead of admitting that German ships had violated Argentina's neutral status. Argentine officials, however, accepted the German story without question.[75]

After Mackie had submitted his initial report, however, more evidence emerged that corroborated the German story. Mackie interviewed a man from Sierra Leone who had been a crewman on *Eleonora Woermann* and had witnessed the action between *Carmania* and *Cap Trafalgar.* He confirmed that *Eleonora Woermann* had acted as a depot and collier for *Cap Trafalgar* and SMS *Dresden.* The German merchant ship *Pontos* and the American ship *Berewind* had also helped resupply the German raiders. *Eleonora Woermann* had rescued survivors of the battle between *Carmania* and *Cap Trafalgar* and transported them to Buenos Aires. The Argentines permitted a coal barge to replenish the vessel, despite its having four holds full of coal.[76] An Admiralty memorandum in early 1915 also concluded that *Eber* had armed *Cap Trafalgar* at sea on September 1, 1914.[77] A letter from an engineer on the Hamburg-America Line's SS *Sleiermark* to a friend on the auxiliary cruiser SMS *Berlin* confirmed that *Eber* had picked up naval reserve personnel at Luderizbucht, German Southwest Africa. *Eber* then steamed directly across the Atlantic to rendezvous with several German merchant ships a few days' journey from South America. This source confirmed that the ships had coaled there without mentioning whether a transfer of weapons occurred. *Eber,* however, proceeded directly into Bahia harbor, where it was interned.[78]

Contrary to what Mackie and Norman thought, Argentina had not violated its neutral status with respect to *Cap Trafalgar*. Nevertheless, the information that emerged concerning the activities of *Eleonora Woermann* and *Pontos* provided British diplomats with ample leverage to pressure Argentina into interning the German vessels and their crews. The Foreign Office directed its agent in New York, C. Bennet, to watch *Berewind.* Spring Rice, the British ambassador to the

United States, brought *Berewind*'s activities to the U.S. government's attention. Spring Rice made his case in Washington that *Berewind* had departed New York on August 5, 1914, with a load of coal bound for Buenos Aires. The ship never arrived in Argentina, but instead had entered Rio de Janeiro, Brazil, with an empty hold. The ambassador asserted that *Berewind* was engaged in supplying German raiders and that the United States should take action to detain the vessel should it attempt to depart again with a cargo of fuel.[79]

Although Brazil permitted *Berewind* to enter and leave Rio de Janeiro, when British vessels in convoy arrived at Pernambuco, the German chargé d'affaires protested, and Brazilian authorities sought to detain them. Mr. Robertson, a British civil servant stationed in Brazil, suggested that the Brazilian government treat the ships as men-of-war and grant them twenty-four hours to depart under existing neutrality rules, stipulating that the ships could not return to a Brazilian port for a period of three months. Brazil agreed to the suggestion and released the ships. Robertson stressed to Grey that the Foreign Office raise no protest because Brazil's precedent enhanced London's diplomacy and would do more to stop German ships from resupplying raiders.[80]

Brazil's policy to treat all supply ships accompanying men-of-war as warships, if extended to other nations, could disrupt Germany's Etappen system. If treated as a warship, any raider's supply ship could only receive enough fuel to reach the nearest port of its own nationality, could stay only twenty-four hours, and could not revisit a port in that country for three months. The Foreign Office and Admiralty contrived to send Brazil's neutrality decree to all coastal nations urging them to adopt the measure as their own. All accredited diplomats and agents in foreign ports were to promptly report all arrivals and departures of German vessels, the cargoes loaded and discharged, and any observed deviation from ships' documents. In this way, the Foreign Office built a case against German ships for violations of neutrality that it presented to foreign governments. Armed with documented evidence, British diplomats pressed local officials to intern the offending ships.[81]

Several months later, Spring Rice received a telegram from the Admiralty notifying him of a German ship, *Prinz Eitel Friedrich,* that had arrived in Newport News seeking repairs. According to the Admiralty, *Prinz Eitel Friedrich* received some repair to its bottom, which was also cleaned and painted. This maintenance exceeded what was strictly required for the ship to depart for sea and improved the raider's fighting capacity by increasing its speed. The telegram noted that the shipyard's actions violated neutrality rules established by the Hague conventions and urged Spring Rice to press the Americans to have the ship interned. The ambassador did as requested and reported to Foreign Secretary Grey that the Americans agreed to intern the German ship.[82]

The day before the war began, the merchant vessel *Kronprinz Wilhelm* had left New York for Buenos Aires. It met SMS *Karlsruhe,* commanded by Lieutenant Commander Erich Köhler, at sea near Bermuda on August 6, where the steamer received the guns, officers, and seamen necessary to commission it as an auxiliary cruiser. Lieutenant Commander Paul Thierfelder took command of the new raider. The sudden appearance of several Royal Navy cruisers, however, interrupted the festivities, forcing *Kronprinz Wilhelm* to flee with only a small quantity of ammunition.[83]

The British cruisers elected to pursue the fleeing *Karlsruhe.* After a short nighttime engagement with HMS *Bristol,* the newer and faster *Karlsruhe* escaped undamaged. *Karlsruhe* coaled in Puerto Rico on August 9 and again at Willemstadt, Curaçao, and then patrolled the Brazilian coast. Köhler refueled from *Patagonia* and also from the German-chartered ships *Rio Negro* and *Indrani.* Cruising in company with *Indrani* and *Rio Negro, Karlsruhe* consistently evaded its pursuers while capturing sixteen British merchant ships. Köhler's rampage ended catastrophically on November 4, when an underwater explosion ripped his ship in half. *Rio Negro* picked up survivors, and, slipping through the British blockade, returned to Germany on December 6, 1914. When wreckage from *Karlsruhe* washed ashore at Grenada, newspapers published accounts of a sea battle. The Admiralty, however, could not confirm an engagement had taken place. In March 1915, Royal Navy intelligence induced that the German raider had sunk. At that point, Royal Navy cruisers ceased searching for the enemy cruiser.[84]

The British ship *Indian Prince* became *Kronprinz Wilhelm*'s first capture on September 4. The vessel surrendered without *Kronprinz Wilhelm* firing a shot. The German raider removed the crew and detonated charges near the keel to sink the ship. Thierfelder took his second prize on October 7, when *La Correntina* hove into view. *La Correntina* was armed for self-defense but had been in port when the war broke out. As a consequence, it had no ammunition. Moreover, the vessel's crew failed to render the ship's guns inoperable prior to capture. *Kronprinz Wilhelm* took *La Correntina*'s guns and mounted them on the aft deck. The Germans also took sixty tons of frozen meat and eight hundred tons of coal from its victim and then sank the *La Correntina,* as it had done with the *Indian Prince.* In December 1914, *Kronprinz Wilhelm* had only a few days' worth of coal remaining when it captured *Bellevue.* The prize, laden with coal, bought the raider more time on the seas. *Bellevue* also carried a large quantity of whiskey that *Kronprinz Wilhelm* seized prior to sinking it.

Kronprinz Wilhelm eventually transferred *La Correntina*'s crew to the German merchant ship *Sierra Cordoba,* which carried the prisoners to Montevideo, Uruguay. Authorities in Montevideo determined that *Sierra Cordoba* carried falsified papers, interned the ship, and released the British crew. *Kronprinz Wilhelm* sent *Bellevue*'s crew to Las Palmas, Canary Islands, on board *Otari.*[85] In Brazil, Mr. W. F. Nicholson responded immediately to the news of *Otari.* The ship had also brought in the crews of *Monte Angel* and *Anne de Bertagne.* Nicholson ascertained, probably from the captives, that *Otari* joined *Kronprinz Wilhelm* on December 4 and remained in company until December 21. During that time, *Otari* provided the raider with coal, stores, and fresh water. Nicholson argued that sufficient cause existed that *Otari* had violated neutrality laws in Brazil, which created a clear case to petition the Spanish government to intern the ship if it failed to depart within the time allowed for warships. The Foreign Office acted on Nicholson's evidence, and the Spanish government complied.[86]

Thierfelder and crew lived off of material captured from Allied ships. The French ship *Guadeloupe* provided cloth, buckles, and shoes that Thierfelder used to make uniforms for his crew. *Kronprinz Wilhelm* managed to manufacture ammunition for the guns taken from *La Correntina* and repeatedly refueled on the coal taken from captured ships. Providing for captured crews became difficult, so Thierfelder risked divulging his presence by summoning German ships to pick up the prisoners. The German steamers then released the captives at various ports—Buenos Aires, Rio de Janario, Pernambuco, and Santos—along the South American coast. *Kronprinz Wilhelm* eventually succumbed to lack of supplies. Without provisions, particularly fresh vegetables, the crew and prisoners became ill with beri-beri. Thierfelder explained that only one German supply ship, *Otari,* had met the raider. He had hoped to meet more, but none arrived.[87] Radio transmissions from Royal Navy cruisers revealed that the Americans had interned *Prinz Eitel Friedrich* at Newport News, Virginia.

At sea for two hundred fifty-five days, the crew exhausted and sick, the ship low on fuel, Thierfelder evaded Allied cruisers and proceeded to Newport News to join his fellow raider and accept internment.[88]

Kronprinz Wilhelm presents an interesting case for several reasons. First, the vessel seemed to refute the logic that a commerce raider could not operate for long on scarce intelligence and no fixed logistical support. Nearly nine months is an exceedingly long time for a vessel to remain at sea. Second, despite Thierfelder sending captives ashore on several occasions, thus divulging *Kronprinz Wilhelm*'s primary area of operation, naval intelligence never located the marauder. Without the fortunate capture of *Bellevue* and its coal, however, *Kronprinz Wilhelm* would have succumbed to lack of fuel at the beginning of December 1914. The raider would not have been at sea to meet *Otari,* the only supply ship to have rendezvoused with Thierfelder during his long voyage. Even with an exceptionally long run of good luck, the exhaustion of crew endurance ultimately spelled the end of *Kronprinz Wilhelm*'s cruise. Men are only temporary inhabitants of the sea. Without a safe refuge for rest and refitting, the fate of the commerce raiders was sealed. The duration of any single raider's cruise and the number of captures it might take was not knowable, but the marauder could not remain at sea indefinitely.

The Admiralty made it a standard policy to rigorously question recovered British crews. This gained them intelligence on the enemy and ensured that ships insured under the government scheme complied with Admiralty direction. If the captains did not follow Admiralty orders, the insurance policy might not pay out. The method proved effective on both counts. Moreover, the intelligence gleaned through interrogation aided the Admiralty in issuing sensible orders for ships to evade capture while also providing details on how Germany armed and supplied its raiders.

Based on information gathered from released prisoners, naval intelligence concluded by February 1915 that none of the German ships acting as an armed merchant cruiser had armament on board when war broke out. *Kronprinz Wilhelm* had been armed from the cruiser *Karlsruhe, Cap Trafalgar* from the gunboat *Eber. Prinz Eitel Friedrich* outfitted as a raider at Tsingtao before departing, and *Kaiser Wilhelm der Grosse* received its guns at Bremen. Therefore, the Admiralty believed that with Germany's overseas cruisers and gunboats accounted for, no other merchant ships currently holed up in foreign harbors could be converted at sea.[89] German ships might still escape from internment in foreign harbors and become depot ships for raiders, but the vessels could not become auxiliary cruisers themselves. For example, *Holge* escaped from internment in Pernambuco, Brazil, in early January 1915. The German steamer slipped out of harbor without papers. In response to the escape, Brazilian authorities dismissed the captain of *Tymbira* and Pernambuco's port captain, the two individuals responsible for detaining interned ships. *Holge*'s activities remained unknown. The ship, however, entered Buenos Aires at the beginning of March. Argentine authorities immediately interned it.[90]

The German steamer *Patagonia* arrived at Recife (in Pernambuco), Brazil, on September 11. The ship had cargo destined for SMS *Dresden.* Moreover, the steamer had a crew of sixty-four men and two captains on board, one commissioned in the naval reserve. The ship's normal complement was twenty-eight men. The funnel had been painted from its original yellow to black. The ship no longer chartered cargo for the Hamburg–South America Line. *Patagonia* even flew a naval reserve flag, indicating that the German government had commandeered the vessel and put it under naval orders. *Patagonia* had intended to proceed to Buenos Aires, but had been instructed by Brazilian port authorities not to leave. Although the steamer agreed to comply, it weighed anchor and departed as soon as Brazilian officials left the immediate vicinity. A Brazilian frigate gave chase, but the German ship was fast and easily outpaced its pursuer. Because similar incidents with German ships had already occurred, the Brazilian government began interning all German vessels. At sea, the German steamer intercepted radio transmissions from patrolling Royal Navy cruisers and decided to proceed to Bahia Blanca, Argentina, instead of Buenos Aires.[91]

Reginald T. Tower, Britain's chargé d'affaires in Argentina, pressed Foreign Minister José Luis Murature to intern *Patagonia.* Murature agreed that the vessel had acted suspiciously, but believed that London's arguments for internment lacked any legal basis. The local minister for marine at Bahia Blanca also provided a lead that turned up the fact that *Patagonia* had visited Saint Thomas in the Danish West Indies and cleared the port on August 12 with papers indicating a journey to the Azores. Argentina, however, wished to maintain good relations with Germany, so it simply placed the suspect vessel under watch. Back in the Foreign Office, Grey was incensed. Grey's correspondence with the Admiralty on the subject revealed his ire as he "purposed to instruct Sir

R. Tower to press the Argentine government to intern [that] vessel," because it was, with the exception of a formal declaration that the ship would issue after it put to sea, "incorporated in the German fleet and has long overstayed the limits of neutral hospitality to a fleet auxiliary." Although the Admiralty received information that *Patagonia* departed Bahia Blanca on November 23, other, reliable information indicates that the German steamer was interned and remained in Bahia Blanca for the duration of the war.[92]

THE SITUATION IN GERMANY AND REVISED PLANS TO ATTACK BRITISH TRADE

An unidentified American businessman who frequented Germany reported in early 1915 that the Teutonic nation was united in support of the war. Some socialist groups desired an immediate peace, but their voice was small and did not represent public thinking. The socialists could not produce enough dissent to affect the Reichstag vote on war funding. The public believed that a defeat in the war spelled the end of the German empire.

Ordinary Germans expected to win the war by defeating Russia and France. Both opponents, the Germans believed, would be hammered physically by the German army and financially crushed so that each would make a separate peace favorable to Germany. The German people would punish Russia, leaving its army in shambles and the state financially destitute. Paradoxically, German public opinion toward France was sympathetic. The average person believed that France had entered the war only to honor its commitment to Russia and regain Alsace and Lorraine. Therefore Germany would offer easy terms to Paris, probably returning most French territory and paying an indemnity. The American opined that German citizens expected to retain Belgium and portions of the French coast including Calais. When other nations joined the Allies, Germans believed they did so to rob Germany of its wealth. One hundred German liners had holed up in Lisbon, Portugal, at the beginning of the war. German citizens asserted that Portugal later entered the war simply to steal Germany's ships.

Germans remained convinced that they could not be starved out, and the American admitted that if Germany were experiencing economic hardship, it was not apparent. Trains ran on schedule, and people traveled regularly. Prices were higher than before the war, but remained reasonable and stable. The American noted that meat was plentiful, but attributed this to farmers slaughtering much of their livestock to avoid paying to feed them over the winter. Most tables served low-grade war bread, but white bread remained available.

Germany fully realized the difficulty in defeating Great Britain. Nevertheless, Berlin was fully committed to the objective. Moreover, the American believed that the average German overestimated the power of the kaiser's fleet relative to that of the Royal Navy. Germans counted on zeppelins and submarines to weaken the Royal Navy's Grand Fleet so that their country could prevail in a final great struggle.

Romania traded oil and cereal for Germany's abundant coal. Nevertheless, Germany's gasoline supply remained limited. Taxis, buses, and private cars ran on a mixture of ethanol and benzol, a coal tar product made in Germany. Berlin reserved its petrol for the war effort, but if the gasoline ran out, the ethanol-benzol mixture would be used by the army as well. Shortages of grain, gasoline, rubber, and other imported goods would eventually show, but the Germans believed that Russia and France would run low of these items first. Overall, the American concluded that German plans were thorough and complete and that Berlin was prepared to go the distance in the war.[93]

About a year later, in early 1916, Frederick Smith, a British businessman, passed some disturbing correspondence penned by someone named Crowborough to David Lloyd George, the British prime minister. According to Crowborough, German sources, whom he knew, indicated that the kaiser's government actively sought to conserve resources because the British blockade had imposed serious shortages on the German economy. As a result of the lesson learned from enduring Britain's distant blockade, Germany decided to rely on destroying British trade to create a food crisis in the home islands as a means of ending the war. The war would become a contest of blockades, in which victory would be decided at sea rather than on the battlefields of Europe.[94] The kaiser's planners at the Wilhelmstrasse knew that defeating Great Britain was the key to victory. German strategists also determined that Britain was most vulnerable to a loss of trade—something Whitehall's ministers knew from the outset.

In several European countries, war mobilization drained manpower that would normally have been used to plant and harvest wheat.[95] As a result of lower crop yields, food shortages began to manifest themselves. A smaller harvest was a fact in Great Britain as well. A concerted German attack on British trade would exacerbate the problem in the home islands. Germany had, however, lost the ability to pursue traditional commerce raiding via cruiser warfare. Britain had extinguished Germany's potential overseas bases and centers of intelligence. London's diplomats had also effectively stifled Berlin's Ettapen system. Moreover, Germany no longer had ships, warships or fast merchant liners, outside of the North Sea to use as raiders. Germany required an alternative weapon to use against British trade. Out of desperation, the German navy turned to the submarine.

9 CONCLUSIONS

It is worth reviewing the prewar strategic situation that made the island empire of Great Britain dependent on trade and vulnerable to its interdiction. London devised and executed a naval strategy to protect its trade, which included seizing Berlin's overseas possessions. That strategy, ruthlessly executed, compelled Germany to view the resumption of unrestricted submarine warfare as its only strategic option—even if that meant bringing the United States into the war.

Great Britain maintained its food supply and sustained its economy thanks to the free flow of trade. Britons paid for imports with income from several sources: exports, return on foreign investments, and fees derived from services rendered in shipping, international credit, and maritime insurance. The extent of the British Empire provided many conveniently located harbors for refueling and ship repair, plus a robust communications network of submerged telegraph cables and high-frequency radio. All of these facilities served to promote trade. British shipping companies owned 50 percent of the world's shipping tonnage. Likewise, Britain controlled access to approximately 80 percent of the international communications network. Merchants worldwide procured the preponderance of their credit and purchased insurance in London's exchanges. Had Germany been able to interfere significantly with Allied shipping or financial systems, British trade might have been halted, at least temporarily. At a minimum, such an outcome would have hampered the Allied war effort. Had trade to the United Kingdom been interrupted for several months, the island nation would have had to seek peace. London's ministers understood this before the war began and prepared to prevent that from happening.

Britain generated vast income through shipping, finance, and insurance services to other nations that allowed most other nations to conduct their trade. As a result, if trade flourished, Britain prospered. On the other hand, if as a result of war, trade ceased anywhere, British well-being suffered, irrespective of whether Britain was a belligerent. To prevent most nations from trading, the Royal Navy could have blockaded their ports and attacked their oceangoing commerce. London's dominance in global trade systems also allowed it to hamper any nation's economy. It could refuse to grant credit, withhold insurance, restrict communications, or forbid its merchant marine from carrying cargoes from other countries. To do so, however, would not have been in Great Britain's economic interest. As a result, Whitehall desired that trade follow prewar patterns as closely as possible.

For decades, British ministers exhibited remarkable foresight in acquiring key bases astride the trade routes that allowed the Royal Navy to both operate against enemy trade and protect British commerce. Moreover, many of these sites also provided financial and communications services essential for trade. The communications, financial, and shipping systems all mutually supported each other, and the task of protecting them fell to the Royal Navy. Although the navy matched the strength of the next two naval powers combined, the Admiralty divided its force three ways—to protect international trade, prevent an invasion of the home islands, and protect imperial possessions abroad. The Royal Navy stretched its resources to the limit accomplishing all that was required.

By 1914, Germany had emerged as a major sea power, second in strength only to Great Britain. Kaiser Wilhelm II's aggressive foreign policy also netted several overseas colonies, where Germany built ports and modern, high-frequency radio communications. As with the British Empire, Germany's colonies supported the nation's trade, but they also supported the German navy, making it more capable of commerce raiding.

Not only had Germany built a strong navy, but Admiral Alfred von Tirpitz had also designed a strategy that called for keeping the bulk of the fleet in the North Sea, where it constituted a threat to the British homeland. As Tirpitz intended, Germany's High Seas Fleet compelled Great Britain to concentrate major portions of the Royal Navy in its home waters. The Admiralty responded with a compromise solution by keeping the Channel Fleet as modern as possible and keeping the Home Fleet stationed at Gibraltar, where it could swing east to respond to trouble in the Mediterranean or north to assist the Channel Fleet. At most times, however, the Royal Navy was only thinly represented in the Mediterranean Sea, South Atlantic, Indian Ocean, and Pacific Ocean.

In addition to expanding the German navy, Berlin's ministers along the Wilhelmstrasse also implemented plans to turn some German merchant vessels into auxiliary cruisers designated to raid enemy commerce in the event of war and others into support ships using its elaborate Etappen system to sustain the commerce raiders. German naval initiatives, when combined, presented a serious threat to Britain's world trade and the security of Great Britain. Any defeat of the British fleets guarding the home islands would mean that invasion could soon follow.

The threat Germany posed to British security caused London to abandon its long-standing policy of remaining aloof from continental affairs. In the first twelve years of the twentieth century, Great Britain had completely altered its grand strategy. First, London formed an alliance with Tokyo. The security agreement with Japan allowed Britain to transfer warships from the Pacific back to home waters, where they buttressed the fleet poised to counter the main German naval threat. Next, Sir Edward Grey, the foreign secretary, settled Britain's differences with France, Russia, and the United States. Grey's diplomacy succeeded to the point where the British cabinet no longer contemplated a war against any of these traditional rivals. War planning in Whitehall instead focused on the threat posed by Germany.

Because Great Britain's Committee of Imperial Defence studied the vulnerability of the nation's trade to interdiction, Whitehall's ministers probed senior managers of major shipping firms about actions their companies contemplated taking in the event of war with another major power. The executives explained that private insurance that covered war risks was impossible to obtain, so the companies had formed their own self-insuring war risk clubs. Their plan consisted of providing insurance to ships already at sea so that the steamers were covered in order to proceed to the nearest British or neutral port and wait out the war. Vessels in port at the outset of hostilities were to remain where they were. If the shippers implemented this plan, however, all British trade would cease in the event of war with a major power such as Germany. The voluntary trade interruption would produce exactly the effect an enemy desired on the British economy. This constituted an outcome unacceptable for Whitehall.

The government and the shippers agreed that merchant vessels could be induced to continue their voyages if they could get adequate insurance. To provide shippers the incentive to complete voyages, the government prepared a national guarantee insurance scheme to cover the value of the vessels. This scheme, administered for the government by the insurance clubs, commenced immediately at the declaration of war. Whitehall initiated another insurance scheme to shore up commercial insurance on cargoes. Under this plan, commercial insurers provided coverage, but if the price rose above a predetermined level, an alternative, government insurance would be offered as a more affordable option, acting as a ceiling on insurance prices. The government, however, became financially liable whenever it participated in an insurance policy for shipping and cargo losses inflicted by the enemy. The Royal Navy, responsible for protecting trade, also indirectly protected the government's financial stake.

In late 1911, the Admiralty began to seriously reconsider how the navy would protect trade. At that time, the Naval Intelligence Division drafted a plan to collect information on all foreign warships and fast merchant liners capable of operating as auxiliary cruisers. The Admiralty used the information during the war to warn merchant vessels of known enemy raiders' locations and reroute the traders around the threat.[1] Assisting cargo ships to evade marauders proved a more effective method to prevent capture than did attempting to protect trade routes with constant patrols. British shipping companies also took advantage of navy-provided guns to arm their ships for self-defense.

The Admiralty issued revised orders in July 1914 that corrected many flaws in previous planning. The Admiralty Staff believed that destruction of the enemy's commerce raiders provided the best protection for British ships, which could then continue to bring food and supplies home. Any German merchant ship that evaded the Royal Navy in the open ocean still had to get past the blockade at the entrance to the North Sea, so British cruisers focused on hunting down commerce destroyers as a higher priority and halted enemy cargo vessels only as a secondary operation.

Prewar exercises, and actual war experience, taught the Admiralty that German commerce raiders more often than not could successfully avoid their hunters. The Admiralty recognized that British merchant vessels could use tactics similar to those employed by enemy marauders to evade capture. Once an enemy raider's location became known, naval intelligence projected the marauder's possible position several days into the future. British shore posts and naval vessels directed British commerce to steer clear of the raider's range of possible positions. Meanwhile, Royal Navy cruisers attempted to relentlessly tighten a noose around commerce destroyers. Cruisers and armed merchants taken for naval service worked in squadrons of three or four ships so that engagements with the enemy tilted heavily in the Allies' favor.

When war erupted, the Offensive Sub-Committee of the Committee of Imperial Defence determined that expeditions to seize Germany's overseas ports and wireless stations would aid the Royal Navy in securing the sea-lanes. This would be the case because seizing these known locations would deprive Germany's commerce raiders of logistics and intelligence. Without the necessary support, the marauders would eventually have to cease their activities.

As the overseas expeditions gained success, the range of options for German naval forces to replenish commerce raiders increasingly narrowed. Samoa, all of German New Guinea, and Germany's island territories in the Pacific had surrendered to the Allies by the middle of September 1914. The Japanese blockaded Tsingtao in late August, and the German garrison there surrendered on November 7, 1914. As a result, the German East Asia squadron had limited means to replenish and gain intelligence in the western Pacific Ocean. If Vice Admiral Maximilian Graf von Spee remained in the Pacific, his squadron would have to sustain itself by relying on supplies taken from captured merchant vessels, and that would be a matter of sheer luck. Von Spee elected instead to flee toward South America and escape into the Atlantic, eventually rejoining the German High Seas Fleet in the North Sea.

During the same period, overseas expeditions aimed at Germany's African colonies began producing results. On August 8, 1914, Governor Heinrich Schnee agreed to keep the German East African cities of Tanga and Dar es Salaam neutral to prevent Royal Navy cruisers from shelling them. As a result, the two cities ceased providing logistical support to the German cruiser SMS *Königsberg.* In addition, Togoland surrendered August 26, 1914, and the Allies took the port of Duala, in the Cameroons, on September 27.

By the end of September, the only African ports Germany retained were Luderitzbucht and Swakopmund, in German Southwest Africa. The two southwest African ports remained open because the ongoing rebellion in South Africa gave the German colony a temporary reprieve from invasion by its southern neighbor. What remained of Germany's elaborate Etappen system resided in neutral countries, mostly in North America and South America. This tended to drive Germany's remaining commerce destroyers into waters around South America. As a result, the Royal Navy established firm control over its two most important trade routes—the North Atlantic and the Oriental.

German commerce raiders reacted by fleeing to where they could obtain the best logistical and intelligence support. That consideration led the bulk of the German marauders to southern waters and tied them to logistics lines emanating from neutral South American ports. Thus, South American waters became the hotbed of commerce raider activity. HMS *Carmania* encountered SMS *Cap Trafalgar* while it was resupplying from depot ships. *Cap Trafalgar* attempted to escape, but *Carmania,* the swifter ship, pursued and sank the raider on September 14, 1914, after a fierce battle near Trinidad. During October and November 1914, the cruisers SMS *Dresden* and *Karlsruhe* operated in South American waters, as did SMS *Kronprinz Wilhelm*, a steamer converted to auxiliary cruiser.

Logistics problems also led to the German East Asia squadron's downfall. Because von Spee needed to replenish the squadron, it had stopped along the way to South America at the Marquesas and Galapagos Islands. Finally, it replenished at Valparaíso, Chile. Various agents, British steamships, and intercepted radio transmissions provided an intelligence trail that allowed the Royal Navy to close in. Admiral Christopher Cradock's squadron engaged the German East Asia squadron near Coronel, Chile, on November 1, but lost the duel. As a result, the Royal Navy lost control of the South American trade route, the island nation's third most important commercial artery. Nevertheless, von Spee required additional fuel to make the trek home across the Atlantic Ocean. When von Spee attempted to raid the Falkland Islands on December 8 to obtain coal for his ships, Admiral Charles Doveton Sturdee's much larger squadron forced him into a battle in which the German East Asia squadron met its demise. This important battle eliminated the danger to commerce traveling around South America.

When Royal Navy cruisers located enemy commerce raiders and support ships using neutral ports as bases of operation, London's diplomats first attempted to prompt the nations involved to enforce their neutrality rights and intern the enemy ships. By doing so, London's diplomats consistently chipped away at Germany's Etappen system. Whenever diplomacy failed, the Admiralty allowed its cruisers to enforce British rights and attack the enemy within a neutral power's territorial waters.[2] The German raiders *Dresden, Kaiser Wilhelm der Grosse,* and *Königsberg* were all in neutral harbors awaiting resupply when the Royal Navy trapped and destroyed them.

The zeal with which the Royal Navy's captains engaged the enemy in neutral waters generated protests with which the Foreign Office had to contend. The Admiralty directed its naval forces to press the attack on *Königsberg* in spite of the fact that the German cruiser had taken shelter up the Rafiji River, inside Portuguese territory. Chile and Spain lodged formal protests over the Royal Navy's sinking of German ships inside their harbors. German raiders chose to replenish at remote locations inside Chilean and Spanish territory because neither neutral power had the capacity to effectively prevent them from doing so. Great Britain had little to fear from Chile, Portugal, and Spain with respect to reprisals. Nevertheless, London and the parties it offended all sought to maintain cordial relations. The fact, however, that Great Britain accepted the risk of alienating neutral nations for the sake of sinking German marauders demonstrates how important protecting trade figured in the cabinet's strategic calculations.

In the war's initial months, it looked as though the British might not be able to beat Germany's Ettapen system. In late October 1914, the Royal Navy, spread thin and stressed nearly to its breaking point, considered which operations it might have to suspend. Soon thereafter, relief arrived. On October 31, Royal Navy cruisers located and trapped SMS *Königsberg* in the Rafiji River. Tsingtao fell on November 7. The cruiser HMAS *Sydney* caught and sank SMS *Emden* on November 9. After Admiral Sturdee sank von Spee's squadron, the naval situation worldwide tilted heavily in Britain's favor. Only a few raiders remained prowling the oceans. SMS *Karlsruhe* had actually exploded and sank on November 4, but the Admiralty did not know this until March 1915. The cruisers HMS *Glasgow* and *Kent* sank SMS *Dresden* in battle on March 14, 1915. *Kronprinz Wilhelm* accepted internment in Newport News, Virginia, a month later, on April 11.

The Royal Navy had succeeded in ridding the trade routes of German commerce destroyers, which freed Great Britain to bring troops from Australia,

New Zealand, and Canada across the oceans to support the French army on the continent. British trade also proceeded normally, and British finance remained secure. Despite London's ruthless methods, it would portray Berlin as a flagrant and constant transgressor of international law, particularly when the latter initially attempted submarine warfare. By doing so, the United Kingdom gained access to American finance and tacit U.S. support.

As the sun set on Germany's cruiser campaign against British trade, the imperial German government proclaimed the open ocean surrounding Great Britain and Ireland a war region. The declaration announced that from February 18, 1915, every enemy merchant vessel entering those waters would be destroyed. If that were the extent of the declaration, the world likely would have accepted its edict. Germany also informed the nations, however, that it would not always be possible to warn the crews and passengers prior to attacking the ships. Moreover, neutral ships also incurred danger by entering the war zone because, Germany's High Command reasoned, belligerents misused neutral flags to disguise their ships.[3] Germany also implied that it intended to use submarines to halt Britain's trade; it had no other vessels capable of the task that could evade the Royal Navy's distant blockade.

President Woodrow Wilson sharply rebuked the German government for the new policy. In a February 10 letter to the kaiser, Wilson stated that he viewed the possibility of sinking unarmed merchant ships without warning with grave concern. He reminded the Wilhelmstrasse that by international law, a belligerent only had the right to board and search neutral vessels on the high seas. Attacking a vessel because it entered a prescribed body of water without first determining its nationality and inspecting its cargo for contraband constituted an act unprecedented in warfare. Wilson understood that belligerents might abuse the flag of neutral nations to mask the identity of a merchant ship; nations, however, recognized the right of visit and search precisely so that a fleet enforcing a blockade could determine a vessel's nationality and the character of its cargo. Wilson warned the kaiser that should German naval vessels harm American shipping and citizens, the U.S. government would hold Germany accountable and take the steps necessary to safeguard American property and lives on the high seas.[4]

Over the next months, Germany sank two American vessels, *Cushing* with an airplane attack and *Gulflight* by submarine torpedo. The latter attack caused the deaths of two American citizens. In addition, an American citizen died when a German submarine torpedoed the British steamer *Cabala*. Another 128 Americans lost their lives May 7, 1915, after the German submarine U-20 torpedoed and sank the British steamer *Lusitania,* provoking another exchange of letters between the U.S. and German governments. In the third of Wilson's letters, dated July 21, 1915, the president warned that the United States would consider any further infringement on the rights of American vessels to conduct neutral trade as a deliberately hostile act.

Nearly a year later, on March 24, 1916, the German submarine UB-29 torpedoed the French passenger ferry *Sussex* in the English Channel. Although *Sussex* remained afloat and limped to Boulogne, several American citizens died in the attack. On April 18, President Wilson condemned unrestricted submarine warfare, warned that the United States would not tolerate Germany's continuation of the practice, and demanded the German government revoke the policy. The kaiser backed down. German prime minister Gottlieb von Jagow announced on April 24, 1916, that in the future German naval vessels would clearly warn merchant ships prior to attack. Shortly thereafter, Germany's naval high command suspended unrestricted submarine warfare.[5]

Admiral John A. Fisher had warned prior to the war that the submarine presented a threat to trade and that Germany would use the new weapon to sink unarmed merchant vessels. First Sea Lord Winston Churchill countered that no civilized nation would resort to such a tactic, and that even if Berlin did attempt to destroy commerce with submarines, worldwide reaction to the practice would soon force Germany back into accepted norms of cruiser warfare.[6] Jagow's promise to Wilson seemed to vindicate Churchill's view.

Nevertheless, Germany needed to alter the status quo in the North Sea in order to regain essential trade. The German High Seas Fleet's increased activity eventually led to the Battle of Jutland in May 1916. Although Germany scored a tactical victory—having sunk three British battle cruisers, three armored cruisers, and seven destroyers while losing a battle cruiser, a pre-dreadnought battleship, four light cruisers, and five destroyers from its own fleet—the kaiser's navy failed to alter the strategic situation.[7] Britain's blockade remained as tight as ever, suffocating German trade.

The Wilhelmstrasse also initiated a major land offensive against the French army at Verdun. By summer 1916, the German army's offensive had faltered.

This was in part because the British army had initiated its own offensive at the Somme to relieve pressure on the French army. Moreover, Austria-Hungary neared collapse, and Romania (siding with its Russian ally) declared war. British pressure forced General Erich von Falkenhayn, chief of the German General Staff, to shift troops from Verdun to stabilize Germany's front at the Somme and to prop up Austria-Hungary. With the German army in crisis, Kaiser Wilhelm II lost confidence in Falkenhayn and summoned Field Marshal Paul von Hindenburg and General Erich Ludendorff to replace him.[8]

The French army had been bludgeoned by the battle for Verdun, but held its position and could still fight, although only defensively. The Royal Navy's North Sea blockade continued to stifle German trade. Great Britain also supplied the Allies with a steady stream of war items and credit and therefore emerged as the Central Powers' chief foe. Ludendorff assessed the situation at the end of 1916 and concluded that Allied material strength would soon exceed what the Central Powers could muster. He and Hindenburg began earnestly preparing defensive positions behind the front and training the German army in defensive tactics. The German high command believed that if the public continued to support the war and defensive positions were properly established, an Allied victory could be forestalled. An outright German victory obtained by force of arms on the continent, however, appeared unrealistic. The problem turned on convincing London to accept a negotiated end to the war with terms favorable to Germany.[9]

The German naval high command presented Ludendorff with the Kalkmann Report, which argued that resuming unrestricted submarine warfare would produce the greatest harm to Britain's economy and in turn compel the island nation to seek peace terms. At first, Ludendorff found the argument unconvincing. After reading the report's details, however, the general reconsidered. Ludendorff believed that if unrestricted submarine warfare were the only method capable of compelling London to seek peace terms, it was his military duty to enact that policy. Nevertheless, German foreign secretary Arthur Zimmermann insisted that negotiating peace must be attempted prior to declaring a war zone in the oceans surrounding the British Isles. For planners at the German high command, synchronizing these two initiatives became critical.[10]

Initially, Germany attempted to persuade President Wilson to mediate peace negotiations. Wilson, however, made his November 1916 reelection a higher priority. He did not make up his mind about whether to mediate peace or respond to Germany's initiative.[11] The German staff believed that for successful negotiations to take place, the Allied powers must believe that Germany offered peace from a position of strength, not out of necessity due to weakness. If Berlin had to resort to unrestricted submarine warfare, the campaign needed to commence by February 1917 to have the greatest impact on Britain's food supply. Therefore, Ludendorff could not wait long for Wilson to take the lead in peace talks. With time running out, Germany made its own direct appeal for peace to the Allied powers in December 1916.[12]

Berlin, starting from an initially strong negotiating position, having thwarted the offensive at Somme and defeated Romania, presented its proposal for peace negotiations to the Allies. While the French army was capable of only defensive operations for another year, the British Expeditionary Force retained a strong offensive capability. The Allies were far from beaten. British prime minister Lloyd George simply rejected Germany's overture. The action did, however, prompt President Wilson to initiate mediation. Wilson urged all belligerents to make their terms for an end to the war known and to seek terminating the war without naming a victor or vanquished. Germany spelled out its requirements and again proposed meeting with the Allies to end the war. In London, the cabinet viewed the terms as too harsh because they included retaining Belgium and significant portions of northern France.[13] London rejected the terms and the remaining Allied powers followed suit, declining to even counter with terms of their own.[14]

Whether Germany's appeals were sincere or not, the peace question was settled. German leadership realized in late 1916 that their path to winning the war lay in defeating Great Britain. The German army had failed to defeat the Allied armies. Germany had to stifle British trade. The success Great Britain realized with its overseas expeditions and its diplomatic efforts to disrupt Germany's Etappen system constrained the kaiser's options. Without cruisers, a merchant marine, and logistics outside of the North Sea, unrestricted submarine warfare, according to Ludendorff, constituted "the only means left to secure, in any reasonable time, a victorious end to the war."[15] Despite knowing that returning to unrestricted submarine operations would mean war with the United States, Germany resumed sinking merchant vessels within the blockade zone. German planners calculated that Britain would succumb to lack of food and trade before the United States could make its industrial might felt on Europe's battlefields.[16]

Berlin was nearly correct. German submarines devastated British shipping. The number of ships sunk per month peaked in April 1917. Britain's economy rapidly declined. Without loan guarantees from the United States, nationalization of the British economy, assistance from U.S. Navy destroyers, and help organizing convoys, Whitehall would have undoubtedly had to seek peace terms. With those extreme measures, and a massive shipbuilding program, by April 1918 the Allies had begun producing ships at a greater rate than German submarines could sink them.[17] Historian C. Ernest Fayle, chronicler of the official history of British trade during the war, explained, "It was, in no small measure, the success with which British trade was brought through the first few months of war which enabled it at [this] later period to surmount [the] still more dangerous crisis."[18] The British hung on, and the tide slowly turned while the United States moved its forces across the ocean. The German army attempted to crush Great Britain on the western front by launching an offensive before the U.S. army could fully organize by launching Operation Michael on March 18. When that attack was blunted, Ludendorff shifted his line of attack four times in order to break through the Allied line. When those failed in mid-July 1918, Germany had no more alternatives and sought an armistice.[19]

Historians have postulated various arguments for why Britain elected to seize Germany's overseas colonies. One theory holds that London desired to add territory to the empire and the war provided a ready excuse. A second explanation argues that Great Britain aimed to hold Germany's colonies in order to occupy a position of relative strength over its alliance partners. At war's end, London's negotiators could use those colonies as bargaining chips to control the tenor and pace of the end-of-war negotiations. Despite historians' divergent opinions on why Britain's cabinet decided to embark on offensive operations overseas, scholars have agreed that the expeditions rated only as minor adjuncts to the battles in Europe during the Great War.[20] The evidence presented in this book, however, suggests that Britain's overseas expeditions shaped the Great War in significant ways.

Some historians also argue that the Battle of Jutland, although a tactical victory for Germany, constituted a strategic victory for Britain. These historians base their conclusion on the fact that the outcome of the battle did not alter the strategic situation.[21] After the battle, the Royal Navy remained in control of the oceans, with the German High Seas Fleet trapped in the North Sea. The Royal Navy had achieved nearly total control of the sea, Captain Alfred Thayer Mahan's theoretical goal for all navies. It is important to note, however, that the Battle of Jutland did not produce the Royal Navy's strategic dominance, but merely upheld it. What historians who fixate on the significance of Jutland fail to realize is that British naval strategy, successfully executed during the first year of the war, elevated the Royal Navy to a dominant position.

Mahan defined sea power as the combination of a nation's maritime trade and its navy.[22] Without credit and appropriate insurance, British commerce would have ground to a halt. The government insurance scheme covered the ships and cargoes against wartime loss, thereby providing the necessary incentive to free up credit and induce the vessels to risk transiting oceans prowled by hostile cruisers. Without this critical financial move, Great Britain would have had little trade for the Royal Navy to protect. Nevertheless, sea control remained beyond the reach of the Royal Navy. Persistent naval activity, however, combined with land forces occupying the enemy's ports, stripped the enemy of its access to the world's oceans. In this sense, Mahanian naval theory, which holds that sea power shapes the outcome of events on land, was turned on its head. Events on land in Germany's colonies, i.e., the loss of port facilities, determined the outcome of naval events.

To be sure, the numbers of soldiers involved, the resultant casualties, and chances for glory paled in comparison to the clash of massive armies on the European continent. On the other hand, the Royal Navy remained fully engaged globally in pursuit of its three main tasks: preventing an invasion of the home islands, supporting the army on the continent, and protecting Britain's empire and trade. After some overseas expeditions succeeded, however, the Royal Navy steadily mastered its German adversary. By March 1915, Germany had lost the bulk of its merchant vessels and crews to internment, and hundreds of other vessels and their cargoes had been captured.[23] The cumulative effects of naval warfare and diplomacy allowed Whitehall to sweep the Kaiser's commerce destroyers from the seas. As a result, the Royal Navy dominated the ocean's highways outside of the North Sea. Moreover, British naval dominance secured Britain's colonies and dominions from attack. The Admiralty could therefore concentrate its warships in the waters surrounding Great Britain, rendering an invasion improbable while fully supporting the Allied armies in France.

When the war concluded, Prime Minister Lloyd George ensured that Germany's High Seas Fleet no longer posed a threat to the home islands by interning its warships at Scapa Flow. Yet victory demanded its price; Germany's defeat did not mean that trade reverted to prewar patterns. Millions of tons of shipping had been destroyed, sunk by German submarines.[24] Unrestricted submarine warfare did not win the war, but it demonstrated its awesome potential. Whitehall had to consider the possibility of commerce destruction in future wars not only by traditional cruiser methods, but also with the ruthless efficiency provided by the submarine. Naval intelligence prepared maps demonstrating the threat posed to trade if Germany retained its overseas colonies and built naval bases.[25] Lloyd George accordingly stripped Germany of its colonies to ensure the threat against British trade that existed at war's outbreak would not recur in a future war.

The victorious powers held the kaiser's territories as mandates under the League of Nations. London readily accepted dividing Germany's former colonies among the Allies, which indicates that the overseas expeditions were not designed to simply add territory to the British Empire. Initially, London only intended to seize ports, submerged telegraph cable junctions, and wireless transmission stations that provided logistical support, plus command and control, for commerce raiders. After several years of war, the Allied powers endorsed stripping Germany of all its imperial possessions because doing so prevented Germany from posing a future threat to global commerce.

While discussing General William Tecumseh Sherman's march to the sea in the U.S. Civil War, historian Mark Grimsley noted that the soldiers involved in destroying the Confederacy's war-making capacity were unaware of the significance of their actions. The few lines officers recorded in their official reports about the devastation demonstrated how blasé Sherman's army grew about the tremendous destruction it wrought on Dixie. In contrast, even a minor skirmish between Union and Confederate forces garnered a lengthy description in a report. One Union officer, Colonel John Flynn, observed that unless a serious clash of arms between opposing forces occurred, nothing of significance happened.[26] Similarly, the colonial campaigns of the Great War may seem minor sideshows, but they are nevertheless strategically important.

Historians have claimed that the advent of unrestricted submarine warfare nearly defeated Great Britain. Without U.S. naval support, including assistance to facilitate effective convoys, Germany could have emerged the victor.[27] Had London not acted early and taken prudent steps to protect its overseas empire and trade, however, it could have lost the war by early 1915. The national guarantee insurance scheme, effective diplomacy, and successful overseas expeditions shut down that possibility.

Britain's overseas offensives, when viewed as attempts to enlarge the empire, or enhance London's negotiating position, dwindle in importance. This is because the operations had little impact on improving the scale or geography of the British Empire. Germany's colonies also proved small leverage in complicated negotiations involving the whole of the European continent. When the expeditions are considered as a key piece in a campaign to protect Britain's vast global trade, however, their significance assumes a wholly different character. Reflecting on the naval situation following the Battle of the Falkland Islands, Churchill penned, "The public, though gratified by the annihilating character of the victory, was quite unconscious of its immense importance to the whole naval situation."[28] In Tirpitz' memoirs, the German admiral reminisced over how gallantly the overseas cruisers did their duty. Despite well-prepared plans by Germany's naval staff, the war against British commerce could not last long due to the lack of overseas bases. He believed that as long as German prestige held, neutral nations would have continued to work with Germany's agents to procure supplies and coal. The loss at the Falklands, however, obliterated what esteem the German navy had gained through its victory at Coronel.[29] In four more months, Germany's cruiser warfare ended when *Kronprinz Wilhelm* steamed into the harbor at Newport News, Virginia. Churchill's reaction to the defeat of Germany's commerce raiders highlights the crucial importance of the campaign:

> Its consequences were far-reaching, and affected simultaneously our position in every part of the globe. The strain was everywhere relaxed. All our enterprises, whether of war or commerce, proceeded in every theater without the slightest hindrance. . . . For the first time we saw ourselves possessed of immense surpluses of ships of certain classes, of trained men and of naval supplies of all kinds, and were in a position to use them to the best advantage.[30]

ABBREVIATIONS

ADM	Records of the Admiralty
CAB	Records of the Cabinet
CHAR	Winston Churchill Papers, Churchill Archives Centre, Churchill College, Cambridge
CO	Records of the Colonial Office
FISR	Fisher Papers, Churchill Archives Centre, Churchill College, Cambridge
FO	Records of the Foreign Office
Harcourt MSS	Lewis Harcourt manuscripts collection, Bodleian Library, Oxford
Asquith MSS	Asquith Manuscripts, Bodleian Library, Oxford University
NA	National Archives, United Kingdom
PRO	Public Records Office
WO	Records of the War Office

NOTES

INTRODUCTION

1. Sir Edward Grey (speech, Parliament, House of Commons, London, August 3, 1914).
2. Avner Offer, *The First World War: An Agrarian Interpretation* (Oxford: Clarendon Press, 1989), 217–23.
3. Royal Commission on the Supply of Food and Raw Material in Time of War, "The Report of the Royal Commission on the Supply of Food and Raw Material in Time of War," *Economic Journal* 15 (December 1905): 610–11.
4. Daniel Yergin, *The Prize: The Epic Quest for Oil, Money, and Power* (New York: Simon and Schuster, 1991), 156.
5. Offer, *Agrarian Interpretation,* 83.
6. Winston Churchill, *World Crisis, 1911–1918* (New York: Free Press, 2005), 602.
7. J. M. Bourne, *Britain and the Great War, 1914–1918* (London: Edward Arnold, 1989), 6.
8. Yergin, *Prize,* 155–56 and 160.
9. Note by the Secretary, Maurice P. A. Hankey, Committee of Imperial Defence, in "Attack on the British Isles from Overseas," October 3, 1914, National Archives of the United Kingdom (NA): Public Records Office (PRO), Records of the Cabinet (CAB) 38/28, no. 44, Kew.
10. Alfred Thayer Mahan, *Naval Strategy Compared and Contrasted with the Principles and Practice of Military Operations on Land* (Boston: Little, Brown and Co., 1911), 198–99.
11. F. J. Moberly, *Military Operations: Togoland and the Cameroons, 1914–1916,* History of the Great War (London: Longmans, Green and Co., 1931), 3.

12. For a general discussion of the disadvantages of these various options, see Brian Ranft, "The Protection of British Seaborne Trade," in *Technical Change and British Naval Policy, 1860–1939,* ed. Bryan Ranft (New York: Holmes and Meier, 1977), 5–6.
13. Yergen, *Prize,* 150–73, general discussion.
14. Holger H. Herwig, *"Luxury" Fleet: The Imperial German Navy, 1888–1918* (London: Allen and Unwin, 1980), 36–37.
15. Julian Corbett, *To the Battle of the Falklands, December 1914,* vol. 1, *Naval Operations,* History of the Great War (London: Longmans, Green and Co., 1920), 132.
16. Moberly, *Togoland and the Cameroons,* 2–3.
17. "Operations in the Union of South Africa and German South West Africa," Lewis Harcourt manuscripts, 508:48, Bodleian Library, Oxford (hereafter Harcourt MSS); "Operations against Samoa," Harcourt MSS, 508:175; "Operations against the German Possessions in New Guinea and the Bismarck Archipelago," Harcourt MSS, 508:187; Lewis Harcourt to Governor-General of Australia Ronald Ferguson, telegram, August 6, 1914, 7:30 p.m., NA: PRO Records of the Colonial Office (CO) 616/1, no. 31; Lewis Harcourt to the Officer Administering the Union of South Africa, John H. de Villiers, telegram, August 6, 1914, 6:35 p.m., NA: PRO CO 616/10, no. 5; Lewis Harcourt to Governor of New Zealand, telegram, August 6, 1914, 7:15 p.m., NA: PRO CO 616/14, no. 4.
18. A. J. Barker, *The Bastard War: The Mesopotamian Campaign of 1914–1918* (New York: Dial Press, 1967), 35.
19. Moberly, *Togoland and the Cameroons,* 11–17.
20. Ibid., 71.
21. Byron Farwell, *The Great War in Africa, 1914–1918* (New York: W. W. Norton, 1986), 77.
22. S. S. Mackenzie, *The Australians at Rabaul: The Capture and Administration of the German Possessions in the Southern Pacific,* The Official History of Australia in the War of 1914–1918 (Sydney: Angus and Robertson, 1942), 5–6.
23. Ibid., 79.
24. Hew Strachan, *The First World War,* vol. 1, *To Arms* (Oxford: Oxford University Press, 2001), 456–59.
25. Wolfgang Wegener, *The Naval Strategy of the World War,* trans. and ed. by Holger H. Herwig (Annapolis: Naval Institute Press, 1989), 151–54.
26. Corbett, *To the Battle of the Falklands,* 132.
27. Ibid., 132.
28. Ibid., 402.
29. Michael Howard, *The First World War* (Oxford: Oxford University Press, 2002), v.
30. Ibid., 49–50.
31. James L. Stokesbury, *A Short History of World War I* (New York: William Morrow, 1981), 181–82.

32. David French, *British Strategy and War Aims, 1914–1916* (London: Allen and Unwin, 1986), 27.
33. Ibid., 27–28.
34. Strachan, *First World War*, 694.
35. Ibid., 695.
36. Niall Ferguson, *Pity of War* (New York: Basic Books, 1999), 444.
37. Ibid., 442.

CHAPTER 1. THE BRITISH EMPIRE'S DEPENDENCE ON GLOBAL TRADE IN 1914

1. Avner Offer, *The First World War: An Agrarian Interpretation* (Oxford: Clarendon Press, 1989) 218; Angus Ross, "Losing the Initiative in Mercantile Warfare: Great Britain's Surprising Failure to Anticipate Maritime Challenges to Her Global Trading Network in the First World War," *International Journal of Naval History* 1 (April 2002); Andrew Lambert, "Economic Power, Technological Advantage, and Imperial Strength: Britain as a Unique Global Power, 1860–1890," *International Journal of Naval History* 5 (August 2006).
2. Paul M. Kennedy, *The Rise and Fall of British Naval Mastery* (New York: Scribner, 1976), 206; Nicholas A. Lambert, "Transformation and Technology in the Fisher Era: The Impact of the Communications Revolution," *Journal of Strategic Studies* 27 (June 2004): 285; Lambert, "Economic Power, Technological Advantage, and Imperial Strength."
3. C. Ernest Fayle, *Seaborne Trade*, vol. 1, *The Cruiser Period,* History of the Great War Based on Official Documents (London: John Murray, 1920), 5; Offer, *First World War,* 83.
4. Royal Commission on the Supply of Food and Raw Material in Time of War, "The Report of the Royal Commission on the Supply of Food and Raw Material in Time of War," *Economic Journal* 15 (December 1905): 610–11.
5. Ibid., 613; Offer, *First World War,* 346.
6. R. J. Hammond, "British Food Supplies, 1914–1939," *Economic History Review* 16 (1946): 2.
7. Ibid., 3.
8. Offer, *First World War,* 346.
9. Ibid., 4.
10. Standing Subcommittee of the Committee of Imperial Defence, "Supplies in Time of War," February 28, 1914, NA: PRO CAB 63/2.
11. Ibid., 4, table (A).
12. M. E. Falkus, "Russia and the International Wheat Trade, 1861–1914," *Economica* 33 (November 1966): 11.

13. Standing Subcommittee, "Supplies in Time of War," 5, table (B).
14. Royal Commission, "Supply of Food and Raw Material in Time of War," 609.
15. Ibid., 609–10.
16. Board of Trade, "The Threatened Shortage of Pit Timber," January 11, 1915, Parliamentary Archives, Lloyd George Papers, LG/C/25/4/4; Offer, *First World War,* 81.
17. Standing Subcommittee, "Supplies in Time of War," 6, table (C).
18. A. W. Flux, "British Export Trade," *Economic Journal* 36 (December 1926): 551.
19. Ibid., 553; T. J. Hatton, "The Demand for British Exports, 1870–1913," *Economic History Review* 43 (November 1990): 577–79.
20. Hatton, "Demand for British Exports," 579.
21. Flux, "British Export Trade," 554.
22. H. H. O'Farrell, "British and German Export Trade before the War," *Economic Journal* 26 (June 1916): 164.
23. Hatton, "Demand for British Exports," 579.
24. Flux, "British Export Trade," 555–56.
25. F. W. Taussig, "The Change in Great Britain's Foreign Trade Terms after 1900," *Economic Journal* 35 (March 1925): 4, table, "Foreign Trade of the United Kingdom, 1880–1913."
26. Fayle, *Seaborne Trade,* 2–3.
27. Taussig, "Great Britain's Foreign Trade," 7–8.
28. Fayle, *Seaborne Trade,* 5.
29. Ibid., 26–29.
30. Ibid., 10.
31. Paul M. Kennedy, *The Rise and Fall of the Great Powers: Economic Change and Military Conflict* (New York: Vintage Books, 1989), 230.
32. Fayle, *Seaborne Trade,* 8. See also a general discussion of the trade balance and credit in Halford J. Mackinder, *Britain and the British Seas* (London: Henry Frowde, 1904), 342–48.
33. J. A. Salter, *Allied Shipping Control: An Experiment in International Administration,* Economic and Social History of the World War (Oxford: Clarendon Press, 1921), 7–8, table "Principle Sea Tonnage in Midsummer 1914."
34. Fayle, *Seaborne Trade,* 9–11.
35. Salter, *Allied Shipping Control,* 9–10.
36. Ibid.; Fayle, *Seaborne Trade,* 8.
37. Salter, *Allied Shipping Control,* 13.
38. Ibid., 12.
39. Ibid., 14.
40. Fayle, *Seaborne Trade,* 9–10.
41. Colonial Defence Committee, "Principles of Imperial Defence," July 8, 1910, NA: PRO CAB 38/16/13. In 1911, this committee would be renamed the Overseas Defence Committee.

42. Paul M. Kennedy, "Imperial Cable Communications and Strategy, 1870–1914," *English Historical Review* 86 (October 1971): 729–30.
43. Ibid.
44. Ibid., 738.
45. Ibid., 740–41.
46. Nicholas A. Lambert, "Strategic Command and Control for Maneuver Warfare: Creation of the Royal Navy's 'War Room' System, 1905–1915," *Journal of Military History* 69 (April 2005): 372.
47. R. Henning, "Die deutsche Seekabelpolitik zur Befreiung vom englischen Weltmonopol," *Meereskunde,* no. 6 (Jahrgang, Heft 4), quoted in Kennedy, "Imperial Cable Communications," 748.
48. Bobbie Johnson, "U.S. Relinquishes Control of the Internet," *Guardian,* September 30, 2009.
49. Kennedy, "Imperial Cable Communications," 738–39.
50. Lambert, "Strategic Command and Control," 363; Standing Subcommittee of the Committee of Imperial Defence, "Submarine Cable Communications in Time of War," December 11, 1911, NA: PRO CAB 38/19/56.
51. Kennedy, "Imperial Cable Communications," 740.
52. Ibid., 742.
53. Ibid., 743.
54. Ibid., 743–44.
55. Standing Subcommittee, "Submarine Cable Communications," NA: PRO CAB 38/19/56.
56. Ibid.
57. Report of the Standing Subcommittee for the Committee of Imperial Defence, "The Maintenance of Overseas Commerce in Time of War," February 3, 1913, NA: PRO CAB 38/23/8.
58. Nicholas A. Lambert, "Transformation and Technology in the Fisher Era: the Impact of the Communications Revolution," *Journal of Strategic Studies* 27 (June 2004): 274.
59. Ibid., 282; Lambert, "Strategic Command and Control," 379.
60. Lambert, "Strategic Command and Control," 374.
61. George S. Clarke, "Wireless Telegraphy and the Berlin Conference: Note by the Secretary," July 24, 1906, NA: PRO CAB 38/12/47.
62. Lambert, "Strategic Command and Control," 374.
63. Ibid., 379.
64. Ibid.
65. Lambert, "Transformation and Technology," 284.
66. Norman Friedman, *Network Centric Warfare: How Navies Leaned to Fight Smarter through Three World Wars* (Annapolis: Naval Institute Press, 2009), 24.
67. Lambert, "Strategic Command and Control," 380.

68. Lambert, "Transformation and Technology," 282.
69. Lambert, "Strategic Command and Control," 372.
70. Lambert, "Transformation and Technology," 283; "Methods of Passing Intelligence of Hostile Raids to the Admiralty and War Office," December 23, 1913, NA: PRO CAB 38/25/41; Colonial Defence Committee, "Principles of Imperial Defence," NA: PRO CAB 38/16/13.
71. Lambert, "Strategic Command and Control," 381.
72. Lambert, "Transformation and Technology," 283.
73. Standing Subcommittee, "The Maintenance of Overseas Commerce," NA: PRO CAB 38/23/8.
74. Fayle, *Seaborne Trade,* 29.
75. Ibid., 26; Standing Subcommittee, "The Maintenance of Overseas Commerce," NA: PRO CAB 38/23/8.
76. Colonial Defence Committee, "Principles of Imperial Defence," NA: PRO CAB 38/16/13.
77. Ibid.; Lambert, "Transformation and Technology," 274.
78. Lambert, "Strategic Command and Control," 310, 376.
79. Lambert, "Transformation and Technology," 278–79.
80. Ibid., 276.
81. Ibid., 284.
82. Ibid., 286.
83. Committee of Imperial Defence, "Probable Scales of Attack against Oversea British Ports," April 21, 1914, NA: PRO CAB 38/26/14; Colonial Defence Committee, "Principles of Imperial Defence," NA: PRO CAB 38/16/13.
84. Paul Halpern, "The War at Sea," in *World War I: A History,* ed. Hew Strachan (Oxford: Oxford University Press, 1998), 104.

CHAPTER 2. GERMAN FOREIGN POLICY, 1880 TO 1914

1. Winston Churchill, *World Crisis, 1911–1918* (London: Charles Scribner's Sons, 1931), 7.
2. Wolfgang Petter, "Deutsche Flottenrüstung von Wallenstein bis Tirpitz," in Wolfgang Petter, Rolf Güth, and Jost Dülffer, *Deutsche Marinegeschichte der Neuzeit,* vol. 8, *Handbuch zu deutschen Militärgeschichte, 1648–1939* (Munich: Bernard and Graefe, 1977), 155.
3. W. O. Henderson, *The German Colonial Empire, 1884–1919* (London: Frank Cass, 1993), 39.
4. W. A. Crabtree, "German Colonies in Africa," *Journal of the Royal African Society* 14, no. 53 (October 1914): 9; Kaiserliche Marine, "History of SMS *Nautilus* (1)," http://www.kaiserliche-marine.de.
5. Kaiserliche Marine, "History of SMS *Elisabeth,*" http://www.kaiserliche-marine.de.
6. Herbert Paul Meritt, "Bismarck and the First Partition of East Africa," *English Historical Review* 91 (July 1976): 587–88, 595.

7. Herbert Paul Meritt, "Bismarck and the German Interest in East Africa, 1884–1885," *Historical Journal* 21 (March 1978): 112; "The So-called Helgoland-Zanzibar Treaty of 1890," http://www.deutsche-schutzgebiete.de/helgoland.htm.
8. Crabtree, "German Colonies in Africa," 9.
9. William Churchill, "Germany's Lost Pacific Empire," *Geographical Review* 10 (August 1920): 84–90.
10. Robert K. Massie, *Dreadnought: Britain, Germany, and the Coming of the Great War* (New York: Ballantine Books, 1991), 99.
11. Hartmut Pogge von Strandmann, "Domestic Origins of Germany's Colonial Expansion under Bismarck," *Past and Present,* no. 42 (February 1969): 158; Ieuan Griffiths, "The Scramble for Africa: Inherited Political Boundaries," *Geographical Journal* 152 (July 1986): 211; G. N. Sanderson, "The Anglo-German Agreement of 1890 and the Upper Nile," *English Historical Review* 78 (January 1963): 64–70; Paul M. Kennedy, "The Development of German Naval Operations Plans against England, 1896–1914," *English Historical Review* 89 (January 1974): 48.
12. Petter, "Deutsche Flottenrüstung," 154–57; Alfred von Tirpitz, *My Memoirs* (New York: Dodd, Mead, 1919), 1:77.
13. Paul M. Kennedy, "German World Policy and the Alliance Negotiations with England, 1897–1900," *Journal of Modern History* 45 (December 1973): 606; Fritz Fischer, *Germany's Aims in the First World War* (New York: W. W. Norton, 1967), 20–21; Petter "Deutsche Flottenrüstung," 164–66.
14. John C. G. Röhl, "Admiral von Müller and the Approach of War, 1911–1914," *Historical Journal* 12, no. 4 (1969): 653–56; Tirpitz, *My Memoirs,* 1:89; Kennedy, "Development of German Naval Operations Plans," 49–50.
15. Kennedy, "German World Policy," 608; Tirpitz, *My Memoirs,* 1:121–22.
16. Kennedy, "Development of German Naval Operations Plans," 75; Tirpitz, *My Memoirs,* 1:89.
17. Alfred Thayer Mahan, *The Influence of Sea Power upon History, 1660–1783,* 12th ed. (Boston: Little, Brown and Company, 1918), 136–38.
18. Tirpitz, *My Memoirs,* 1:121; Fischer, *Germany's Aims,* 18.
19. Kennedy, "Development of German Naval Operations Plans," 54–55.
20. Herbert Rosinski, *The Development of Naval Thought: Essays by Herbert Rosinski,* ed. B. Mitchell Simpson III (Newport, RI: Naval War College Press, 1977), 29; Holger H. Herwig, *"Luxury" Fleet: The Imperial German Navy, 1888—1918* (London: Allen and Unwin, 1980), 92 and 139.
21. Tirpitz, *My Memoirs,* 1:159–60; Rosinski, *Development of Naval Thought,* 54–55; Kennedy, "Development of German Naval Operations Plans," 55; Herwig, *Luxury Fleet,* 91.
22. Kennedy, "German World Policy," 608–13; Tirpitz, *My Memoirs,* 1:133–34.
23. Tirpitz, *My Memoirs,* 1:88–89; Petter, "Deutsche Flottenrüstung,"145–47.
24. Colonial Defence Committee, "Principles of Imperial Defence," July 8, 1910, TNO: PRO CAB 38/16/13.

25. James Arthur Salter, *Allied Shipping Control: An Experiment in International Administration* (Oxford: Clarendon Press, 1921), 8.
26. C. Ernest Fayle, *Seaborne Trade*, vol. 1, *The Cruiser Period,* History of the Great War Based on Official Documents (London: John Murray, 1920), 11.
27. Alfred Thayer Mahan, *Naval Strategy Compared and Contrasted with the Principles and Practice of Military Operations on Land* (Boston: Little, Brown and Co., 1911), 250.
28. Tirpitz, *My Memoirs,* 1:159; Churchill, *World Crisis,* 10.
29. Tirpitz, *My Memoirs,* 1:76, 118–20 and 162.
30. Terrell D. Gottschall, *By Order of the Kaiser: Otto von Diederichs and the Rise of the Imperial German Navy, 1865–1902* (Annapolis: Naval Institute Press, 2003), 134.
31. Ibid., 136–62; Tirpitz, *My Memoirs,* 1:90.
32. Gottschall, *By Order of the Kaiser*, 136–62.
33. R. W. Seton-Watson, *Britain in Europe, 1789–1914* (Cambridge: Cambridge University Press, 1938), 582; Paul M. Kennedy, *The Rise of the Anglo-German Antagonism, 1860–1914* (London: George Allen and Unwin, 1980), 234.
34. J. A. Cramb, *German and England* (New York: E. P. Dutton, 1914), 50–51; R. B. Mowat, "Great Britain and Germany in the Early Twentieth Century," *English Historical Review* 46 (July 1931): 423; Kennedy, "German World Policy," 612–13.
35. Kennedy, "German World Policy," 608; Kennedy, *Rise of the Anglo-German Antagonism,* 412; Tirpitz, *My Memoirs,* 1:244.
36. Tirpitz, *My Memoirs,* 1:233–34 and 254–62; Kennedy, "Development of German Naval Operations Plans," 55; Petter, "Deutsche Flottenrüstung," 255.
37. Kennedy, "German World Policy," 611.
38. Fischer, *Germany's Aims,* 20, and 24.
39. Tirpitz, *My Memoirs,* 1:269–70.
40. John H. Maurer, "The Anglo-German Naval Rivalry and Informal Arms Control, 1912–1914," *Journal of Conflict Resolution* 36 (June 1992): 287; Tirpitz, *My Memoirs,* 1:155–62.
41. Seton-Watson, *Britain in Europe,* 586; Murrell Marris, *Right Honorable Joseph Chamberlain: The Man and the Statesman,* 2nd ed. (New York: E. P. Dutton, 1900), 366–67; Kennedy, *Rise of the Anglo-German Antagonism,* 239; Tirpitz, *My Memoirs,* 1:158–59.
42. Kennedy, *Rise of the Anglo-German Antagonism,* 236; Fischer, *Germany's Aims,* 38–39; Tirpitz, *My Memoirs,* 1:287.
43. Kennedy, "German World Policy," 618–19; Tirpitz, *My Memoirs,* 1:159–60, and 221.
44. Röhl, "Müller and the Approach of War," 656; Seton-Watson, *Britain in Europe,* 587; Kennedy, *Rise of the Anglo-German Antagonism,* 243–46; Tirpitz, *My Memoirs,* 1:290–91.
45. Seton-Watson, *Britain in Europe,* 587; Kennedy, *Rise of the Anglo-German Antagonism,* 243–46; Petter, "Deutsche Flottenrüstung," 238–39.

46. Fischer, *Germany's Aims,* 21.
47. "Declaration between the United Kingdom and France Respecting Egypt and Morocco, Together with the Secret Articles Signed at the Same Time, 8 April 1904," Parliamentary Papers, London, Cd. 5969 (1911); Eugene N. Anderson, *The First Moroccan Crisis, 1904–1906* (Hamden: Archon Books, 1966), 88–92.
48. Massie, *Dreadnought,* 353–56; Churchill, *World Crisis,* 18.
49. Massie, *Dreadnought,* 357–59; Anderson, *First Moroccan Crisis,* 397.
50. Anderson, *First Moroccan Crisis,* 219 and 230.
51. "Declaration between United Kingdom and France," Cd. 5969.
52. Churchill, *World Crisis,* 19.
53. Massie, *Dreadnought,* 364–67.
54. Tirpitz, *My Memoirs,* 1:276; Churchill, *World Crisis,*19; Anderson, *First Moroccan Crisis,* 397–405.
55. Germany Navy "German Hochseeflotte, Battleships," http://www.german-navy.de/hochseeflotte/ships/battleships/index.html.
56. Tirpitz, *My Memoirs,* 1:262–68; Churchill, *World Crisis,* 24; Herwig, *Luxury Fleet,* 69–71; Samuel P. Huntington, "Arms Races: Prerequisites and Results," *Public Policy: The Yearbook of the Graduate School of Public Administration, Harvard University,* ed. Carl J. Friedrich and Seymour E. Harris (Cambridge, MA: Harvard University Press, 1958), reprinted in Richard K. Betts, ed., *Conflict after the Cold War: Argument on Causes of War and Peace,* 2nd ed. (New York: Pearson Longman, 2005), 372.
57. Fischer, *Germany's Aims,* 26; Mowat, "Great Britain and Germany," 426.
58. Fischer, *Germany's Aims,* 23; Churchill, *World Crisis,* 21–22.
59. Churchill, *World Crisis,* 21–22.
60. Ibid.; Fischer, *Germany's Aims,* 22.
61. Churchill, *World Crisis,* 22.
62. Data derived from German Navy, "German Hockseeflotte," http://www.german-navy.de/hochseeflotte/ships/battleships/index.html.
63. Ima Christina Barlow, *The Agadir Crisis* (Chapel Hill: University of North Carolina Press, 1940), 169–70.
64. Foreign Office in London to Ambassador in Berlin, telegram, July 21, 1911, no. 164, NA: PRO CAB 37/107/81.
65. Barlow, *Agadir Crisis,* 123–52, 217–18.
66. Ibid., 235; F. Bertie to Edward Grey, telegram, July 9, 1911, no. 92, NA: PRO CAB 37/107/75.
67. Edward Grey to Foreign Office [for Prime Minister?], memorandum, August 9, 1911, no. 86, NA: PRO CAB 37/107/102; Edward Grey to Foreign Office [for Prime Minister?], telegram, September 4, 1911, no. 242, NA: PRO CAB 37/107/106; Barlow, *Agadir Crisis,* 232; Churchill, *World Crisis,* 26; Tirpitz, *My Memoirs,* 1:275.

68. Herwig, *Luxury Fleet,* 73; Röhl, "Müller and the Approach of War," 653.
69. Fischer, *Germany's Aims,* 25; Tirpitz, *My Memoirs,* 1:275–76.
70. Churchill, *World Crisis,* 26–27.
71. Foreign Office in London to Ambassador in Berlin, telegram, July 21, 1911, no. 164, NA: PRO CAB 37/107/81; Churchill, *World Crisis,* 26–27; Barlow, *Agadir Crisis,* 218.
72. Paul G. Halpern, *A Naval History of World War I* (Annapolis: Naval Institute Press, 1994), 8 and 19; Petter, "Deutsche Flottenrüstung," 255.
73. Halpern, *Naval History,* 29.
74. Ibid., 31; Röhl, "Müller and the Approach of War," 655.
75. Churchill, *World Crisis,* 34.
76. Herwig, *Luxury Fleet,* 73–74; Röhl, "Müller and the Approach of War," 654; Tirpitz, *My Memoirs,* 1:277–82.
77. Edward Grey to F. Bertie, memorandum, February 7, 1912, no. 58, NA: PRO CAB 37/109/16; Röhl, "Müller and the Approach of War," 656–57; Massie, *Dreadnought,* 800–805; Frederick Maurice, *Haldane, 1856–1915: The Life of Viscount Haldane of Cloan,* vol. 1 (Westport, CT: Greenwood Press, 1970), 291–92; Röhl, "Müller and the Approach of War," 657–58.
78. Massie, *Dreadnought,* 810–12; Churchill, *World Crisis,* 60–62; Maurice, *Haldane,* 1:295 and 309–314; Tirpitz, *My Memoirs,* 1:282–96.
79. Churchill, *World Crisis,* 61.
80. Massie, *Dreadnought,* 820; Tirpitz, *My Memoirs,* 1:294.
81. Churchill, *World Crisis,* 62–63; Massie, *Dreadnought,* 812–14; Tirpitz, *My Memoirs,* 1:277–78.
82. Churchill, *World Crisis,* 62–63; Massie, *Dreadnought,* 815–16; Maurice, *Haldane,* 1:299; Röhl, "Müller and the Approach of War," 658; Fischer, *Germany's Aims,* 27.
83. Massie, *Dreadnought,* 816–17.
84. Churchill, *World Crisis,* 64; Massie, *Dreadnought,* 829–30; Tirpitz, *My Memoirs,* 1:305–6.
85. R. J. Crampton, *The Hollow Détente: Anglo-German Relations in the Balkans, 1911–1914* (London: George Prior Publishers; Atlantic Highlands, NJ: Humanitarian Press, 1979?), 171–72; Fischer, *Germany's Aims,* 31.
86. Ivo Nikolai Lambi, *The Navy and German Power Politics* (Boston: Allen and Unwin, 1984), 392–98.
87. Kennedy, "Development of German Naval Operations Plans," 75.
88. Lambi, *Navy and German Power Politics,* 392–98.
89. Mowat, "Great Britain and Germany," 428; Maurice, *Haldane,* 316–19; Fischer, *Germany's Aims,* 40–41.
90. Fischer, *Germany's Aims,* 53.
91. Massie, *Dreadnought,* 848; Tirpitz, *My Memoirs,* 1:306.
92. Sean M. Lynn-Jones, "Détente and Deterrence: Anglo-German Relations, 1911–1914," *International Security* 11 (Autumn 1986): 141; Fischer, *Germany's Aims,* 58.

93. Massie, *Dreadnought,* 827.
94. Henderson, *German Colonial Empire,* 103; S. S. MacKenzie, *The Australians at Rabaul: The Capture and Administration of the German Possessions in the Southern Pacific,* Official History of Australia in the War of 1914–18, vol. 10 (Sidney: Angus and Robertson, 1927), 2–5.
95. John Walter, *The Kaiser's Pirates: German Surface Raiders in World War One* (Annapolis: Naval Institute Press, 1994), 35.
96. MacKenzie, *Australians at Rabaul,* 5.
97. Lambi, *Navy and German Power Politics,* 408–11; Kurt Aßmann, ed., *Die Kämpfe der Kaiserlichen Marine in den Deutchen Kolonienm,* Der Krieg zur See 1914–1918 (Berlin: E. S. Mittler, 1935), 1–7.
98. Lambi, *Navy and German Power Politics,* 408–11; Aßmann, *Kämpfe der Kaiserlichen Marine,*132–34.
99. Lambi, *Navy and German Power Politics,* 408–11.
100. Ibid.
101. Tirpitz, *My Memoirs,* 2:85–87.
102. Walter, *Kaiser's Pirates,* 35; Rolf Güth, "Die Organisation der deutschen Marine in Krieg und Frieden, 1913–1933," in *Deutsche Marinegeschichte der Neuzeit,* vol. 8, *Handbuch zu deutschen Militärgeschichte, 1648–1939* (Munich: Bernard and Graefe, 1977), 299; Fritz Otto Busch and Georg Günter Freiherr von Forstner, *Unsere Marine im Weltkrieg* (Berlin: Brunnen-Verlag, Willi Bischoff, 1934), 231–33.
103. Ernst Bischoff, *Die Leistungen der deutschen Flotte im Weltkrieg (The Performance of the German Fleet in the World War)* (Zurich: Orell Füssli, 1918), 37–38.

CHAPTER 3. THE BRITISH RESPOND TO GERMAN POWER

1. Ellery C. Stowell, *The Diplomacy of the War of 1914: The Beginnings of the War* (Boston and New York: Houghton Mifflin, 1915), 7–9.
2. R. P. Dua, *Anglo-Japanese Relations during the First World War* (New Delhi: S. Chand and Co., 1972), 29–30.
3. Dua, *Anglo-Japanese Relations,* 44.
4. Ibid., 38–41; Massie, *Dreadnought,* 339.
5. Henry Lansdowne and Hayashi Tadasu, "The Anglo-Japanese Alliance, January 30, 1902," Japanese Center for Asian Historical Records, http://www.jacar.go.jp/nichiro/uk-japan.htm.
6. Ibid.
7. Ian Nish, "Politics, Trade and Communications in East Asia: Thoughts on Anglo-Russian Relations, 1861–1907," *Modern Asian Studies* 21, no. 4 (1987): 677.
8. Jon Tetsuro Sumida, "Geography, Technology, and British Naval Strategy in the Dreadnought Era," *Naval War College Review* 59, no. 3 (2006): 92.
9. Kennedy, *Rise and Fall of the Great Powers: Economic Change and Military Conflict* (New York: Vintage Books, 1989), 251.

10. Ibid., 251–54; Winston Churchill, *World Crisis, 1911–1918* (New York: Free Press, 2005), 11.
11. Jon Tetsoro Sumida, "Geography, Technology, and British Naval Strategy in the Dreadnought Era," *Naval War College Review* 59 (2006): 92.
12. Beryl J. Williams, "The Strategic Background to the Anglo-Russian Entente of August 1907," *Historical Journal* 9, no. 3 (1966): 362–63.
13. Ibid., 369.
14. Ibid., 362.
15. John P. MacKintosh, "The Role of the Committee of Imperial Defence before 1914," *English Historical Review* 77, no. 304 (July 1962): 493–94, 502–3; Maurice P. Hankey, *The Supreme Command, 1914–1918* (London: George Allen and Unwin, 1961), 45–50.
16. Committee of Imperial Defence, "Probable Scales of Attack against Overseas British Ports," April 21, 1914, NA: PRO CAB 38/26/14; Colonial Defence Committee, "Principles of Imperial Defence," NA: PRO CAB 38/16/13; Winston Churchill, Admiralty, "Notes by the First Lord of the Admiralty on Overseas Attacks from Germany," April 18, 1913, NA: PRO CAB 37/115/24.
17. Williams, "Strategic Background to the Anglo-Russian Entente," 373.
18. Ibid., 371–72.
19. "1905 Anglo Japanese Renewal," http://navalhistory.flixco.info/H/180236x54372/8330/a0.htm.
20. "Agreement Concerning Persia August 31, 1907," http://www.gwpda.org/1914m/anglruss.html; also at Parliamentary Papers, London, vol. 125, Cd. 3750 (1908).
21. See Ministerial Declaration in "Abridged Text of the Triple Alliance, May 20, 1882," http://www.firstworldwar.comsource/triplealliance.htm; Bernadotte E. Schmitt, "Triple Alliance and Triple Entente, 1902–1914," *American Historical Review* 29, no. 3 (April 1924): 452.
22. Henry Wilson, "Appreciation of the Political and Military Situation in Europe," September 20, 1911, NA: PRO WO 106/47 E 2.26.
23. Churchill, *World Crisis,* 8.
24. Bryan Ranft, *Technical Change and British Naval Policy, 1860–1939* (New York: Holmes and Meier, 1977), 5.
25. Ranft, *Technical Change,* 8.
26. "Treaty between Her Majesty and the United States of America, for the Amicable Settlement of all Causes of Difference between the two Countries ("Alabama" Claims; Fisheries; Claims of Corporations, Companies or Private Individuals; Navigation of Rivers and Lakes; San Juan Water Boundary; and Rules Defining Duties of a Neutral Government during War), Signed at Washington, May 8, 1871" (hereafter Treaty of Washington, 1871), http://www.intfish.net/treaties/bilaterals/texts/can-usa/1871.htm.

27. "Encl. B, Short account of *Alabama;* Cruise and Remarks on Federal Efforts to Capture *Alabama,*" in "Functions of Armed Merchantile Cruisers on Trade Routes," April 14, 1914, NA: PRO ADM 1/8374/103.
28. Treaty of Washington, 1871, art. 6.
29. Ibid.
30. U.S. Department of State, "The *Alabama* Claims," http://future.state.gov/when/timeline/1861_timeline/alab_claims.html.
31. Committee of Imperial Defence, "The Hague Conference: Notes on Subjects Which Might be Raised by Great Britain or by Other Powers," October 26, 1905, NA: PRO CAB 38/10/76.
32. James Brown Scott, ed., *The Declaration of London: London International Naval Conference, 1908–1909* (London: Oxford University Press, 1919), 105.
33. Committee for Furthering the Ratification of the Declaration of London, "Statement of Committee Member on Why It Is Important to Create International Law Governing Rights of Merchants and Definitions of Contraband," NA: PRO FO 800/91/322–3.
34. Committee of Imperial Defence, "Overseas Commerce in War: Replies of the Chairman of the British Shipowners' Association and of the Chairman of Lloyd's to Two Questions Addressed to Them by Colonel Seely," May 1912, NA: PRO CAB 38/20/20.
35. Standing Subcommittee of the Committee of Imperial Defence, "Insurance of British Shipping in Time of War," April 30, 1914, NA: PRO CAB 38/27/16; Standing Subcommittee of the Committee of Imperial Defence, "Insurance of British Shipping in Time of War: Revised for Presentation to Parliament," April 30, 1914, NA: PRO CAB 38/27/17.
36. Standing Committee for the Committee of Imperial Defence, "Report of the Standing Committee for the Committee of Imperial Defence on Maintenance of Oversea Commerce in Time of War," February 3, 1913, NA: PRO CAB 38/23/8.
37. Committee of Imperial Defence, "Minutes from the 122d meeting of the Committee of Imperial Defence," February 6, 1913, NA: PRO CAB 38/23/9.
38. Ibid.
39. Ibid.
40. Ibid.
41. Winston Churchill, "Oil Fuel Supply for His Majesty's Navy," June 1913, NA: PRO CAB 37/115/39.
42. "Agreement Between the Anglo-Persian Oil Company and the Commissioners for Executing the Office of Lord High Admiral of the United Kingdom of Great Britain and Ireland," May 20, 1914, NA: PRO ADM 116/4668.
43. Nicholas A. Lambert, "Transformation and Technology in the Fisher Era: The Impact of the Communications Revolution," *Journal of Strategic Studies* 27 (June 2004): 277.

44. Nicholas A. Lambert, "Strategic Command and Control for Maneuver Warfare: Creation of the Royal Navy's 'War Room' System, 1905–1915," *Journal of Military History* 69 (April 2005): 369.
45. Ibid., 381.
46. Standing Subcommittee of the Committee of Imperial Defence, "Report of the Standing Subcommittee of the Committee of Imperial Defence on the Maintenance of Overseas Commerce in Time of War," February 3, 1913, NA: PRO CAB 38/23/8.
47. Lambert, "Strategic Command and Control," 382.
48. Ibid., 392.

CHAPTER 4. GREAT BRITAIN'S STRATEGIC OPTIONS IN THE COMING WAR

1. David Lloyd George, *War Memoirs of David Lloyd George,* vol. 1 (London: Ivor Nicholson and Watson, 1933), 59–60.
2. Ibid., 66.
3. Ibid., 72–73.
4. Ibid., 67.
5. James Brown Scott, "Lord Haldane's Diary of Negotiations between Germany and England in 1912," *American Journal of International Law* 12 (July 1918): 593.
6. Winston Churchill, *World Crisis, 1911–1918* (New York: Free Press, 2005), 29.
7. Sir Edward Grey, Foreign Secretary in London, to Sir E. Goschen, Ambassador in Berlin, telegram, July 29, 1914, no. 253, in George Peabody Gooch and Harold William Temperley, eds., *British Documents on the Origins of the War, 1898–1914* vol. 11 (London: Her Majesty's Stationery Office, 1926), item 286; a note at the end of the entry indicates that the telegram was drafted but not sent.
8. "Copies of the Treaty Relative to the Netherlands signed at London, Nov. 15, 1831 with translation, the Treaty Relative to the Netherlands and Belgium signed at London, April 19, 1839, and the Treaty Relative to the Grand Duchy of Luxemburg signed at London, May 11, 1867," printed August 4, 1870, Parliamentary Archives, Lloyd George Papers, LG/C/125/7/1.
9. Committee of Imperial Defence, *Belgian Neutrality in 1870,* July 1914, NA: PRO CAB 37/120/95.
10. Jonathan Steinberg, "A German Plan for the Invasion of Holland and Belgium, 1897," *Historical Journal* 6, no. 1 (1963): 107–8 and 119.
11. The Hague, "Chapter 1, The Rights and Duties of Neutral Powers," *Convention 5, Respecting the Rights and Duties of Neutral Powers and Persons in Case of War on Land,* October 18, 1907, http://www.icrc.org/ihl.nsf/FULL/200?OpenDocument.
12. Churchill, *World Crisis,* 96–97.
13. Sir E. Goschen to Sir Edward Grey, telegram, July 29, 1914, no. 102, Gooch and Temperley, *British Documents,* item 293.
14. Ibid.

15. Niall Ferguson, *The Pity of War* (New York: Basic Books, 1999), 46.
16. Ibid., 168–70 and 444.
17. Sir E. Goschen to Sir Edward Grey, telegram, July 29, 1914, no. 102, Gooch and Temperley, *British Documents,* item 293.
18. Harry F. Young, "The Misunderstanding of August 1, 1914," *Journal of Modern History* 48 (December 1976): 652–53 and 664.
19. Churchill, *World Crisis,* 104; James Brown Scott, "Proposed Neutrality of France and the Beginning of the War," *American Journal of International Law* 12 (April 1918): 376.
20. Committee of Imperial Defence, "The Violation of the Neutrality of Belgium during a Franco-German War," September 29, 1905, NA: PRO CAB 38/10/73.
21. Committee of Imperial Defence, "Our Position as Regards the Low Countries," August 8, 1907, NA: PRO CAB 18/24.
22. War Office, memorandum, October 1910, NA: PRO WO 106/47 E 2.20.
23. War Office, correspondence between the War Office and the Board of Trade concerning the effects of a blockade on the Triple Alliance, November 29, 1909, NA: PRO WO 106/47 E 2.7.
24. Henry Wilson, War Office, memorandum concerning England's position should Germany attack France, August 11, 1911, NA: PRO WO 106/47 E 2.23.
25. Ibid.
26. Ibid.
27. Churchill remarked how much he had learned from Henry Wilson about the strategic and military situation in Europe: Churchill, *World Crisis,* 33.
28. Ibid., 35–36.
29. Maurice Hankey, *The Supreme Command, 1914–1918* (London: George Allen and Unwin, 1961), 78–82.
30. Henry Wilson, War Office, "Appreciation of the Political and Military Situation in Europe," September 20, 1911, TNA: PRO WO 106/47 E 2.26. The paper also resides in the CID's bound records, printed in April 1912.
31. Ibid.
32. Ibid.
33. War Office, memoranda concerning British support to Denmark and Holland in the event of a war with Germany, NA: PRO WO 106/47 E 2.20; WO 106/47 E 2.22; WO 106/47 E 2.26; WO 106/47/16; WO 106/47/19; WO 106/47/22; NA: PRO CAB 18/24; CAB 38/10/73.
34. Lewis Harcourt to Herbert Gladstone, September 12, 1911, British Library, Viscount Gladstone Papers, vol. 13, ADD MSS 45997.
35. Hankey, *Supreme Command,* 78–82.
36. Standing Subcommittee for the Committee of Imperial Defence, *Coordination of Departmental Action on the Outbreak of War* (London: Her Majesty's Stationery Office, 1912), NA: PRO CAB 15/3; *Coordination of Departmental Action on the*

Outbreak of War, second annual report (London: Her Majesty's Stationery Office, 1913), NA: PRO CAB 15/4; *Coordination of Departmental Action on the Outbreak of War,* third annual report (London: Her Majesty's Stationery Office, 30 June 1914, printed 10 July 1914), NA: PRO CAB 15/5.

37. Herbert H. Asquith and Alexander Mackintosh, *Memories and Reflections, 1852–1927,* vol. 2 (Boston: Little, Brown, 1928), 12.
38. Ibid.
39. Herbert H. Asquith to Andrew Bonar Law, August 2, 1914, Parliamentary Archives, Bonar Law Papers, BL/34/3/3.
40. Henry Wilson, NA: PRO WO 106/47 E 2.23; David French, "Chapter 1, Allies, Rivals and Enemies: British Strategy and War Aims during the First World War," in *Britain and the First World War,* ed. John Turner (London: Unwin Hyman, 1988), 23.
41. Asquith, *Memories and Reflections,* 11–15.
42. Roy Pryce, "Italy and the Outbreak of the First World War," *Cambridge Historical Journal* 11, no. 2 (1954): 224.

CHAPTER 5. AVOIDING DEFEAT

1. Maurice Hankey, *The Supreme Command, 1914–1918* (London: Allen and Unwin, 1961), 94.
2. Admiralty, "Admiralty Notes," NA: PRO CAB/37/115/23.
3. Committee of Imperial Defence, "Minutes of the 126 Meeting of the Committee of Imperial Defence," May 14, 1914, NA: PRO CAB 38/27/23.
4. Ibid.
5. Admiralty, "Admiralty Notes," NA: PRO CAB/37/115/23.
6. Winston Churchill, *World Crisis, 1911–1918* (New York: Free Press, 2005), 286–87.
7. Winston Churchill to First Sea Lord, Admiral John Fisher, January 15, 1915, Fisher Papers (Henceforth FISR), Churchill Archives Centre, Churchill College, Cambridge, 1/18/920.
8. "Admiralty Notes," April 1913, NA: PRO CAB 37/115/23.
9. Wolfgang Petter, "Deutsche Flottenrüstung von Wallenstein bis Tirpitz," in Wolfgang Petter, Rolf Güth, and Jost Dülffer, *Deutsche Marinegeschichte der Neuzeit,* vol. 8, *Handbuch zu deutschen Militärgeschichte, 1648–1939* (Munich: Bernard and Graefe, 1977), 233–36.
10. Wolfgang Wegenger, *The Naval Strategy of the World War,* trans. Holger Herwig (Annapolis: Naval Institute Press, 1989,) xxii–xxiv.
11. Ibid., xxvii.
12. Ibid., 14.
13. Admiralty to Commander in Chief, Home Fleets, telegram, July 28, 1914, no. 270, Winston Churchill Papers (Henceforth CHAR), Churchill Archives Centre, Churchill College, Cambridge, United Kingdom, 13/36/35.

14. Admiralty to Vice Admirals for 2nd and 3rd Fleets, and Commander in Chief, Home Fleets, telegram, August 2, 1914, CHAR 13/36/37.
15. Admiralty to All Ships, telegram, August 4, 1914, CHAR 3/36/42.
16. Admiralty, "War Orders no. 1 (for War with Germany), to Commander in Chief, Home Fleets," December 31, 1913, NA: PRO ADM 137/818/2.
17. Julian S. Corbett, *Some Principles of Maritime Strategy* (1911, repr., Annapolis: Naval Institute Press, 1988), 184–86.
18. Admiralty, "War Orders no. 1 (for War with Germany), to Commander in Chief, Home Fleets," December 31, 1913, NA: PRO ADM 137/818/2.
19. Admiralty, "War Plans (War with Germany), Part I: General Instructions," April 14, 1914, NA: PRO ADM 137/818/7.
20. Paul Halpern, *A Naval History of World War I* (Annapolis: Naval Institute Press, 1994), 35.
21. Richard Hough, *Louis and Victoria: The Family History of the Mountbattens,* 2nd ed. (London: Weidenfeld and Nicolson, 1984), 317.
22. Vice Admiral Cecil Burney to Admiral John Fisher, November 8, 1914, FISR 1/16/836.
23. Strachan, *First World War,* vol. 1, *To Arms* (Oxford: Oxford University Press, 2001), 673.
24. Ulrich Trumpener, "Turkey's War," in *World War I: A History,* ed. Hew Strachan (Oxford: Oxford University Press, 1998), 80; Churchill, *World Crisis,* 276.
25. Churchill, *World Crisis,* 276; Strachan, *First World War,* 670 and 673.
26. Churchill, *World Crisis,* 276–77.
27. Trumpener, "Turkey's War," 80; Strachan, *First World War,* 676.
28. Churchill, *World Crisis,* 277; Strachan, *First World War,* 673.
29. Strachan, *First World War,* 673–74.
30. Ibid., 674–75; India Office, "Precis of Correspondence Regarding the Mesopotamia Expedition—Its Genesis and Development," NA: PRO WO 106/52.
31. Strachan, *First World War,* 688–89; Fischer, *Germany's Aims,* 126–27; Erich Georg Anton Sebastian von Falkenhayn, *The German General Staff and Its Decisions, 1914–1916* (New York: Dodd, Mead and Co., 1920), 53–57.
32. Churchill, *World Crisis,* 282–83.
33. Wegener, *Naval Strategy of the World War,* 56.
34. Churchill, "Oil Fuel Supply for His Majesty's Navy," June 1913, NA: PRO CAB 37/115/39.
35. Fritz Fischer, *Germany's Aims in the First World War* (New York: W. W. Norton, 1967), 127; Tirpitz Alfred von Tirpitz, *My Memoirs,* vol. 2 (New York: Dodd, Mead, 1919), 82.
36. Churchill, "Oil Fuel Supply for His Majesty's Navy," June 1913, NA: PRO CAB 37/115/39; James Brown Scott, *The Declaration of London: London International Naval Conference, 1908–1909* (London: Oxford University Press, 1919), 105;

"Laws of War: The Rights and Duties of Neutral Powers in Naval War (Hague 13), October 18, 1907," http://avalon.law.yale.edu/20th_century/hague13.asp.

37. Daniel Yergin, *The Prize: The Epic Quest for Oil, Money, and Power* (New York: Simon and Schuster, 1991), 173; Churchill, "Oil Fuel Supply," NA: PRO CAB 37/115/39.
38. Strachan, *First World War,* 687.
39. Ibid., 678; Churchill, *World Crisis,* 277.
40. Hankey, *Supreme Command,* 181.
41. Fischer, *Germany's Aims,* 127–28; Tirpitz, *My Memoirs,* 2:83–84.
42. Churchill, *World Crisis,* 285.
43. Ibid., 286; Wegener, *Naval Strategy of the World War,* 70.
44. Winston Churchill to Lord John A. Fisher, January 1, 1914, FISR 1/14/763; Lord Selborne to Lord Fisher, March 18, 1914, FISR 1/15/800; Captain S. S. Hall to Lord Fisher, April 26, 1914, FISR 1/15/803; Lord John A. Fisher "Memorandum to Prime Minister (Mr. Asquith) Before Meeting of the Committee of Imperial Defence Held on May 14, 1914," FISR 1/15/804.
45. Churchill to Fisher, January 1, 1914, FISR 1/14/763.
46. Standing Committee for the Committee of Imperial Defence, "Report of the Standing Committee for the Committee of Imperial Defence on Maintenance of Overseas Commerce in Time of War," February 3, 1913, NA: PRO CAB 38/23/8.
47. Rolf Güth, "Die Organisation der deutschen Marine in Krieg und Frieden, 1913–1933," in Petter, Güth, and Dülffer, *Deutsche Marinegeschichte der Neuzeit,* 8:299; Fritz Otto Busch and Georg Günter Freiherr von Forstner, *Unsere Marine im Weltkrieg* (Berlin: Brunnen-Verlag, Willi Bischoff, 1934), 231–33; Ernst Bischoff, *Die Leistungen der deutschen Flotte im Weltkrieg* (Zurich: Orell Füssli, 1918), 37–38; Falkenhayn, *German General,* 78; Tirpitz, *My Memoirs,* 2:83, 85–87; R. K. Lochner, *The Last Gentleman-of-War: The Raider Exploits of the Cruiser Emden,* trans. Thea and Harry Lindauer (Annapolis: Naval Institute Press, 1988), 48–50; Franz Joseph Hohenzollern, *Emden: My Experiences in SMS Emden* (London: Herbert Jenkins, 1928), 30–32.
48. Standing Committee, "Maintenance of Oversea Commerce in Time of War," February 3, 1913, NA: PRO CAB 38/23/8.
49. Committee of Imperial Defence, "Minutes from the 122d Meeting," NA: PRO CAB 38/23/9; David Lloyd George, "Statement on War Risks in House by Lloyd George," August 4, 1914, Asquith Manuscripts (henceforth Asquith MSS), Bodleian Library, Oxford University, United Kingdom, Asquith MSS 26, folio 5.
50. David Lloyd George, "Statement on War Risks in House by Lloyd George," MSS Asquith 26, folio 5.
51. Committee of Imperial Defence, "Minutes from the 122d Meeting," NA: PRO CAB 38/23/9.

52. Maurice P. A. Hankey and Sir John Simon to Prime Minister Asquith, August 1, 1914, Asquith MSS 25, fol. 201.
53. Ibid.
54. Winston Churchill, "War Standing Order for Vessels Engaged in the Protection of Trade and War Order for Cruiser Forces," memorandum, April 14, 1914, NA: PRO ADM 137/818/9.
55. Committee of Imperial Defence, "Minutes from the 122d Meeting," NA: PRO CAB 38/23/9.
56. Churchill, "Vessels Engaged in the Protection of Trade," NA: PRO ADM 137/818/9.
57. Ibid.
58. Committee of Imperial Defence, "Minutes from the 122d Meeting," NA: PRO CAB 38/23/9; James Arthur Salter, *Allied Shipping Control: An Experiment in International Administration* (Oxford: Clarendon Press, 1921), 8.
59. Churchill, "Vessels Engaged in the Protection of Trade," NA: PRO ADM 137/818/9.
60. Admiralty, "War Standing Orders for Vessels Employed in Protection of Trade," July 14, 1914, NA: PRO ADM 137/818/14.
61. Herbert H. Asquith to His Majesty, King George V, November 4, 1914, NA: PRO CAB 41/35/57.
62. Churchill, *World Crisis,* 240 and 286.
63. Ibid., 285–87.

CHAPTER 6. A STRATEGY EMERGES

1. Julian S. Corbett, *Some Principles of Maritime Strategy* (1911, repr, Annapolis: Naval Institute Press, 1988), 91, 224; Alfred Thayer Mahan, *The Influence of Sea Power upon History, 1660–1783,* 12th ed. (Boston: Little, Brown and Co., 1890), 398–99.
2. Corbett, *Principles of Maritime Strategy,* 157–58; Mahan, *Influence of Sea Power,* 15–18.
3. Carl von Clausewitz, *On War,* ed. and trans. Michael Howard and Peter Paret (Princeton: Princeton University Press, 1976), 357–59.
4. For a general discussion of this idea, see Corbett, *Principles of Maritime Strategy,* 239.
5. Winston Churchill to First Sea Lord, Admiral John Fisher, January 26, 1915, Fisher Papers, series 1, file 18, item 920, Churchill Archives Centre, Churchill College, Cambridge, UK (hereafter FISR 1/18/920).
6. Arthur J. Balfour, remarks about a conversation the previous night, note 170, August 5, 1914, Balfour Papers, Additional Collection of Manuscripts, 49724 (ADD MSS 49724), British Library, London.
7. Ibid.; Arthur Balfour to Richard B. Haldane, August 4, 1914, Bonar Law Papers, Parliamentary Archives, BL/34/3/8.

8. Arthur J. Balfour, remarks about a conversation the previous night, note 170, August 5, 1914, Balfour Papers, Additional Collection of Manuscripts, 49724 (ADD MSS 49724), British Library, London.
9. Nigel Hawkins, *The Starvation Blockades* (Barnsley: Leo Cooper, 2002), 25.
10. Committee of Imperial Defence, "Minutes from the 122d Meeting," NA: PRO CAB 38/23/9.
11. Corbett, *Principles of Maritime Strategy*, 270–76.
12. Mahan, *Influence of Sea Power*, 30–31.
13. Committee of Imperial Defence, "Proceedings of a Joint Naval and Military Subcommittee for the Consideration of Combined Operations in Foreign Territory," October 6, 1914, NA: PRO CAB 38/28/45.
14. Julian Corbett, *To the Battle of the Falklands, December 1914*, vol. 1, *Naval Operations*, History of the Great War (London: Longmans, Green and Co., 1920), 132.
15. Committee of Imperial Defence, "Combined Operations in Foreign Territory," NA: PRO CAB 38/28/45.
16. Ibid.
17. Prime Minister Henry H. Asquith to the Sovereign, George V, August 6, 1914, NA: PRO CAB 41/35/26.
18. Lewis Harcourt, "Operations in Togoland," Harcourt Manuscripts, series 508, page 27 (hereafter Harcourt MSS 508/27), Bodleian Library, Oxford.
19. Secretary of State for Colonies Lewis Harcourt to Officer Administering the Government of South Africa, telegram, August 6, 1914, NA: PRO CO 616/10/5; Lewis Harcourt, "Operations in the Union of South Africa and German Southwest Africa," Harcourt MSS 508/47; Secretary of State for the Colonies Lewis Harcourt to Governor of New Zealand, telegram, August 6, 1914, NA: PRO CO 616/14/4; Lewis Harcourt, "Operations against Samoa," Harcourt MSS 508/175; Secretary of State for the Colonies Lewis Harcourt to Governor General of Australia, telegram, August 6, 1914, NA: PRO CO 616/1/31; Lewis Harcourt, "Operations against the German Possessions in New Guinea and the Bismarck Archipelago and the Islands of Nauru, Yap, Angaur, and Feys," Harcourt MSS 508/186.
20. Harcourt, "Operations in the Union of South Africa and German Southwest Africa," Harcourt MSS 508/47.
21. Harcourt, "Operations against Samoa," Harcourt MSS 508/175.
22. Harcourt, "Operations against the German Possessions in New Guinea and the Bismarck Archipelago and the Islands of Nauru, Yap, Angaur, and Feys," Harcourt MSS 508/186.
23. Secretary of State for the Colonies Louis Harcourt to Governor General Commonwealth of Australia, telegram, August 18, 1914, Harcourt MSS 507/7/1.
24. Harcourt, "Operations in East Africa," Harcourt MSS 508/301.
25. Committee of Imperial Defence, "Combined Operations in Foreign Territory," NA: PRO CAB 38/28/45; Harcourt, "Operations in Nigeria and Cameroons," Harcourt MSS 508/218.

26. Harcourt, "Operations in Nigeria and Cameroons," Harcourt MSS 508/218.
27. Foreign Secretary Sir Edward Grey to British Ambassador at Tokyo, Japan, telegram, August 3, 1914, no. 36, NA: PRO FO 262/1161/47.
28. British Embassy, Tokyo, to Sir Edward Grey, telegram, August 2, 1914, no. 57, NA: PRO FO 262/1162/71.
29. British Embassy, Tokyo, to Sir Edward Grey, telegram, August 3, 1914, no. 58, NA: PRO FO 262/1162/72.
30. Foreign Secretary Sir Edward Grey to British Ambassador at Tokyo, Japan, telegram, August 6, 1914, no. 40, NA: PRO FO 262/1161/55.
31. British Embassy, Tokyo, to Sir Edward Grey, telegram, August 2, 1914, no. 58, NA: PRO FO 262/1162/72.
32. British Embassy, Tokyo, to Sir Edward Grey, telegram, August 8, 1914, no. 66, NA: PRO FO 262/1162/83.
33. Foreign Secretary Sir Edward Grey to British Ambassador at Tokyo, Japan, telegram, August 11, 1914, no. 46, NA: PRO FO 262/1161/65.
34. British Embassy, Tokyo, to Sir Edward Grey, telegram, August 8, 1914, no. 67, NA: PRO FO 262/1162/84.
35. Foreign Secretary Sir Edward Grey to British Ambassador at Tokyo, Japan, telegram, August 9, 1914, no. 44, NA: PRO FO 262/1161/63.
36. British Embassy, Tokyo, to Sir Edward Grey, telegram, August 7, 1914, no. 65, NA: PRO FO 262/1162/82.
37. Foreign Secretary Sir Edward Grey to British Ambassador at Tokyo, Japan, telegram, August 10, 1914, no. 43, NA: PRO FO 262/1161/62.
38. Foreign Secretary Sir Edward Grey to British Ambassador at Tokyo, Japan, telegram, August 10, 1914, no. 45, NA: PRO FO 262/1161/64; Foreign Secretary Sir Edward Grey to British Ambassador at Tokyo, Japan, telegram, August 11, 1914, no. 47, NA: PRO 262/1161/67–69; Foreign Secretary Sir Edward Grey to British Ambassador at Tokyo, Japan, telegram, August 14, 1914, no. 59, NA: PRO 262/1162/86–88.
39. British Embassy, Tokyo, to Sir Edward Grey, telegram, August 11, 1914, no. 75, NA: PRO FO 262/1162/95.
40. Foreign Secretary Sir Edward Grey to British Ambassador at Tokyo, Japan, telegram, August 11, 1914, no. 47, NA: PRO FO 262/1161/67–69.
41. Foreign Secretary Sir Edward Grey to British Ambassador at Tokyo, Japan, telegram, August 12, 1914, no. 49, NA: PRO FO 262/1161/73; Foreign Secretary Sir Edward Grey to British Ambassador at Tokyo, Japan, telegram, August 13, 1914, no. 55, NA: PRO FO 262/1161/81; Foreign Secretary Sir Edward Grey to British Ambassador at Tokyo, Japan, telegram, August 15, 1914, no. 63, NA: PRO FO 262/1161/92; Foreign Secretary Sir Edward Grey to British Ambassador at Tokyo, Japan, telegram, August 22, 1914, no. 70, NA: PRO FO 262/1161/100; Foreign Secretary Sir Edward Grey to British Ambassador at Tokyo, Japan, telegram, August 24, 1914, no. 91, NA: PRO FO 262/1161/124.

42. Foreign Secretary Sir Edward Grey to British Ambassador at Tokyo, Japan, telegram, August 16, 1914, no. 65, NA: PRO FO 262/1161/94.
43. Foreign Secretary Sir Edward Grey to British Ambassador at Tokyo, Japan, telegram, August 17, 1914, no. 686, NA: PRO FO 262/1161/97.
44. British Embassy, Tokyo, to Sir Edward Grey, telegram, August 17, 1914, no. 88, NA: PRO FO 262/1162/111.
45. British Embassy, Tokyo to Sir Edward Grey, telegram, August 18, 1914, no. 92, NA: PRO FO 262/1162/115; Takaaki Kato to British Ambassador at Tokyo, Japan, August 18, 1914, NA: PRO FO 262/1162/116; British Embassy, Tokyo, to Sir Edward Grey, telegram, August 19, 1914, no. 94, NA: PRO FO 262/1162/118; and British Embassy, Tokyo, to Sir Edward Grey, telegram, August 19, 1914, no. 95, NA: PRO FO 262/1162/120.
46. Foreign Secretary Sir Edward Grey to British Ambassador at Tokyo, Japan, telegram, August 21, 1914, no. 84, NA: PRO FO 262/1161/116 and FO 262/1161/117.
47. Foreign Secretary Sir Edward Grey to British Ambassador at Tokyo, Japan, telegram, September 2, 1914, no. 108, NA: PRO FO 262/1161/149.
48. British Embassy, Tokyo, to Sir Edward Grey, telegram, August 23, 1914, no. 109, NA: PRO FO 262/1162/135; British Embassy, Tokyo, to Sir Edward Grey, telegram, August 2, 1914, no. 119, NA: PRO FO 262/1162/151.
49. British Embassy, Tokyo, to Sir Edward Grey, telegram, August 22, 1914, no. 108, NA: PRO FO 262/1162/134.
50. Military Department, India Office, "Precis of Correspondence Regarding the Mesopotamian Expedition: Its Genesis and Development," NA: PRO WO 106/52.
51. H. H. Asquith and Alexander Mackintosh, *Memories and Reflections, 1852–1927,* 2 vols. (Boston: Little, Brown and Co., 1928), 1:31.
52. Lewis Harcourt, "The Spoils," March 25, 1915, NA: PRO CAB 63/3.
53. Winston Churchill, *World Crisis, 1911–1918* (New York: Free Press, 2005), 171–72.
54. Mahan, *Influence of Sea Power,* 12–13.
55. John Fisher to Prime Minister Asquith, "The Submarine," in "Lord Fisher's correspondence with the Prime Minister Regarding the War," March 1914?, FISR 8/33/4901, p. 17.

CHAPTER 7. WORLD WAR I IN THE COLONIES

1. Governor General Australia to Secretary of State for Colonies, "War Between Great Britain, France, Russia, and Japan Against Germany and Austria, 1914: Participation by the Seagoing Fleet in the Operations," September 6, 1914, NA: PRO CO 881/14/9/17.
2. Ibid.

3. Rear Admiral Sir George Patey, "Royal Australian Navy Operation Order no. 1," August 9, 1914, Great War Primary Documents Archive, http://www.gwpda.org/naval/ranopo1.htm.
4. Governor General Australia, "War Against Germany," NA: PRO CO 881/14/9/17.
5. Ibid.
6. Ibid.
7. Governor Fiji, Ernest Bickham Sweet-Escott, to Secretary of State for Colonies, Lewis Harcourt, August 30, 1914, NA: PRO CO 616/2/103.
8. Governor General Australia, "War Against Germany," NA: PRO CO 881 /14/9/17.
9. Governor New Zealand, Liverpool, to Secretary of State for the Colonies, Harcourt, telegram, August 30, 1914, NA: PRO CO 616/2/104; Commander in Chief, Admiral Patey, HMAS *Australia* to Admiralty, August 30, 1914, NA: PRO CO 616/10/30.
10. Governor General Australia, "War Against Germany," NA: PRO CO 881/14/9/17.
11. Commander in Chief, China, to Admiralty, telegram, August 18, 1914, NA: PRO CO 616/10/17.
12. Foreign Secretary Grey to Colonial Secretary Harcourt, August 14, 1914, NA: PRO CO 616/10/17.
13. Secretary of State for Colonies to Governor General Australia, telegram, August 19, 1914, NA: PRO CO 616/10/17.
14. Governor General Australia, "War Against Germany," NA: PRO CO 881/14/9/17.
15. Foreign Secretary Grey to British Embassy, Tokyo, Telegram, August 22, 1914, NA: PRO FO 262/1161/122.
16. British Embassy, Tokyo, to Sir Edmond Grey, telegram, August 15, 1914, NA: PRO FO/1162/105.
17. Rear Admiral Patey, Commanding Australia Squadron, to Admiralty, telegram, September 9, 1914, NA: PRO CO 616/10/46; Rear Admiral Patey, Commanding Australia Squadron, to Admiralty, telegram, September 23, 1914, NA: PRO CO 616/10/46.
18. Rear Admiral Patey, Commanding Australia Squadron, to Admiralty, telegram, September 12, 1914, NA: PRO CO 616/10/38; Rear Admiral Patey, Commanding Australia Squadron, to Admiralty, telegram, September 13, 1914, NA: PRO CO 616/10/46; Rear Admiral Patey, Commanding Australia Squadron, to Admiralty, telegram, September 24, 1914, NA: PRO CO 616/10/47; Governor General Australia, "War Against Germany," NA: PRO CO 881/14/9/17.
19. Admiralty to Undersecretary of State Colonial Office, September 21, 1914, NA: PRO CO 616/10/45.
20. Governor General Australia, "War Against Germany," NA: PRO CO 881/14/9/17.
21. Admiralty to Undersecretary of State Colonial Office, September 27, 1914, NA: PRO CO 616/10/50; Ibid.

22. Hew Strachan, *The First World War,* vol. 1, *To Arms* (Oxford: Oxford University Press, 2001), 462–65; "Battles: The Siege of Tsingtao, 1914," FirstWorld War.com, http://www.firstworldwar.com/battles/tsingtao.htm; Colin Denis, "Tsingtao Campaign," World War I Document Archive, http://www.gwpda.org/naval/tsingtao.htm .
23. Keith Steward, "Lieutenant Colonel F. C. Bryant, CMG, CBE, DSO, Gold Coast Regiment and the Short Campaign in Togo, August 11 to 26, 1914," http://www.britishcolonialafrica.com/PDFS/10_LIEUT_COLONEL_BRYANT_8_Single_20_3.pdf.
24. Acting Governor William Clark Flemming Robertson to Secretary of State for Colonies, "War With Germany: Submits a Brief Summary of Action Taken from Receipt of Warnings to Prepare for a State of War," August 12, 1914, NA: PRO CO 91/547/650.
25. Steward, "Lieutenant Colonel F. C. Bryant," http://www.britishcolonialafrica.com/PDFS/10_LIEUT_COLONEL_BRYANT_8_Single_20_3.pdf.
26. Alfons Stoher, Sergeant Major of the Reserve Force (Germany), "An Account of the Military Operations in Togoland," September 9, 1914, NA: PRO CAB 45/111.
27. Acting Governor, Robertson, "War With Germany," NA: PRO CO 91/547/650.
28. Committee of Imperial Defence, "Operations in Togoland," 1914, NA: PRO CAB 45/110; "Brief Narrative of Events and Operations in Togoland from August 5, 1914; Compiled from Telegrams and Dispatches," 1914, NA: PRO WO 106/1533.
29. Acting Governor, Robertson, "War With Germany," NA: PRO CO 91/547/650.
30. Ibid.
31. Committee of Imperial Defence, "Operations in Togoland," NA: PRO CAB 45/110; Stoher, "Military Operations in Togoland," NA: PRO CAB 45/111; "Brief Narrative of Events," NA: PRO WO 106/1533; Frederick James Moberly, *Military Operations: Togoland and the Cameroons, 1914–1916,* History of the Great War (London: Longmans, Green and Co., 1931), 38.
32. Lt. Col. Bryant to Secretary of State for Colonies, August 27, 1914, NA: PRO CO 343/29.
33. Prime Minister Asquith to the Sovereign, King George V, August 26, 1914, NA: PRO CAB 41/35/36.
34. "The Operations in the Cameroons from August 2, 1914, to January 27, 1915," NA: PRO CAB 45/112.
35. Sir Francis Bertie, Ambassador to Paris, to Foreign Office, telegram, no. 435, August 20, 1914, NA: PRO CO 537/590/1.
36. Eyre A. Crowe, Foreign Office to Undersecretary of State, Colonial Office, August 23, 1914, NA: PRO CO 537/590/1.
37. "Operations in the Cameroons," NA: PRO CAB 45/112.

38. Moberly, *Togoland and the Cameroons,* 129.
39. Secretary of State for the Colonies, Lewis Harcourt, to Secretary of State for War, Lord Kitchener, March 30, 1915, NA: PRO WO 159/19.
40. Moberly, *Togoland and the Cameroons,* xxii.
41. Admiralty to Undersecretary of State, Colonial Office, November 5, 1914, NA: PRO CO 616/10/71; SS *Kamerun* at "Hamburg-America Line," http://www.theshipslist.com/ships/lines/hamburg.shtml; SS *Max Brock* at "German East Africa Line," The Ships List, http://www.theshipslist.com/ships/lines/woermann.shtml.
42. "The Campaign in German Southwest Africa from August 1, 1914, to July 9, 1915; Narrative of Events with Composition of Forces," July 1915[?], NA: PRO CAB 45/112.
43. Lord Paul Sanford Methuen, General Commanding Forces in South Africa, to War Office, March 8, 1909, WO 106/49 E2 6.
44. Officer Administering the Government of the Union of South Africa, John H. DeVilliers, to Secretary of State for the Colonies, Mr. Lewis Harcourt, telegram, August 26, 1914, NA: PRO CO 616/2/83.
45. Commander in Chief, Cape to Admiralty, telegram, October 23, 1914, CHAR 13/38/19; Prime Minister Asquith to the Sovereign, King George V, September 30, 1914, NA: PRO CAB 41/35/48; "Campaign in German Southwest Africa," NA: PRO CAB 45/112.
46. Prime Minister Asquith to the Sovereign, King George V, October 30, 1914, NA: PRO CAB 41/35/55.
47. Prime Minister Asquith to the Sovereign, King George V, November 3, 1914, NA: PRO CAB 41/35/56.
48. "Campaign in German Southwest Africa," NA: PRO CAB 45/112.
49. Committee of Imperial Defence, "German East Africa, Brief History," August 1915, NA: PRO CAB 37/133/16.
50. Prime Minister Asquith to the Sovereign, King George V, September 14, 1914, NA: PRO CAB 41/35/45.
51. General Sir Edmond G. Barrow, Military Secretary, India Office, in connection with the Colonial Office, "Expedition Against German East Africa," September 28, 1914, NA: PRO CAB 38/28/42.
52. General Sir Edmond G. Barrow, G.C.B., Military Secretary, India Office, "Expedition Against German East Africa," September 14, 1914, NA: PRO CAB 38/28/41.
53. Ibid.; Major General A. E. Aiken, Commanding IEF B, to the Secretary, War Office, London, "Status in East Africa and Report on Tanga," December 1, 1914, NA: PRO CAB 37/123/59.
54. Aiken, "Report on Tanga," NA: PRO CAB 37/123/59.
55. Strachan, *First World War,* 579–84.

56. Admiralty to HMS *Chatham,* telegram, November 4, 1914, CHAR 13/38/61; Admiralty to HMS *Chatham,* telegram, November 4, 1914, CHAR 13/38/63; Admiralty to HMS *Chatham,* telegram, November 6, 1914, CHAR 13/38/68; Senior Naval Officer, Mombasa to Admiralty, telegram, November 7, 1914, CHAR 13/38/69; Strachan, *First World War,* 576.
57. Strachan, *First World War,* 600–603; Winston Churchill, *World Crisis, 1911–1918* (New York: Free Press, 2005), 463–73.
58. Viceroy to Secretary of State for India, February 10, 1915, NA: PRO PRO 30/57/69 WO/12.
59. Undersecretary of State for India to Viceroy, n.d., NA: PRO PRO 30/57/69 WO/1; Frederick James Moberly, *The Campaign in Mesopotamia, 1914–1918,* 4 vols., History of the Great War (London: His Majesty's Stationery Office, 1927), 1:161, 167–68.
60. Viceroy to Undersecretary of State for India, February 10, 1915, NA: PRO PRO 30/57/69 WO/10; Moberly, *Campaign in Mesopotamia,* 1:168.
61. Viceroy to Secretary of State for India, February 10, 1915, NA: PRO PRO 30/57/69 WO/12; Moberly, *Campaign in Mesopotamia,* 1:177–78.
62. Viceroy to Secretary of State for India, February 10, 1915, NA: PRO PRO 30/57/69 WO/12; Moberly, *Campaign in Mesopotamia,* 1:220–21.
63. Moberly, *Campaign in Mesopotamia,* 1:223, 246; 2:1–5, 62–125, 157, 182–83.
64. Ibid., 2:191, 264, 352–54.
65. Ibid., 3:1–36, 24.

Chapter 8. Diplomacy and the Strategy's Effects

1. Ernst Bischoff, *Leistungen der Deutschen Flotte im Weltkrieg* (Zurich: Orell Füssli, 1918), 39.
2. Ibid., 39–40.
3. United Kingdom, "World War I at Sea: British Merchant Ships Lost at Sea Due to Enemy Action," extracted from *British Vessels Lost at Sea, 1914–1918* (London, HMSO, 1919), http://www.naval-history.net/WW1LossesaContents.htm.
4. Bischoff, *Deutschen Flotte im Weltkrieg,* 38.
5. Ibid., 24.
6. John Alexander Clinton Gray, *Amerika Samoa: A History of American Samoa and Its United States Naval Administration* (Annapolis: U.S. Naval Institute, 1960), 184–85; Franz Joseph Hohenzollern, *Emden: My Experiences in SMS Emden* (London: Herbert Jenkins, 1928), 19.
7. Admiralty to Undersecretary of State Foreign Office, September 4, 1914, NA: PRO CO 616/10/31.
8. Admiralty to Commander in Chief East Indies (via Aden and Bombay), Commander in Chief, China, Vice Admiral embarked HMAS *Australia* (via Melbourne), Naval Ottawa, Rear Admiral embarked HMS *Good Hope* (via Montevideo), telegram, September 30, 1914, FISR 1/15/834.

9. "Vice Admiral Graf Spee's Cruiser Squadron," World War I Naval Combat, http://www.worldwar1.co.uk/GrafSpee.html; Paul G. Halpern, *A Naval History of World War I* (Annapolis: Naval Institute Press, 1994), 89.
10. R. K. Lochner, *The Last Gentleman-of-War: The Raider Exploits of the Cruiser Emden,* trans. Thea and Harry Lindauer (Annapolis: Naval Institute Press, 1988), 48–50; Admiralty to Intelligence Officer, Montevideo, October 5, 1914, FISR 1/15/834; Admiralty to Intelligence Officer, Montevideo, October 7, 1914, FISR 1/15/834; Gray, *Amerika Samoa*, 184–85.
11. "History of SMS *Dresden* (Nr. 1)," http://www.kaiserlich-marine.de; "Dresden Class Light Cruiser," World War I Naval Combat, http://www.worldwar1.co.uk/cruisers/sms-dresden.html; "Vice Admiral Graf Spee's Cruiser Squadron," World War I Naval Combat, http://www.worldwar1.co.uk/GrafSpee.html.
12. Admiralty to Rear Admiral, HMS *Good Hope,* via British Minister, Rio de Janeiro, telegram, September 14, 1914, FISR 1/15/834; Rear Admiral Cradock, 4th Cruiser Squadron (via Montevideo) to Admiralty, telegram, October 11, 1914, FISR 1/15/834; Rear Admiral Cradock, 4th Cruiser Squadron (via Montevideo) to Admiralty, telegram, October 12, 1914, FISR 1/15/834; Admiralty to Intelligence Officer, Montevideo, October 14, 1914, FISR 1/15/834; Mr. Watson, Iquique, to Admiralty, telegram, November 2, 1914, FISR 1/15/834; Mr. Cooper, Coronel to Admiralty, telegram, November 3, 1914, FISR 1/15/834; Commonwealth Naval Board of Administration, Melbourne, to Admiralty, telegram, November 3, 1914, FISR 1/15/834; Mr. McLean, Valparaiso, to Admiralty, telegram, November 2, 1914, FISR 1/15/834; Mr. McLean, Valparaiso, to Admiralty, telegram, November 3, 1914, 10:00 p.m., FISR 1/15/834; Mr. McLean, Valparaiso, to Admiralty, telegram, November 3, 1914, 12:30 p.m., FISR 1/15/834; Mr. McLean, Valparaiso, to Admiralty, telegram, November 3, 1914, 6:10 p.m., FISR 1/15/834.
13. Prime Minister Asquith to the Sovereign, King George V, November 4, 1914, NA: PRO CAB 41/35/57; HMS *Glasgow*, Magellan Straits, to Admiralty, telegram, November 4, 1914, FISR 1/15/834; First Lord to Commander in Chief, Home Fleet (via Pembroke), telegram, November 5, 1914, FISR 1/15/834; Tirpitz, *My Memoirs,* 2 vols. (New York: Dodd, Mead, 1919), 1:83.
14. Admiralty to Undersecretary of State, Colonial Office, November 12, 1914, NA: PRO CO 616/10/75; Secretary of State for Colonies, Harcourt, to Governor General Union of South Africa, telegram, November 13, 1914, NA: PRO CO 616/10/75.
15. Petty Officer Plötz, "Plötz's Diary: The Cruise of the SMS *Emden*," trans. Captain A. Gordon, NA: PRO ADM 137/1020/46; Captain Glossop, HMAS *Sydney* to Admiralty, November 15, 1914, NA: PRO ADM 137/1020/42.
16. Secretary of State for Colonies, Harcourt, to Governor General Australia, telegram, November 17, 1914, NA: PRO CO 616/10/79; Admiralty to Naval Board,

Melbourne, telegram, November 7, 1914, CHAR 13/38/45; Admiralty to Commander in Chief, HMAS *Australia,* at Fanning Island, telegram, November 12, 1914, CHAR 13/38/50.

17. Vice Admiral Sturdee (via Intelligence Office, Montevideo) to Admiralty, telegram, December 11, 1914, FISR 1/16/866; Gray, *Amerika Samoa*, 184–85.
18. Admiralty to HMS *Dartmouth,* telegram, December 9, 1914, CHAR 13/38/38; Prime Minister Asquith to the Sovereign, King George V, December 10, 1914, NA: PRO CAB 41/35/63.
19. Admiralty to Commonwealth Naval Board, Melbourne, telegram, December 12, 1914, CHAR 13/38/53.
20. Sir Edward Grey to Mr. Lewis Harcourt, November 23, 1914, NA: PRO FO 800/91/481.
21. Foreign Secretary Grey to British Embassy, Tokyo, telegram, August 22, 1914, no. 88, NA: PRO FO 262/1161/120.
22. Admiralty to Undersecretary of State Foreign Office, October 11, 1914, NA: PRO CO 616/10/62.
23. Admiralty to Commander in Chief, Cape, telegram, October 31, 1914, CHAR 13/38/20; Prime Minister Asquith to the Sovereign, King George V, November 3, 1914, NA: PRO CAB 41/35/56; Cabinet, "Summary of Notes of a Meeting of a War Council held at 10 Downing Street," January 28, 1915, Asquith MSS 132: 225 Bodleian Library, Oxford.
24. Edwin P. Hoyt, *The Germans Who Never Lost* (New York: Funk and Wagnalls, 1968), 16 and 19; Edward Paice, *Tip and Run: The Untold Tragedy of the Great War in Africa* (New York: Weidenfeld and Nicolson, 2007), 145–46.
25. Hoyt, *Germans Who Never Lost,* 22–25 and 39.
26. Admiralty to Commander in Chief, East Indies, telegram, August 12, 1914, CHAR 13/38/1; Commander in Chief, East Indies, at Aden to Admiralty, telegram, September 8, 1914, CHAR 13/28/2; Admiralty, "Remarks on Escorts in the Indian Ocean," CHAR 13/38/3–7; Admiralty to Commander in Chief, East Indies, telegram, September 20, 1914, CHAR 13/38/8.
27. "History of SMS *Königsberg* (Nr. 1)," http://www.kaiserlich-marine.de.
28. Hew Strachan, *First World War,* vol. 1, *To Arms* (Oxford: Oxford University Press, 2001), 576; Hoyt, *Germans Who Never Lost,* 47–48.
29. Hoyt, *Germans Who Never Lost,* 32, 39, and 42; "History of SMS *Königsberg* (Nr. 1)."
30. "History of SMS *Königsberg* (Nr. 1)."
31. Admiralty to British Consul General Lorenzo Marques, telegram, October 13, 1914, CHAR 13/38/55; British General Consul to Admiralty, telegram, October 13, 1914, CHAR 13/38/56; Admiralty to HMS *Chatham* info Commander in Chief, Cape, telegram, November 1, 1914, CHAR 13/38/57.
32. R. A. Burt, *British Battleships 1889–1904* (Annapolis: Naval Institute Press, 1988), 158; Steven Schoenherr, "War in Africa," http://history.sandiego.edu/gen/ww1/

africa.html (no longer accessible); Senior Naval Officer, HMS *Fox*, Zanzibar, to Admiralty, telegram, November 29, 1914, NA: PRO ADM 8404/451.

33. HMS *Chatham* to Admiralty, telegram, November 11, 1914, CHAR 13/38/84; HMS *Chatham* to Admiralty, telegram, no. 14, November 24, 1914, CHAR 13/38/105.
34. Hoyt, *Germans Who Never Lost,* 143–45.
35. Prime Minister Asquith to the Sovereign, King George V, November 25, 1914, NA: PRO CAB 41/35/61.
36. Hawkins, *Starvation Blockades,* 25.
37. Louis Guichard, *The Naval Blockade, 1914–1918,* trans. and ed. Christopher R. Turner (New York: D. Appleton & Co., 1930), 21–22.
38. Nigel Hawkins, *Starvation Blockades: The Naval Blockades of WWI* (Barnsley: Leo Cooper, 2002), 81–82; Guichard, *Naval Blockade,* 7–8.
39. Prime Minister Asquith to the Sovereign, King George V, August 15, 1914, NA: PRO CAB 41/35/30; Prime Minister Asquith to the Sovereign, King George V, August 20, 1914, NA: PRO CAB 41/35/34.
40. Governor General, Canada, to Secretary of State for Colonies, telegram, August 13, 1914, NA: PRO CO 616/1/93.
41. Admiralty to Secretary of State for Colonies, August 29, 1914, NA: PRO CO 323/629/309.
42. Governor of New Zealand, Liverpool, to Secretary of State for Colonies, Harcourt, telegram, August 4, 1914, NA: PRO 616/1/22; Admiralty to Secretary of State for Colonies, August 4, 1914, NA: PRO 616/1/22.
43. Guichard, *Naval Blockade,* 20–22.
44. Hawking, *Starvation Blockades,* 83–84.
45. Guichard, *Naval Blockade,* 22.
46. Hawking, *Starvation Blockades,* 13–14.
47. Ibid., 60.
48. Ibid., 62–63.
49. Guichard, *Naval Blockade,* 28–32.
50. Hawkins, *Starvation Blockades*, 63.
51. Ibid., 64–65.
52. Hawkins, *Starvation Blockades*, 64–65.
53. Marion C. Siney, *The Allied Blockade of Germany, 1914–1916* (Westport, CT: Greenwood Press, 1973), 24–25; Guichard, *Naval Blockade,* 35–37.
54. Sir Edward Grey to distribution list, telegram, no. 4 commercial, August 21, 1914, NA: PRO FO 262/1121/115.
55. Governor New Zealand, Liverpool, to Secretary of State for the Colonies, Harcourt, telegram, August 13, 1914, NA: PRO CO 616/1/99; Governor, New Zealand, Liverpool, to Secretary of State for the Colonies, Harcourt, telegram, August 17, 1914, NA: PRO CO 616/2/6; Governor New Zealand, Liverpool,

to Secretary of State for the Colonies, Harcourt, telegram, August 24, 1914, NA: PRO CO 616/2/62.

56. Governor of Newfoundland, Davidson, to Secretary of State for the Colonies, Harcourt, telegram, August 14, 1914, NA: PRO CO 616/1/102.
57. Admiralty to Undersecretary of State Colonial Office, September 10, 1914, NA: PRO CO 616/10/36.
58. Board of Trade to Admiralty, Director of Transports, August 24, 1914, NA: PRO CO 616/10/23.
59. W. F. Nicholson, Admiralty, to Lewis Harcourt, Secretary of State for Colonies, October 15, 1914, NA: PRO CO 537/596; Secretary of State for Colonies to Governor General Australia, telegram, October 5, 1914, NA: PRO CO 616/10/58.
60. Admiralty War Staff, Trade Division, "Operations of the *Emden*: Trade Routes during War," October 17, 1914, NA: PRO CAB 37/121/123.
61. Admiralty, "Overdue List," August 18, 1914, NA: PRO ADM 137/1013/9.
62. Admiralty, "British Shipping Losses, Corrected to September 23, 1914," NA: PRO ADM 137/1013/18.
63. Winston Churchill, "Cover Note and Report Prepared by the Trade Division of the Admiralty on Wheat Prices and Food Supplies," January 25, 1915, Lloyd George Papers, LG/C/25/3/1, Parliamentary Archives, London.
64. Walter Runciman, "The Capture of Enemy Trade: Board of Trade Exchange Exhibitions and Leipzig Fair," December 31, 1914, Lloyd George Papers, LG/C/25/4/3, Parliamentary Archives, London.
65. War Office to Secretary of State for the Colonies, August 25, 1914, NA: PRO CO 616/14/29.
66. Governor General Australia, Ferguson, to Secretary of State for Colonies, Harcourt, telegram, August 21, 1914, NA: PRO CO 612/2/53.
67. Sir Edward Grey to Sir Francis Stronge, telegram, March 11, 1915, no. 21 treaty, NA: PRO ADM 137/1023/31; Sir Edward Grey to Sir Francis Stronge, telegram, March 11, 1915, no. 22 treaty, NA: PRO ADM 137/1023/31; Sir Francis Stronge to Sir Edward Grey, telegram, March 11, 1915, NA: PRO ADM 137/1023/31.
68. "SMS *Dresden* (Nr. 1)," http://www.kaiserliche-marine.de.
69. Chilean Minister in London to Sir Edward Grey, Foreign Office, March 26, 1915, NA: PRO ADM 137/1023/35.
70. Sir Francis Stronge to Sir Edward Gray, telegram, March 30, 1915, NA: PRO ADM 137/1023/37.
71. "SMS *Kaiser Wilhelm der Grosse,*" http://www.kaiserliche-marine.de; Admiralty, to Undersecretary of State, Foreign Affairs, memorandum, December 12, 1914, NA: PRO ADM 137/1023/33.
72. Sir Francis Stronge to Sir Edward Grey, telegram, March 23, 1915, NA: PRO ADM 137/1023/35; Foreign Office to Chilean Ambassador, London, unsigned and undated draft, NA: PRO ADM 137/1023/37.

73. Lloyd's of London, "Prizes of War and Vessels and Cargoes Detained," NA: PRO CO 323/629/252, 255, and 289–95.
74. H. Norman to Sir Edward Grey, August 5, 1914, NA: PRO ADM 137/1014/5.
75. Sir Reginald T. Tower, Buenos Aires, to Sir Edward Grey, October 9, 1914, no. 24 treaty, NA: PRO ADM 137/1019/13.
76. Mr. H. G. Mackie, Buenos Aires, to Sir Reginald T. Tower, October 8, 1914, NA: PRO ADM 137/1019/13.
77. Admiralty memorandum, February 12, 1915, NA: PRO ADM 137/1019/55.
78. B. Konrad, 4th Engineer, SS *Sleiermark,* Hamburg-America Line, Bahia, Brazil, to Engineroom Petty Officer Hans Rudolph, Auxilary Cruiser SMS *Berlin,* Trondheim, Norway, July 7, 1915, NA: PRO ADM 137/1019/18.
79. Sir Reginald T. Tower, Buenos Aires, to Sir Edward Grey, October 9, 1914, no. 24 treaty, NA: PRO ADM 137/1019/13; Foreign Office to Sir Cecil Spring Rice, British Ambassador to the United States, Washington, D.C., November 19, 1914, no. 178 treaty, NA: PRO ADM 137/1019/13; Sir Cecil Spring Rice, British Embassy, Washington, D.C., to Robert Lansing, Acting Secretary of State, November 20, 1914, no. 391, NA: PRO ADM 137/1019/14.
80. Mr. Robertson to Sir Edward Grey, telegram, September 19, 1914, NA: PRO ADM 137/1027/32; Mr. Robertson to Sir Edward Grey, telegram, October 6, 1914, NA: PRO ADM 137/1027/34.
81. Foreign Office to Admiralty, memorandum, October 13, 1914, no. 54262/14, NA: PRO ADM 137/1025/7; Admiralty to Foreign Office, memorandum, November 5, 1914, no. m02642, NA: PRO ADM 137/1025/7.
82. Vice Admiral, Commander in Chief, North America and West Indies, Bermuda, to Admiralty, telegram, March 27, 1915, NA: PRO ADM 137/1019/61; Cecil Spring Rice to Sir Edward Grey, April 16, 1915 NA: PRO ADM 137/1019/64.
83. Admiralty memorandum, February 12, 1915, NA: PRO ADM 137/1019/55; Commanding Officer, HMS *Coronia,* to Rear Admiral, Commanding North American Station, "Information Taken from Two New Ratings Who Were Former Crew Members on British Merchant Vessels *La Correntina* and *Bellevue,* Which Were Captured by *Kronprinz Wilhelm,"* March 2, 1915, NA: PRO ADM 137/1019/39.
84. "History of SMS *Karlsruhe* (Nr. 1)"; "SMS *Karlsruhe,"* World War I, Naval Combat, http://www.worldwar1.co.uk/karlsruhe.html; "Saw Naval Battle; *Karlsruhe* Sunk?; Night Fight Off Grenada, B.W. I., Nov. 25, Lasted Four Hours, Solitary Observer Writes. *Karlsruhe* Relics Ashore and Fishermen Report Seeing Floating Bodies and Wreckage—No Such Battle Before Reported," *New York Times,* January 13, 1915, http://query.nytimes.com/mem/archive-free/pdf?_r=1&res=9E0DE6DE1538E633A25750C1A9679C946496D6CF.
85. Admiralty memorandum, February 12, 1915, NA: PRO ADM 137/1019/55; Commanding Officer, HMS *Coronia,* to Rear Admiral, Commanding North

American Station, "Information Taken from Two New Ratings Who Were Former Crew Members on British Merchant Vessels *La Correntina* and *Bellevue,* Which Were Captured by *Kronprinz Wilhelm,*" March 2, 1915, NA: PRO ADM 137/1019/39.

86. W. F. Nicholson, Brazil, to Under Secretary of State, Foreign Office, January 5, 1915, NA: PRO ADM 137/1019/27; Foreign Office to Sir A. Hardinge, Madrid, telegram, January 6, 1915, NA: PRO ADM 137/1019/28; Sir A. Hardinge to Sir Edward Grey, telegram, January 9, 1915, NA: PRO ADM 137/1019/30.
87. Admiralty memorandum, taken from the *Weser Zeitung*, May 8, 1915, NA: PRO ADM 137/1019/55.
88. Ibid.
89. Admiralty memorandum, February 12, 1915, NA: PRO ADM 137/1019/55.
90. M. Robertson to Sir Edward Grey, telegram, January 8, 1915, NA: PRO ADM 137/1019/29; Sir Reginald T. Tower to Sir Edward Grey, telegram, March 2, 1915, NA PRO ADM 137/1019/36.
91. Minister for Foreign Affairs, Rio de Janeiro, to British chargé d'affaires, September 16, 1914, NA: PRO ADM 137/1027/39; British Consul, Buenos Aires, to Dr. Don Jose Luis Murature, September 25, 1914, NA: PRO ADM 137/1027/40.
92. Dr. Jose Luis Murature, Buenos Aires, to Sir Reginald T. Tower, October 8, 1914, NA: PRO ADM 137/1027/41; Foreign Office to Admiralty, November 21, 1914, no. 70154/14, NA: PRO ADM 137/1027/41; Admiralty note, November 23, 1914, NA: PRO ADM 137/1027/41; "Hamburg-America Line," *The Ship's List,* http://www.theshipslist.com/ships/lines/hamburg.html.
93. "Present Conditions in Germany," February 9, 1915, Creedy (K.) papers; Lord Kitchner's Strategical, Political and Miscellaneous Papers, January–May 1915, NA: PRO WO 159/3/18.
94. Crowborough to David Lloyd George c/o Sir Frederick Smith, May 5, 1916, Northcliffe Papers, ADD MSS 62157, British Library, London.
95. C. W. Fielding to Bonar Law, August 13, 1914, Bonar Law Papers, BL/34/3/38, Parliamentary Archives, London; C. W. Fielding to Bonar Law, August 26, 1914, Bonar Law Papers, BL/34/4/75.

CHAPTER 9. CONCLUSIONS

1. Nicholas Lambert, "Strategic Command and Control for Maneuver Warfare: Creation of the Royal Navy's 'War Room' System, 1905–1915," *Journal of Military History* 69 (April 2005): 392.
2. Admiralty, "War Standing Orders for Vessels Employed in Protection of Trade," July 14, 1914, NA: PRO ADM 137/818/14.
3. Admiral Hugo von Pohl, Chief of Marine Staff, "German Declaration of Naval Blockade of Britain, February 4, 1915," http://www.firstworldwar.com/source/pohl_uboatwar1915.htm.

4. United States Government to Imperial German Government, February 10, 1915, http://www.firstworldwar.com/source/wilsonwarningfeb1915.htm.
5. William Jennings Bryan, United States Secretary of State, to Gottilieb von Jagow, German Foreign Minister, May 13, 1915, http://www.firstworldwar.com/source/bryanlusitaniaprotes.htm; Gottilieb von Jagow to William Jennings Bryan, May 28, 1915, http://www.firstworldwar.com/source/lusitania_germanresponse.htm; Bryan to Jagow, July 21, 1915, http://www.firstworldwar.com/source/lusitania 3rdprotest.htm; Woodrow Wilson to Jagow, April 18, 1916, http://www.first worldwar.com/source/uboat1916_usultimatum.htm; "Sinking of the Sussex" http://www.firstworldwar.com/atoz/sussex.htm.
6. Winston Churchill to Lord John A. Fisher, January 1, 1914, FISR 1/14/768.
7. Paul G. Halpern, "The War at Sea," in *World War I,* vol. 1, *A History,* ed. Hew Strachan (Oxford: Oxford University Press, 1998), 116.
8. Churchill, *World Crisis, 1911–1918* (New York: Free Press, 2005), 669–70.
9. Erich von Ludendorff, *"Ludendorff's Own Story: The Great War from the Siege of Liege to the Signing of the Armistice as Viewed from the Grand Headquarters of the German Army,* 2 vols. (New York: Harper and Brothers, 1919), 1:364–66.
10. Ibid., 369; Representative of the Admiralty Staff, General Headquarters East, memorandum, no. 2597, September 10, 1916, in Erich von Ludendorff, *The General Staff and Its Problems: The History of the Relations between High Command and the German Imperial Government as Revealed by Official Documents,* 2 vols., trans. F. A. Holt (New York: E. P. Dutton and Co., 1920), 1:275–79; Arthur Zimmermann to Baron von Lersner, telegram, no. 1612, December 21, 1916, Ludendorff, *General Staff and Its Problems,* 1:289.
11. Ludendorff, *Ludendorff's Own Story,* 1:366.
12. Theobald von Bethmann-Hollweg, Imperial German Chancellor, to His Majesty the Kaiser and King, telegram, September 23, 1916, in Ludendorff, *General Staff and Its Problems,* 1:279; Ludendorff, "Notes for My Summary," in Ludendorff, *General Staff and Its Problems,* 1:285–87.
13. Michael Howard, *The First World War* (Oxford: Oxford University Press, 2002), 84; David Stevenson, "War Aims and Peace Negotiations," in Strachan, *World War I,* 204–209.
14. Ludendorff, *Ludendorff's Own Story,* 1:367–69; Ludendorff to Zimmermann, December 20, 1916, in Ludendorff, *General Staff and Its Problems,* 1:288.
15. Ludendorff, *Ludendorff's Own Story,* 1:369.
16. John Lee, *The Warlords: Hindenburg and Ludendorff* (London: Weidenfeld and Nicolson, 2005), 113–15.
17. Martin Gilbert, "British Merchant Ship Losses, 1917–1918," in *The Routledge Atlas of the First World War,* 2nd ed. (Glasgow: Bell and Bain, 2002), 85.
18. Fayle, *Seaborne Trade,* vol. 1, *The Cruiser Period,* History of the Great War Based on Official Documents (London: John Murray, 1920), 410.

19. Halpern, "War at Sea," 114–18; Holger Herwig, "The German Victories, 1917–1918," in Strachan, *World War I*, 259–64.
20. Stokesbury, *A Short History of World War I* (New York: William Morrow, 1981), 181–82; David French, *British Strategy and War Aims, 1914–1916* (London, Boston: Allen and Unwin, 1986), 27; Howard, *First World War* (Oxford: Oxford University Press, 2002), 40–50.
21. Halpern, "The War at Sea," 115–16.
22. Alfred Thayer Mahan, *The Influence of Sea Power upon History, 1660–1783* (New York: Dover Publications, 1987), 28.
23. Martin Gilbert, "Allied Blockades, 1914–1918," *The Routledge Atlas of the First World War*, 2nd ed. (Glasgow: Bell and Bain, 2002), 76; Lloyds of London, "Prizes of War and Vessels and Cargoes Detained," NA: PRO CO 323/629/32613.
24. Gilbert, "British Merchant Ship Losses, 1917–1918,"*Atlas of the First World War*, 85.
25. Naval Staff, Intelligence Division, "Maritime Trade Routes of the World Which Could Be Rendered Inoperative by German Commerce Attackers Based on Duala in the Cameroons, Dar es Salaam in German East Africa, Rabaul in German New Guinea, and on German Samoa," October 1918, NA: PRO FO 925/36116.
26. Mark Grimsley, *The Hard Hand of War: Union Military Policy toward Southern Civilians, 1861–1865* (Cambridge: Cambridge University Press, 1995), 205.
27. Halpern, "The War at Sea," 116.
28. Churchill, *World Crisis*, 250.
29. Alfred von Tirpitz, *My Memoirs*, 2 vols. (New York: Dodd, Mead, 1919), 1:85.
30. Churchill, *World Crisis*, 250.

BIBLIOGRAPHY

PRIMARY SOURCES

Manuscripts

Bodleian Library, Oxford University, Oxford
- Asquith Manuscripts
- Harcourt Manuscripts

British Library, London
- Balfour Papers
- Northcliffe Papers

Churchill Archives Centre, Churchill College, Cambridge University
- Winston Churchill Papers
- Fisher Papers

National Archives, Public Record Office, Kew Gardens
- Horatio Herbert Kitchener, 1st Earl Kitchener of Khartoum, Papers, PRO 30/57

Parliamentary Archives, House of Lords Record Office, London
- Bonar Law Papers
- Lloyd George Papers

Public Documents

"Agreement Concerning Persia, August 31, 1907." Parliamentary Papers, vol. 125, Cd. 3750. London, 1908. The World War I Document Archive, http://www.gwpda.org/1914m/anglruss.html.

"Anglo-Japanese Alliance, January 30, 1902." Japan Center for Asian Historical Records. http://www.jacar.go.jp/nichiro/uk-japan.htm.

"British Vessels Lost at Sea, 1914–1918." Naval-History.Net, http://www.naval-history.net/WW1LossesaContents.htm. Originally published London, Her Majesty's Stationery Office, 1919.

"Convention 5, Respecting the Rights and Duties of Neutral Powers and Persons in Case of War on Land." The Hague. October 18, 1907. International Humanitarian Law: Treaties and Documents. International Committee of the Red Cross. http://www.icrc.org/ihl.nsf/FULL/200?OpenDocument.

"Convention 13, Concerning the Rights and Duties of Neutral Powers in Naval War, The Hague." October 18, 1907. International Humanitarian Law: Treaties and Documents. International Com-mittee of the Red Cross. http://www.icrc.org/ihl.nsf/FULL/200?OpenDocument.

"Renewal of the Anglo-Japanese Alliance, August 12, 1905." Naval History. http://navalhistory.flixco.info/H/180236x54372/8330/a0.htm.

Schlachten des Weltkrieges / in Einzeldarstellungen Bearb. und Hrsg. im Auftrage des Reichsarchivs. Reichsarchiv, Germany. 36 vols. Berlin, 1921.

"Treaty between Her Majesty and the United States of America, for the Amicable Settlement of all Causes of Difference between the Two Countries, Signed at Washington, May 8, 1871." Open Library. http://openlibrary.org/books/OL24159101M/The_Treaty_of_Washington.

United Kingdom, Parliament. "Agreement Concerning Persia, August 31, 1907." Parliamentary Papers, vol. 125, Cd. 3750 (1908). Parliamentary Archives. House of Lords Record Office, London.

United Kingdom, Public Record Office. Kew Gardens, London.

———. Records of the Admiralty. ADM 116, 137, and 8404.

———. Records of the Cabinet. CAB 9, 15, 18, 37, 38, 41, 45, 62, and 63.

———. Records of the Colonial Office. CO 91, 96, 323, 343, 537, 616, and 881.

———. Records of the Foreign Office. FO 262, 800, and 925.

———. Records of the Public Record Office. PRO 30.

———. Records of the War Office. WO 106 and 159.

United Kingdom, War Office. *Naval and Military Dispatches Relating to Operations in the War: September, October and November, 1914.* 2 vols. London: Her Majesty's Stationery Office, 1914.

United States, Department of State. "The *Alabama* Claims." http://future.state.gov/when/timeline/1861_timeline/alab_claims.html.

"World War I: Conventions and Treaties." World War I Document Archive. http://wwi.lib.byu.edu/index.php/Conventions_and_Treaties.

World War I Document Archive. http://wwi.lib.byu.edu/index.php/Main_Page.

Books and Articles

Asquith, H. H., and Alexander Mackintosh. *Memories and Reflections, 1852–1927.* 2 vols. Boston: Little, Brown and Co., 1928.

Bethmann Hollweg, Theobald von. *Betrachtungen zur Weltkriege.* 2nd ed. Edited by Jost Duelffer. Essen: Hoblin, 1989.

Churchill, Winston S. *World Crisis, 1911–1918.* London: Charles Scribner's Sons, 1931. Reprinted with introduction by Martin Gilbert. New York: Free Press, 2005. Page references are to the 2005 edition.

Clausewitz, Carl von. *On War.* Translated by Peter Paret. Princeton: Princeton University Press, 1977.

Corbett, Julian S. *Some Principles of Maritime Strategy.* London: Longmans, Green and Co., 1911. Reprinted, Annapolis: Naval Institute Press, 1988. Page references are to the 1988 edition.

Donohoe, M. H. *With the Persian Expedition.* London: Edward Arnold, 1919.

Downes, W. D. *With the Nigerians in German East Africa.* London: Nethuen and Co., 1919.

Falkenhayn, Erich Georg Anton Sebastian von. *The German General Staff and Its Decisions, 1914–1916.* New York: Dodd, Mead and Co., 1920.

Fisher, John Arbuthnot. *Fear God and Dread Naught: The Correspondence of Admiral of the Fleet Fisher of Kilverstone.* Edited by Arthur Marder. London: Cape, 1952–59.

———. *Memories and Records.* 2 vols. New York: George H. Doran Co., 1920.

Geiss, Immanuel. *July 1914: The Outbreak of the First World War: Selected Documents.* London: Batsford, 1967.

Germany, Auswärtiges Amt. *German Diplomatic Documents, 1871–1914.* Translated by Edgar Trevelyan Stratford Dugdale. London: Methuen and Co., 1928–31.

Gooch, George Peabody, and Harold William Temperley, eds. *British Documents on the Origins of the War, 1898–1914.* 11 vols. London: Her Majesty's Stationery Office, 1926.

Hankey, Maurice. *The Supreme Command, 1914–1918.* 2 vols. London: Allen and Unwin, 1961.

Hindenburg, Paul von. *Hindenburg-Worte: Briefe, Drahtungen, Reden und Gespräche des Generalfeldmarschalls von Hindenburg.* Edited by Hans Wohltmann. Munich: J. F. Lehmann, 1918.

———. *Out of My Life.* Translated by F. A. Holt. London: Cassell, 1920.

Hohenzollern, Franz Joseph. *Emden: My Experiences in SMS Emden.* London: Herbert Jenkins, 1928.

Jellicoe, John Rushworth. *The Grand Fleet, 1914–1916: Its Creation, Development, and Work.* London: Cassell, 1919.

Kock, Nis. *Blockade and Jungle.* Edited by Christen P. Christensen. Translated by Eleanor Arkwright. Classic History of the Great War, Battery Press Great War Series. Nashville: Battery Press, 2003.

Lee, John. *The Warlords: Hindenburg and Ludendorff.* London: Weidenfeld and Nicolson, 2005.

Lettow-Vorbeck, Paul von. *My Reminiscences of East Africa.* London: Hurst and Blackett, 1920.

Lloyd George, David. *War Memories of David Lloyd George*. 6 vols. London: I. Nicholson and Watson, 1933–36.

Ludendorff, Erich. *The Coming War*. London: Faber and Faber, 1931.

———. *Der Total Kreig*. Munich: Ludendorff Verlag, 1937.

———. *The General Staff and Its Problems: The History of the Relations between High Command and the German Imperial Government as Revealed by Official Documents*. 2 vols. Translated by F. A. Holt. New York: E. P. Dutton and Co., 1920.

———. *Ludendorff's Own Story: August 1914–November 1918. The Great Siege of Liege to the Signing of the Armistice as Viewed from the Grand Headquarters of the German Army*. 2 vols. New York: Harper and Bros., 1919–20.

———. *Meine Kreigserinnerungen, 1914–1918*. Berlin: E. S. Mittler and Sohn, 1919.

Mackinder, Halford John. *Britain and the British Seas*. New York: Appleton, 1902.

Mahan, Alfred Thayer. *The Influence of Sea Power upon History, 1660–1783*. Boston: Little, Brown and Co., 1890. Reprinted, New York: Dover Publications, 1987. Page references are to the 1987 edition.

———. *Naval Strategy Compared and Contrasted with the Principles and Practice of Military Operations on Land*. Boston: Little, Brown and Co. 1911.

Muller, Admiral Georg Alexander von, and Walter Gorlitz. *The Kaiser and His Court: The Diaries, Note Books, and Letters*. London: MacDonald, 1961.

Royal Commission on the Supply of Food and Raw Material in Time of War. "The Report of the Royal Commission on the Supply of Food and Raw Material in Time of War." *Economic Journal* 15 (December 1905): 609–16.

Schnee, Heinrich. *Deutsch-Ostafrika im Weltkriege: Wie Wir Lebten and Kaempften*. Leipzig: Quelle und Meyer, 1919.

Scott, James Brown, ed. *The Declaration of London: London International Naval Conference, 1908–1909*. London: Oxford University Press, 1919.

Tirpitz, Alfred von. *My Memoirs*. 2 vols. New York: Dodd, Mead, 1919.

Townshend, Charles V. F. *My Campaign in Mesopotamia*. London: Thornton Butterworth, 1920.

United Kingdom, Parliament and Foreign Office. *The Diplomatic History of the War, Including a Diary of the Negotiations and Events in the Different Capitals, the Texts of the Official Documents of the Various Governments, the Public Speeches in the European Parliaments, an Account of the Military Preparations of the Countries Concerned, and Original Matter*. Edited by Price M. Philips (Morgan Philips). London: Allen and Unwin; New York: Scribner's Sons, 1915.

Wegener, Wolfgang. *The Naval Strategy of the World War*. Berlin: E. S. Mittler, 1929. Reprinted with translation, introduction, and notes by Holger H. Herwig. Annapolis: Naval Institute Press, 1989. Page references are to the 1989 edition.

William, Crown Prince of Germany. *Meine Erinnerungen aus Deutschlands Heldenkampf*. Berlin: E. S. Mittler, 1923.

Young, F. Brett. *Marching on Tanga (with General Smuts in East Africa).* London: William Collins Sons, 1919.

SECONDARY SOURCES

Books and Articles

Allard, Dean C. "Anglo-American Naval Differences during World War I." *Military Affairs* 44 (April 1980): 75–81.

Anderson, Eugene N. *The First Moroccan Crisis, 1904–1906.* Hamden: Archon Books, 1966.

Andrew, Christopher. *Théophile Delcassé and the Making of the Entente Cordiale.* New York: Macmillan, 1968.

Asprey, Robert B. *The German High Command at War: Hindenburg and Ludendorff Conduct World War I.* New York: W. Morrow, 1991.

Assmann, Kurt, ed. *Die Kämpfe der Kaiserlichen Marine in den deutschen Kolonien.* Vol. 16. *Der Krieg zur See 1914–1918.* Berlin: E. S. Mittler, 1935.

Balderston, Theo. "War, Finance, and Inflation in Britain and Germany, 1914–18." *Economic History Review* 42 (May 1989): 222–44.

Barker, A. J. *The Bastard War: The Mesopotamian Campaign of 1914–1918.* New York: Dial Press, 1967.

Barlow, Ima Christina. *The Agadir Crisis.* Chapel Hill: University of North Carolina Press, 1940.

Barnett, L. Margaret. *British Food Policy during the First World War.* London: Collins, 1985.

Barraclough, Geoffrey. *From Agadir to Armageddon.* New York: Holmes and Meier, 1982.

Beesley, Patrick. *Room 40: British Naval Intelligence, 1914–1918.* Oxford: Oxford University Press, 1984.

Bennett, Geoffrey M. *The Battle of Jutland.* British Battles Series. London: Batsford, 1964.

———. *Coronel and the Falklands.* British Battles Series. London: Batsford, 1962.

———. *Naval Battles of the First World War.* British Battles Series. London: Batsford, 1968.

Bischoff, Ernst. *Die Leistungen der deutschen Flotte im Weltkrieg.* Zurich: Orell Füssli, 1918.

Boell, Ludwig. *Die Operationen in Ostafrika: Weltkrieg, 1914–1918.* Hamburg: Walter Dachert, 1952.

Boemeke, Manfred, Gerald Feldman, and Elizabeth Glaser, eds. *The Treaty of Versailles: A Reassessment after 75 Years.* Cambridge: Cambridge University Press, 1998.

Bond, Brian, ed. *The First World War and British Military History.* Oxford: Clarendon Press, 1991.

Bourne, J. M. *Britain and the Great War, 1914–1918.* London: Edward Arnold, 1989.

Brown John C. "Imperfect Competition and Anglo-German Trade Rivalry: Markets for Cotton Textiles before 1914." *Journal of Economic History* 55 (September 1995): 494–527.

Burdick, Charles B. *The Japanese Siege of Tsingtao: World War I in Asia.* Hamden, CT: Archon Books, 1976.

Burk, Kathleen. *Britain, America and the Sinews of War, 1814–1918.* London: Collins, 1985.

Burt, R. A. *British Battleships, 1889–1904.* Annapolis: Naval Institute Press, 1988.

Busch, Briton Cooper. *Britain, India, and the Arabs, 1914–1921.* Berkeley: University of California Press, 1971.

Calder, Kenneth. *Great Britain and the Origins of the New Europe, 1914–1918.* Cambridge: Cambridge University Press, 1976.

Cassar, G. H. *Asquith as War Leader.* London: Hambledon, 1994.

Charlewood, C. J. "Naval Actions on the Tanganyika Coast, 1914–1917: Part 1." *Tanganyika Notes and Records* 54 (March 1960): 120.

———. "Naval Actions on the Tanganyika Coast, 1914–1917: Part 2." *Tanganyika Notes and Records* 55 (September 1960): 153–80.

Charmley, John. *Splendid Isolation? Britain, the Balance of Power and the Origins of the World War.* London: Hodder and Stoughton, 1999.

Churchill, Randolph S. *Winston S. Churchill, Young Statesman, 1901–1914.* Boston: Houghton Mifflin, 1967.

———. *Winston S. Churchill.* Companion vol. 2, part 3, *1911–1914.* Boston: Houghton Mifflin, 1969.

Churchill, William. "Germany's Lost Pacific Empire." *Geographical Review* 10 (August 1920): 84–90.

Clifford, Hugh. *The Gold Coast Regiment in the East African Campaign.* Nashville: Battery Press, 1995.

Cohen, Stuart. "Mesopotamia in British Strategy, 1903–1914." *International Journal of Middle East Studies* 9 (April 1978): 171–81.

Coles, Paul. *The Ottoman Impact in Europe.* New York: Harcourt Brace and World, 1968.

Collyer, John Johnson. *The Campaign in German South West Africa, 1914–1915.* Battery Press Great War Series. London: Imperial War Museum Department of Printed Books; Nashville: Battery Press, 1997.

Coogan, John W. *The End of Neutrality: The United States, Britain, and Maritime Rights, 1899–1915.* London: Cornell University Press, 1981.

Copeland, Dale C. "Economic Interdependence and War: A Theory of Trade Expectations." *International Security* 20 (Spring 1996): 5–41.

Corbett, Julian S., and Henry Newbolt. *Naval Operations.* 5 vols. History of the Great War. London: Longmans, Green and Co. 1920–26.

Cowley, Robert, ed. *The Great War: Perspectives on the First World War.* New York: Random House, 2003.

Crabtree, W. A. "German Colonies in Africa." *Journal of the Royal African Society* 14 (October 1914): 1–14.

Craig, Gordon A. "The World War I Alliance of the Central Powers in Retrospect: The Military Cohesion of the Alliance." *Journal of Modern History* 37 (September 1965): 336–44.

Cramb, J. W. *Germany and England.* New York: E. P. Dutton, 1914.

Crampton, R. J. *The Hollow Détente: Anglo-German Relations in the Balkans, 1911–1914.* London: George Prior Publishers; Atlantic Highlands, NJ: Humanitarian Press, [1979?].

Cruttwell, C. R. M. F. *A History of the Great War.* Oxford: Clarendon Press, 1936.

Dane, Edmund. *British Campaigns in Africa and the Pacific, 1914–1918.* London, New York: Hodder and Stoughton, 1919.

———. *Campaigns in the Nearer East, 1914–1918: From the Outbreak of War with Turkey to the Armistice.* 2 vols. London: Hodder and Stoughton, 1919.

Davis, Paul K. *Ends and Means: The British Mesopotamian Campaign and Commission.* Rutherford, NJ: Farleigh Dickinson University Press, 1994.

Dawson, R. MacGregor. "The Cabinet Minister and Administration: A. J. Balfour and Sir Edward Carson at the Admiralty, 1915–1917." *Canadian Journal of Economics and Political Science* 9 (February 1943): 1–38.

———. "The Cabinet Minister and Administration Winston S. Churchill at the Admiralty, 1911–1915." *Canadian Journal of Economics and Political Science* 6 (August 1940): 325–58.

Dearle, Norman Burrell. *An Economic Chronicle of the Great War for Great Britain and Ireland, 1914–1919.* London: H. Milford; Oxford University Press, 1929.

Dewey, Peter. *British Agriculture in the First World War.* London: Routledge, 1989.

Dickinson, Frederick R. "Japan: Declaring War for the Anglo-Japanese Alliance." In *The Origins of World War I*, edited by Richard Hamilton and Holger Herwig. Cambridge: Cambridge University Press, 2003.

Dockrill, Michael, and David French, eds. *Peace without Promise: Britain and the Peace Conferences, 1919–23.* London: Batsford, 1981.

Dua, R. P. *Anglo-Japanese Relations during the First World War.* New Delhi: S. Chand and Co., 1972.

Ellinwood, DeWitt C., and S. D. Pradhan, eds. *India and World War I.* Columbia, MO: South Asia Books, 1978.

Emme, Eugene M. "Technical Change and Western Military Thought, 1914–1945." *Military Affairs* 24 (Spring 1960): 6–19.

Epkenhans, Michael. "Krupp and the Imperial German Navy, 1898–1914: A Reassessment." *Journal of Military History* 64 (April 2000): 335–69.

Evans, R. J. W., and Hartmut Pogge von Strandmann. *The Coming of the First World War.* Oxford: Clarendon, 1988.

Fairbanks, Charles H. "The Origins of the Dreadnought Revolution: A Historiographical Essay." *International History Review* 13 (June 1991): 246–72.

Falkus, M. E. "Russia and the International Wheat Trade, 1861–1914." *Economica* 33 (November 1966): 416–29.

Farrar, Lancelot L. *The Short-War Illusion: German Policy, Strategy and Domestic Affairs, August–December 1914.* Santa Barbara, CA: ABC-CLIO, 1973.

Farwell, Byron. *The Great War in Africa, 1914–1918.* New York, London: W. W. Norton and Company, 1986.

Fayle, C. Ernest. *Seaborne Trade.* Vol. 1, *The Cruiser Period.* History of the Great War Based on Official Documents. London: John Murray, 1920.

Ferguson, Niall. "The Kaiser's European Union: What If Britain Had Stood Aside in August 1914?" In *Virtual History: Alternative and Counterfactuals*, edited by Niall Ferguson. London: Picador, 1997: 228–80.

———. *The Pity of War.* New York: Basic Books, 1999.

Ferris, John. "Before 'Room 40': The British Empire and Signals Intelligence, 1898–1914." *Journal of Strategic Studies* 12 (December 1989): 431–57.

First World War.com. http://www.firstworldwar.com.

Fitzhardinge, L. F. "Australia, Japan, and Great Britain, 1914–1918: A Study in Triangular Diplomacy." *Historical Studies* 14 (April 1970): 250–59.

"The Fleets." The Ship's List. http://www.theshipslist.com/index.html.

Flux, A. W. "British Export Trade." *Economic Journal* 36 (December 1926): 551–62.

Frane, Thomas R. *First In, Last Out: The Navy at Gallipoli.* New South Wales: Kangaroo Press, 1990.

French, David. *British Economic and Strategic Planning, 1905–1915.* London: Unwin, 1982.

———. *British Strategy and War Aims, 1914–1916.* London, Boston: Allen and Unwin, 1986.

Friedman, Norman. *Network Centric Warfare: How Navies Learned to Fight Smarter through Three World Wars.* Annapolis: Naval Institute Press, 2009.

Gardner, Brian. *German East: The Story of the First World War in East Africa.* London: Cassell, 1963.

"German Hochseeflotte." German Naval History. http://www.german-navy.de/hochseeflotte/index.html.

Gibson, Richard Henry, and Maurice Prendergast. *The German Submarine War, 1914–1918.* Forward by Admiral of the Fleet Earl Jellicoe. London: Constable, 1931.

Gilbert, Bentley B. "Pacifist to Interventionist: David Lloyd George in 1911 and 1914. Was Belgium an Issue?" *Historical Journal* 28 (December 1985): 863–85.

Gilbert, Martin. *The Routledge Atlas of the First World War.* 2nd ed. Glasgow: Bell and Bain, 2002.

———. *Winston S. Churchill.* Companion vol. 3, part 1, *July 1914–April 1915.* Boston: Houghton Mifflin, 1973.

Goldrick, James. *The King's Ships Were at Sea: The War in the North Sea, August 1914–February 1915.* Annapolis: Naval Institute Press, 1984.

Gooch, John. *The Plans for War: The General Staff and British Military Strategy c. 1900–1916.* New York: John Wiley and Sons, 1974.

Gordon, Andrew. *The Rules of the Game: Jutland and British Naval Command.* London: Jon Murray, 1997.

Gordon, Donald C. "The Colonial Defence Committee and Imperial Collaboration, 1885–1904." *Political Science Quarterly* 77 (December 1962): 526–45.

Gottschall, Terrell D. *By Order of the Kaiser: Otto von Diederichs and the Rise of the Imperial German Navy, 1865–1902.* Annapolis: Naval Institute Press, 2003.

Gray, John Alexander Clinton. *Amerika Samoa: A History of American Samoa and Its United States Naval Administration.* Annapolis: U.S. Naval Institute, 1960.

"Great War in a Different Light." http://www.greatwardifferent.com/Great_War (no longer accessible).

Griffiths, Ieuan. "The Scramble for Africa: Inherited Political Boundaries." *Geographical Journal* 152 (July 1986): 204–16.

Grimsley, Mark. *The Hard Hand of War: Union Military Policy toward Southern Civilians, 1861–1865.* Cambridge: Cambridge University Press, 1995.

Groos, Otto, and Walter Gladisch. *Der Krieg zur See, 1914–1918.* 7 vols. Berlin: E. S. Mittler. 1920–37.

Guichard, Louis. *The Naval Blockade, 1914–1918.* Translated and edited by Christopher R. Turner. New York: D. Appleton and Co., 1930.

Guinn, Paul. *British Strategy and Politics, 1914–1918.* Oxford: Oxford University Press, 1965.

Haggie, Paul. "The Royal Navy and War Planning in the Fisher Era." *Journal of Contemporary History* 8 (July 1973): 113–31.

Halpern, Paul G. *A Naval History of World War I.* Annapolis: Naval Institute Press, 1994.

Hammond, R. J. "British Food Supplies, 1914–1939." *Economic History Review* 16 (February 1946): 1–14.

Hatton, T. J. "The Demand for British Exports, 1870–1913." *Economic History Review* 43 (November 1990): 576–94.

Hawkins, Nigel. *Starvation Blockades: The Naval Blockades of WWI.* Barnsley: Leo Cooper, 2002.

Haywood, A., and F. A. S. Clarke. *The History of the Royal West African Frontier Force.* Aldershot: Gale and Polden, 1964.

Hazlehurst, Cameron. "Asquith as Prime Minister, 1908–1916." *English Historical Review* 85 (July 1970): 502–31.

Henderson, W. O. *The German Colonial Empire, 1884–1919.* London: Frank Cass, 1993.

Herwig, Holger H. *The First World War: Germany and Austria-Hungary, 1914–1918.* London: Arnold. 1997.

———. "The German Reaction to the Dreadnaught Revolution." *International History Review* 13 (June 1991): 273–83.

———. *"Luxury" Fleet: The Imperial German Navy, 1888–1918.* London: Allen and Unwin, 1980.

———, ed. *The Outbreak of World War I: Causes and Responsibilities.* Boston: Houghton Mifflin, 1997.

Hiery, Hermann Joseph. *The Neglected War: The German South Pacific and the Influence of World War I.* Honolulu: University of Hawaii Press, 1995.

Higham, Robin, ed., with Dennis E. Showalter. *Researching World War I: A Handbook.* Westport, CT: Greenwood Press, 2003.

Hilditch, A. Neville. *Coronel and the Falkland Islands.* London: Oxford University Press, 1915.

Hiley, Nicholas. "Counter-Espionage and Security in Great Britain during the First World War." *English Historical Review* 101 (July 1986): 635–70.

———. "The Failure of British Counter-Espionage against Germany, 1907–1914." *Historical Journal* 28 (December 1985): 835–62.

Hinsley, F. H., ed. *British Foreign Policy under Sir Edward Grey.* Cambridge: Cambridge University Press, 1977.

Hodges, Geoffrey. *The Carrier Corps: Military Labor in the East African Campaign, 1914–1918.* Contributions in Comparative Colonial Studies. New York: Greenwood Press, 1986.

Hordern, Charles. *Military Operations, East Africa.* History of the Great War. London: His Majesty's Stationery Office, 1941.

Hough, Richard. *Louis and Victoria: The Family History of the Mountbattens.* 2nd ed. London: Weidenfeld and Nicolson, 1984.

Howard, Michael. *The First World War.* Oxford: Oxford University Press, 2002.

Howarth, Stephen. *The Fighting Ships of the Rising Sun: The Drama of the Imperial Japanese Navy.* New York: Atheneum, 1983.

Hoyt, Edwin P. *The Germans Who Never Lost.* New York: Funk and Wagnalls, 1968.

Huntington, Samuel P. "Arms Races: Prerequisites and Results." *Public Policy: The Yearbook of the Graduate School of Public Administration, Harvard University.* Edited by Carl J. Friedrich and Seymour E. Harris. Cambridge, MA: Harvard University Press, 1958. Reprinted in Richard K. Betts, ed., *Conflict after the Cold War: Argument on Causes of War and Peace.* 2nd ed. New York: Pearson Longman, 2005.

Irving, John J. C. *Coronel and the Falklands.* London: Philpot, 1927.

Jackson, W. G. F. *The Pomp of Yesterday: The Defence of India and the Suez Canal, 1798–1918.* London: Brassey's, 1995.

Jaffe, Lorna. *The Decision to Disarm Germany: British Policy towards Postwar German Disarmament, 1914–19.* London: Allen and Unwin, 1985.

James, Lawrence. *The Savage Wars: The British Campaigns in Africa, 1870–1920.* New York: St. Martin's Press, 1985.

Joll, James. *The Origins of the First World War.* London: Longman, 1984.

Kaiser, David E. "Germany and the Origins of the First World War." *Journal of Modern History* 55 (September 1983): 442–74.

Kaiserliche Marine: Geschichte und Kriegsschiffe der Kaiserlichen Marine. http://www.kaiserliche-marine.de.

Karsh, Efraim, and Inari Karsh. *Empires of the Sand: The Struggle for Mastery in the Middle East, 1789–1923.* Cambridge, MA: Harvard University Press, 1999.

Katzenellenbogen, W. E. "Southern Africa and the War of 1914–18," *War and Society: Historical Essays in Honor and Memory of J. R. Western, 1928–1971.* Edited by M. R. D. Foot. New York: Barnes and Noble, 1973.

Kearsey, Alexander Horace Cyril. *A Study of the Strategy and Tactics of the Mesopotamia Campaign, 1914–1917, Up To and Including the Capture and Consolidation of Baghdad, April, 1917, Illustrating the Principles of War.* London: Gale and Polden, 1934.

Keegan, John. *The First World War.* New York: Vintage, 1998.

Kennedy, Dane. *Islands of White: Settler Society and Culture in Kenyan and Southern Rhodesia, 1890–1939.* Durham: Duke University Press, 1987.

Kennedy, Paul. "The Development of German Naval Operations Plans against England, 1896–1914." *English Historical Review* 89 (January 1975): 48–76.

———. "German World Policy and the Alliance Negotiations with England, 1897–1900." *Journal of Modern History* 45 (December 1973): 605–25.

———. "Imperial Cable Communications and Strategy, 1870–1914." *English Historical Review* 86 (October 1971): 728–52.

———. *The Rise of the Anglo-German Antagonism, 1860–1914.* London: Unwin, 1980.

———. *The Rise and Fall of British Naval Mastery.* New York: Scribner, 1976.

———. *The Rise and Fall of the Great Powers: Economic Change and Military Conflict.* New York: Vintage Books, 1989.

———, ed. *The War Plans of the Great Powers, 1880–1914.* Boston: Allen and Unwin, 1985.

Killingray, David. "The Idea of a British Imperial African Army." *Journal of African History* 20 (November 1979): 421–36.

Klieman, Aaron S. "Britain's War Aims in the Middle East in 1915." *Journal of Contemporary History* 3, no. 3 (July 1968): 237–251.

Kumar, Ravinder. "The Records of the Government of India on the Berlin-Baghdad Railway Question." *Historical Journal* 5 (March 1962): 70–79.

Lambert, Andrew. "Economic Power, Technological Advantage, and Imperial Strength: Britain as a Unique Global Power, 1860–1980." *International Journal of Naval History* 5 (August 2006).

Lambert, Nicholas A. "British Naval Policy, 1913–1914: Financial Limitation and Strategic Revolution." *Journal of Modern History* 67 (September 1995): 595–626.

———. "'Our Bloody Ships' or 'Our Bloody System'? Jutland and the Loss of the Battle Cruisers, 1916." *Journal of Military History* 62 (January 1998): 27–55.

———. *Sir John Fisher's Naval Revolution.* Columbia: University of South Carolina Press, 1999.

———. "Strategic Command and Control for Maneuver Warfare: Creation of the Royal Navy's 'War Room' System, 1905–1915." *Journal of Military History* 69 (April 2005): 361–410.

———. "Transformation and Technology in the Fisher Era: the Impact of the Communications Revolution." *Journal of Strategic Studies* 27 (June 2004): 272–97.

Lambi, Ivo Nikolai. *The Navy and German Power Politics.* Boston: Allen and Unwin, 1984.

Lautenschlager, Karl. "The Submarine in Naval Warfare, 1901–2001." *International Security* 11 (Winter 1986–87): 94–140.

Lee, John. *The Warlords: Hindenburg and Ludendorff.* London: Weidenfeld and Nicolson, 2005.

Levy, Jack S. "Preferences, Constraints, and Choices in July 1914." *International Security* 15 (Winter 1990–91): 151–86.

Levy, Jack S., Thomas J. Christensen, and Marc Trachtenberg. "Mobilization and Inadvertence in the July Crisis." *International Security* 16 (Summer 1991): 189–203.

Liddell Hart, Basil H. *The Real War, 1914–1918.* Boston: Little, Brown and Co., 1930.

Lochner, R. K. *The Last Gentleman-of-War: The Raider Exploits of the Cruiser Emden.* Translated by Thea and Harry Lindauer. Annapolis: Naval Institute Press, 1988.

Louis, William Roger. "Australia and the German Colonies in the Pacific, 1914–1919." *Journal of Modern History* 38 (December 1966): 407–21.

———. *Great Britain and Germany's Lost Colonies, 1914–19.* Oxford: Oxford University Press, 1967.

Lowe, Peter. *Great Britain and Japan, 1911–1915: A Study of British Far Eastern Policy.* London: Macmillan, 1969.

Lucas, Charles. *The Empire at War.* 5 vols. Oxford: Oxford University Press, 1921–26.

Lynn-Jones, Sean M. "Détente and Deterrence: Anglo-German Relations, 1911–1914." *International Security* 11 (Fall 1986): 121–50.

Mackenzie, S. S. *The Australians at Rabaul: The Capture and Administration of the German Possessions in the Southern Pacific.* The Official History of Australia in the War of 1914–1918. Sydney: Angus and Robertson, 1942.

MacKintosh, John P. "The Role of the Committee of Imperial Defence before 1914." *English Historical Review* 77 (July 1962): 490–503.

Marder, Arthur J. *From the Dreadnought to Scapa Flow: The Royal Navy in the Fisher Era, 1904–1919.* 5 vols. Oxford: Oxford University Press, 1961–70.

Marris, Murrell. *Right Honorable Joseph Chamberlain: The Man and the Statesman.* 2nd ed. New York: E. P. Dutton, 1900.

Massie, Robert K. *Dreadnought: Britain, Germany, and the Coming of the Great War.* New York: Ballantine Books, 1991.

Maurer, John H. "The Anglo-German Naval Rivalry and Informal Arms Control, 1912–1914." *Journal of Conflict Resolution* 36 (June 1992): 284–308.

Maurice, Frederick. *Haldane, 1856–1915: The Life of Viscount Haldane of Cloan.* 2 vols. Westport, CT: Greenwood Press, 1970.

McDermott, J. "Total War and the Merchant State: Aspects of British Economic Warfare against Germany, 1914–1916." *Canadian Journal of History* 21 (April 1986): 61–76.

Mentzel, Heinrich. *Die Kämpfe im Kamerun, 1914–1916: Vorbereitung und Verlauf.* Berlin: Junker und Dünnhaupt, 1936.

Meritt, Herbert Paul. "Bismark and the First Partition of East Africa." *English Historical Review* 91 (July 1976): 585–97.

———. "Bismark and German Interest in East Africa, 1884–1885." *Historical Journal* 21 (March 1978): 97–116.

Miller, Charles. *Battle for the Bundu: The First World War in East Africa.* New York: Macmillan, 1974.

Miller, Roger G. "The Logistics of the British Expeditionary Force: 4 August to 5 September 1914." *Military Affairs* 43 (October 1979): 133–38.

Miller, Ronald. *Death of an Army: The Siege of Kut, 1915–1916.* Boston: Houghton Mifflin, 1970.

Miller, Steven E., Sean M. Lynn-Jones, and Stephen van Evera, eds. *Military Strategy and the Origins of the First World War.* Princeton: Princeton University Press, 1991.

Moberly, Frederick James. *The Campaign in Mesopotamia, 1914–1918.* 4 vols. History of the Great War. London: His Majesty's Stationery Office, 1927.

———. *Military Operations: Togoland and the Cameroons, 1914–1916.* History of the Great War. London: Longmans, Green and Co., 1931.

———. *Operations in Persia, 1914–1919.* History of the Great War. London: His Majesty's Stationery Office. 1929.

Mowat, R. B. "Great Britain and Germany in the Early Twentieth Century." *English Historical Review* 46 (July 1931): 423–41.

Moyer, Laurence. *Victory Must Be Ours: Germany and the Great War, 1914–1918.* New York: Hippocrene Books, 1995.

Neilson, Keith. *Strategy and Supply: The Anglo-Russian Alliance, 1914–1917.* London: Harper Collins, 1984.

Nelson, Harold. *Land and Power: British and Allied Policy on Germany's Frontiers, 1916–1919.* London: Routledge and Kegan Paul, 1963.

Nish, Ian H. *Alliance in Decline: A Study in Anglo-Japanese Relations, 1908–1923.* London: Athlone Press, 1972.

———. "Politics, Trade and Communications in East Asia: Thoughts on Anglo-Russian Relations, 1861–1907." *Modern Asian Studies* 21 (1987): 667–78.

O'Farrell, H. H. "British and German Export Trade before the War." *Economic Journal* 26 (June 1916): 161–67.

Offer, Avner. *The First World War: An Agrarian Interpretation.* Oxford: Clarendon Press, 1989.

———. "Morality and Admiralty: 'Jacky' Fisher, Economic Warfare and the Laws of War." *Journal of Contemporary History* 23 (January 1988): 99–118.

———. "The Working Classes, British Naval Plans and the Coming of the Great War." *Past and Present,* no. 107 (May 1985): 204–226.

Olson, Mancur. *The Economics of Wartime Shortage: A History of British Food Supplies in the Napoleonic Wars and World Wars I and II.* Durham: Duke University Press, 1963.

Olukoju, Ayodeji. "Elder Dempster and the Shipping Trade of Nigeria during the First World War." *Journal of African History* 33 (July 1992): 255–71.

Padfield, Peter. *The Great Naval Race: Anglo-German Naval Rivalry, 1900–14.* London: Hart Davis, 1974.

Paice, Edward. *Tip and Run: The Untold Tragedy of the Great War in Africa.* New York: Weidenfeld and Nicolson, 2007.

Partridge, M. S. "The Royal Navy and the End of the Close Blockade, 1885–1905." *Mariner's Mirror* 75 (May 1989): 119–36.

Peattie, Mark R. *Nanyo: The Rise and Fall of the Japanese in Micronesia, 1885–1945.* Honolulu: University of Hawaii Press, 1988.

Petter, Wolfgang, Rolf Güth, and Jost Dülffer. *Deutsche Marinegeschichte der Neuzeit.* Vol. 8, *Handbuch zur deutschen Militärgeschichte, 1648–1939.* Munich: Bernard and Graefe, 1977.

Pitt, Barrie. *Coronel and Falkland.* London: Cassell, 1960.

———. *Zeebrugge.* New York: Ballantine, 1958.

Pochhamer, Hans. *Before Jutland: Admiral von Spee's Last Voyage. Coronel and the Battle of the Falklands.* London: Jarrolds, 1931.

Prior, Robin, and Trevor Wilson. *The First World War.* London: Cassell, 1999.

Pryce, Roy. "Italy and the Outbreak of the First World War." *Cambridge Historical Journal* 11 (1954): 219–27.

Ranft, Bryan., ed. *Technical Change and British Naval Policy, 1860–1939.* London: Hodder and Stoughton. 1977.

Rathbone, Richard. "World War I and Africa: Introduction." *Journal of African History* 19 (March 1978): 1–9.

Renzi, William A. "Great Britain, Russia, and the Straits, 1914–1915." *Journal of Modern History* 42 (March 1970): 1–20.

Robinson, Ronald, and Jack Gallagher, with Alice Denny. *Africa and the Victorians: The Climax of Imperialism in the Dark Continent.* New York: St. Martin's Press, 1961.

Rolo, P. J. V. *Entente Cordiale: The Origin and Negotiations of the Anglo-French Agreements of 8 April, 1904.* London: Macmillan, 1969.

Ropp, Theodore. *The Development of a Modern Navy: French Naval Policy, 1871–1904.* Annapolis: Naval Institute Press, 1987.

Rosen, Stephen Peter. *Societies and Military Power: India and Its Armies.* Ithaca: Cornell University Press, 1996.

Rosinski, Herbert. *The Development of Naval Thought: Essays by Herbert Rosinski.* Edited by B. Mitchell Simpson III. Newport, RI: Naval War College Press, 1977.

Ross, Angus. "Losing the Initiative in Mercantile Warfare: Great Britain's Surprising Failure to Anticipate Maritime Challenges to Her Global Trading Network in the First World War." *International Journal of Naval History* 1 (April 2002).

Rothwell, Victor Howard. *British War Aims and Peace Diplomacy, 1914–1918.* Oxford: Clarendon Press, 1971.

Sagan, Scott D. "1914 Revisited: Allies, Offense, and Instability." *International Security* 11 (Autumn 1986): 151–75.

Salter, James Arthur. *Allied Shipping Control: An Experiment in International Administration.* Oxford: Clarendon Press, 1921.

Sanderson, G. N. "The Anglo-German Agreement of 1890 and the Upper Nile." *English Historical Review* 78 (January 1963): 49–72.

Schenking, J. Charles. "Bureaucratic Politics, Military Budgets, and Japan's Southern Advance: The Imperial Navy's Seizure of German Micronesia in World War I." *War in History* 5 (July 1998): 308–26.

Schilling, Warner R. "Civil-Naval Politics in World War I." *World Politics* 7 (July 1955): 572–91.

Schmitt, Bernadotte E. "Triple Alliance and Triple Entente, 1902–1914." *American Historical Review* 29 (April 1924): 449–73.

Schoenherr, Steven. "War in Africa." http://history.sandiego.edu/gen/ww1/africa.html (no longer accessible).

Schwarz, Benjamin. "Divided Attention: Britain's Perception of a German Threat to Her Eastern Position in 1918." *Journal of Contemporary History* 28 (January 1993): 103–22.

Scott, James Brown. "Lord Haldane's Diary of Negotiations between Germany and England in 1912." *American Journal of International Law* 12 (July 1918): 589–96.

———. "Proposed Neutrality of France and the Beginning of the War." *American Journal of International Law* 12 (April 1918): 375–78.

Sebald, Peter. *Togo, 1884–1914: Eine Geschichte der Deutschen 'Musterkolonie' auf der Grundlage amtlichen Quellen.* Berlin: Akademie Verlag, 1988.

Seton-Watson, R. W. *Britain in Europe, 1789–1914.* Cambridge: Cambridge University Press, 1938.

Showalter, Dennis. "From Deterrence to Doomsday Machine: The German Way of War, 1890–1914." *Journal of Military History* 64 (July 2000): 679–710.

Siney, Marion C. *The Allied Blockade of Germany, 1914–1916.* Westport, CT: Greenwood Press, 1973.

———. "British Official Histories of the Blockade of the Central Powers during the First World War." *American Historical Review* 68 (January 1963): 392–401.

Smith, C. Jay, Jr. "Great Britain and the 1914–1915 Straits Agreement with Russia: The British Promise of November 1914." *American Historical Review* 70 (July 1965): 1015–34.

Smith, Munroe, Karl Max Furst von Lichnowsky, Gunther Gottlieb Karl Eugen von Jagow, and Henry Fraser Munro. *The Disclosures from Germany.* New York: American Association for International Consolation, 1918.

Spindler, Arno. *Der Handelskreig mit U-boten: Bearbeitet von Arno Spindler.* Berlin: E. S. Mittler and Sohn, 1932.

Spinks, Charles Nelson. "Japan's Entrance into the World War." *Pacific Historical Review* 5 (August 1936): 297–311.

Steinberg, Jonathan. "A German Plan for the Invasion of Holland and Belgium, 1897." *Historical Journal* 6 (1963): 107–119.

Steiner, Zara. *Britain and the Origins of the First World War.* London: Macmillan, 1977.

Steward, Keith. "Lieutenant Colonel F. C. Bryant, CMG, CBE, DSO, Gold Coast Regiment and the Short Campaign in Togo, August 11 to 26, 1914." http://british-colonial-africa-from-1873-to-1955.com/PDFS/10_LIEUT_COLONEL_BRYANT_8_Single_2-_3.pdf.

Stokesbury, James L. *A Short History of World War I.* New York: William Morrow, 1981.

Stowell, Ellery C. *The Diplomacy of the War of 1914: The Beginnings of the War.* Boston and New York: Houghton Mifflin, 1915.

Strachan, Hew. *The First World War.* Vol. 1, *To Arms.* Oxford: Oxford University Press, 2001.

———, ed. *World War I: A History.* Oxford: Oxford University Press, 1998.

Strandman, Hartmut Pogge von. "Domestic Origins of Germany's Colonial Expansion under Bismarck." *Past and Present,* no. 42 (February 1969): 140–59.

Stowell, Ellery C. *The Diplomacy of the War of 1914: The Beginnings of the War.* New York: Houghton Mifflin, 1915.

Sumida, Jon Tetsuro. "British Capital Ship Design and Fire Control in the Dreadnought Era: Sir John Fisher, Arthur Hungerford Pollen, and the Battle Cruiser." *Journal of Modern History* 51 (June 1979): 205–30.

———. "British Naval Administration and Policy in the Age of Fisher." *Journal of Military History* 54 (January 1990): 1–26.

———. "British Naval Operational Logistics, 1914–1918." *Journal of Military History* 57 (July 1993): 447–80.

———. "Geography, Technology, and British Naval Strategy in the Dreadnought Era." *Naval War College Review* 59 (2006): 89–102.

———. *In Defense of Naval Supremacy: Finance, Technology, and British Naval Policy, 1889–1914.* London: Routledge, 1993.

———. "Sir John Fisher and the Dreadnought: The Sources of Naval Mythology." *Journal of Military History* 59 (October 1995): 619–37.

Sweet, David W. "The Baltic in British Diplomacy before the First World War." *Historical Journal* 13 (September 1970): 451–90.

Taussig, F. W. "The Change in Great Britain's Foreign Trade Terms after 1900." *Economic Journal* 35 (March 1925): 1–10.

Taylor, Philip M. "The Foreign Office and British Propaganda during the First World War." *Historical Journal* 23 (December 1980): 875–98.

Thompson, J. Lee. "'To Tell the People of America the Truth': Lord Northcliffe in the USA, Unofficial British Propaganda, June–November 1917." *Journal of Contemporary History* 34 (April 1999): 243–62.

Thornton, Robert. "Invaluable Ally or Imminent Aggressor? Australia and Japanese Naval Assistance, 1914–1918." *Journal of Australian Studies* 12 (June 1983): 5–20.

Towle, Philip. "The Russo-Japanese War and the Defense of India." *Military Affairs* 44 (October 1980): 111–17.

Townshend, Charles. "Military Force and Civil Authority in the United Kingdom, 1914–1921." *Journal of British Studies* 28 (July 1989): 262–92.

Trumpener, Ulrich. "Turkey's Entry into World War I: An Assessment of Responsibilities." *Journal of Modern History* 34 (December 1962): 369–80.

Turner, John, ed. *Britain in the First World War.* London: Unwin Hyman, 1988.

———. *British Politics and the Great War: Coalition and Conflict, 1915–1918.* New Haven: Yale University Press, 1992.

United States Military Academy, Department of History. "Campaign Atlas to the Great War." http://www.westpoint.edu/history/SitePages/WWI.aspx.

Vandervort, Bruce. *Wars of Imperial Conquest in Africa, 1830–1914.* Bloomington: Indiana University Press, 1998.

Vincent, C. Paul. *The Politics of Hunger: The Allied Blockade of Germany, 1915–1919.* Athens: Ohio University Press, 1985.

Wallin, Jeffrey D. *By Ships Alone: Churchill and the Dardanelles.* Durham: Carolina Academic, 1981.

Walter, John. *The Kaiser's Pirates: German Surface Raiders in World War One.* Annapolis: Naval Institute Press, 1994.

Williams, Beryl J. "The Strategic Background to the Anglo-Russian Entente of August, 1907." *Historical Journal* 9 (September 1966): 360–73.

Williams, Rhodri. *Defending the Empire: The Conservative Party and British Defense Policy, 1899–1915.* New Haven: Yale University Press, 1991.

Williamson, Samuel R., Jr. "The Origins of World War I." *Journal of Interdisciplinary History* 18 (Spring 1988): 795–818.

———. *The Politics of Grand Strategy: Britain and France Prepare for War, 1904–1914.* Cambridge, MA: Harvard University Press, 1969.

Wilson, Keith, ed. *Decisions for War, 1914.* New York: St. Martin's Press, 1995.

———. "Imperial Interests in the British Decision for War: The Defense of India in Central Asia." *Review of International Studies* 9 (April 1984): 189–203.

———. *The Policy of the Entente: Essays on the Determinants of British Foreign Policy, 1904–1914.* Cambridge: Cambridge University Press, 1985.

Wilson, Trevor. *The Myriad Faces of War: Britain and the Great War, 1914–18.* Cambridge: Polity Press, 1986.

Wohlforth, William C. "The Perception of Power: Russia in the Pre-1914 Balance." *World Politics* 39 (April 1987): 353–81.

Woodhouse, C. M. *Britain and the Middle East.* Geneva: E. Droz, 1959.

Woodward, David R. "Britain's 'Brass-Hats' and the Question of a Compromise Peace, 1916–1918." *Military Affairs* 35 (April 1971): 63–68.

Woodward, E. L. *Great Britain and the German Navy.* Oxford: Clarendon, 1935.

"World Battleship Lists: Royal Navy Dreadnoughts." Haze Gray and Underway. http://www.hazegray.org/navhist/battleships/rn_dr.htm.

"World War I: The Maritime War." World War I Document Archive. http://www.gwpda.org/naval/n0000000.htm.

World War I Naval Combat. http://www.worldwar1.co.uk.

Yates, Keith. *Flawed Victory: Jutland, 1916.* Annapolis: Naval Institute Press, 2000.

———. *Graf Spee's Raiders Challenge to the Royal Navy, 1914–1915.* London: Cooper, 1995.

Yergen, Daniel, *The Prize: The Epic Quest for Oil, Money, and Power.* Oxford: Clarendon, 1989.

Young, Harry F. "The Misunderstanding of August 1, 1914." *Journal of Modern History* 48 (December 1976): 644–65.

Dissertations

Canning, Craig Noel. "The Japanese Occupation of Shantung during World War I." PhD diss., Stanford University, 1975.

Lambert, Nicholas. "A Revolution in Naval Strategy: The Influence of the Submarine upon Maritime Thought." PhD diss., Oxford University, 1992.

Moon, H. R. "The Invasion of the United Kingdom: Public Controversy and Official Planning, 1888–1918." 2 vols. PhD diss., University of London, 1968.

Randel, Jonathan Clay. "Information for Economic Warfare: British Intelligence and the Blockade, 1914–1918." PhD diss., University of North Carolina, 1993.

Summerton, N. W. "The Development of British Military Planning for a War against Germany 1904–1914." 2 vols. PhD diss., University of London, 1970.

INDEX